CRUISING
IN COMFORT

CRUISING IN COMFORT

Jim Skoog

INTERNATIONAL MARINE PUBLISHING COMPANY
Camden, Maine

Typeset by The Key Word, Inc., Belchertown, Massachusetts
Printed and bound by The Alpine Press, Stoughton, Massachusetts

Published by International Marine Publishing Company
21 Elm Street, Camden, Maine 04843
(207) 236-4342

Library of Congress Cataloging in Publication Data

Skoog, James.
    Cruising in comfort.

    Index.
    1. Sailboat living. 2. Yachts and yachting.
I. Title.
GV811.65.S55 1986   797.1′24   85-23074
ISBN 0-87742-199-4

For Penny—shipmate, friend, wife

▶ Contents

▶ Preface

The roots of this book go back 20 years, and more. It's a composite of lessons learned by building boats and sailing them, by living aboard them, by examining other sailors' vessels and experiences, and by identifying with their aspirations.

I grew up on the waterfront near Seattle, and my whole family was boat crazy. If it floated, at one time or another a member of the family tried it: dugout canoes, rafts, rowboats, outboard hydroplanes, family runabouts, a fire-breathing drag boat, and finally sailboats, when, in the mid 1960s, my brothers and I hankered to circumnavigate the world. We couldn't afford to buy a boat, so we built a 30-foot sloop called *Brinestormer*.

My career in boatbuilding spun off my desire to cruise. Funds were scarce while building *Brinestormer*, and a neighbor introduced me to a pleasure boat manufacturer where I gained employment as a fiberglass laminator. Soon I was installing engines and doing electrical and mechanical work—things I'd learned by tinkering with cars and boats at home.

Brinestormer was a partial victory: she was both reliable and seaworthy, critical attributes for an offshore boat. Nonetheless, some months into our round-the-world voyage it dawned on us that our preconceptions and blue-water reality were two different things. Most cruising people we met along the way were in a similar fix. In those days, only a minority of veterans on second or third voyages had their acts together.

After my stint on *Brinestormer*, I crewed on a 42-foot ketch from Auckland to the Cook Islands. I presupposed the larger vessel would outclass the 30-footer, but it didn't. The ketch lacked offshore capability, to put it mildly, and nearly foundered in a great gale. In harbor, she didn't do much for her crew's morale, either. I noted her failings, adding them to what I'd learned from *Brinestormer*.

Cruising, I concluded, centered on human need and the dictates of the sea, an obvious viewpoint perhaps, but tricky to implement without direct experience. I was convinced sailing could be a comfortable and safe way to live, rather than a hit-or-miss camping trip, once the basics were understood and satisfied.

The episode on the 42-footer fizzled in discontent. I jumped ship, signing on a tramp steamer bound for Fiji, where I stayed aboard a 70-foot schooner owned by Ross and Minine Norgrove, seasoned cruising friends. Ross and I talked boats, and I inspected every inch of his *White Squall II*. As importantly, since I had always admired the Norgroves' lifestyle, I studied how their ship supported it. Not her size so much—a 70-footer was out of my league—but rather the organization and thought that went into her features.

Back in Seattle, I went into partnership with several other experienced offshore sailors and established a boatbuilding company to construct cruising hulls. I had the urge to have another crack at the Pacific with a vessel prepared exactly for the purpose.

The offshoot was a hull design for a heavy-displacement 45-footer, a size I felt was small enough to handle yet large enough to support a fine blue-water existence. A female mold was constructed, and each partner built a GRP and timber hull/deck structure in the shop, transporting it home for completion to individual preference.

As I was recently married, my voyage was to be a family affair, with my wife Penny and her two young children. Our itinerary included remote areas where self-sufficiency would be tested. Safety was paramount, long-term happiness a priority. These considerations shaped our interior layout, deck layout, rig configuration, and the ship's operating systems and equipment.

During the construction of our boat, *Dolphin Queen*, I worked for a yacht dealer commissioning new so-called cruising boats to customer specs. Here I saw much of what is wrong in the world of production boats. They were designed, built, sold, and bought by people who hadn't experienced cruising. The most obvious deficiencies to me—electrical, plumbing, mechanical, rigging—were the least obvious to the customers, who, sooner or later, would have to live with them.

Consequently, I became disenchanted with those selling the cruising dream. This eventually played a part in my motivation to set the record straight with a book.

We finished *Dolphin Queen* and lived aboard from Seattle to New Zealand via Mexico and Polynesia, four years in all. The vessel proved supportive and secure, even in hindsight—the only true yardstick of boats and cruises.

However, many cruising people we met en route were not as fortunate. Although boats and budgets had grown in the intervening years, the basics were as elusive as ever. Many voyages were hardly more than expensive trial runs, a pity for those who wouldn't have a second chance. I was reminded of what I'd learned at the yacht dealership: let the buyer beware!

I crossed paths with Ross Norgrove again in Auckland, in late 1980. By this time, he'd swallowed the anchor and was writing cruising books. He urged me to do likewise. Frankly, I'd shot my bolt building boats; it's regressive to slap them together for others after building them lovingly for oneself. So I changed hats and started writing about them—first, a two-year series of articles for a New Zealand boating magazine, then this book.

The title and theme came naturally. Cruising in comfort is the name of the game, especially for couples and families seeking an alternate lifestyle. It's what I'd always tried to achieve and finally did, and it's what almost everyone I'd met cruising hoped for, too.

My objective was clear: help my readers have a great cruise—even if it's their first.

Jim Skoog
Auckland

▶ Introduction:
At Home—Anywhere in the World

Cruising is living aboard a sailboat on the move. The words *on the move* make cruising a far cry from living aboard at a dock or ashore in a house.

When you cast off on a voyage, you throw away the crutches of civilization, the shoreside amenities, goods, and services dock dwellers and suburbanites lean on to live. While cruising, the boat replaces civilization, for better or worse.

Today's technology and relative affluence contribute much to life afloat. Without hardware, materials, and techniques to resist the oceanic environment *and* support a pleasant way of life, cruising is too much like camping on a wing and a prayer—and damned unattractive to almost everyone!

While rising living standards afloat make cruising more popular by the day, affluence and technology make it more challenging. Today's sailors must wear many hats and wear them well. Ironically, things like sailhandling and navigation have become a less prominent part of cruising. That's not because seamanship is any less a discipline—it's as exacting as ever—but because sailing as an alternative lifestyle has introduced new disciplines. Family life aboard small boats far from civilization is founded on understandings yesterday's hardy adventurers never had to fathom.

WHY THE SIMPLE LIFE?

For ages, the cruising axiom has been *keep it simple*, and some sailors still live by those words. Why? For several reasons, all concerning individual style and prejudice, none concerning boats or the sea.

One faction adheres to the simple life as though it were a religion. While this is unquestionably their privilege, or their problem, depending on your viewpoint, it's not a credible alternative for most of us. Some members of this group say the only trustworthy boat is a basic one. Admittedly, there have been headaches in cruising grounds when boats fall short of expectations. However, these disappointments are not the fault of inanimate things such as machines or electrical wires; they are born of human failings, such as laziness and ignorance. After all, people build boats. Sailors who make it their business to build comfortable boats don't have headaches—just fun!

Other sailors claim the simple life afloat is traditional and therefore the only bona fide way to sail. This group reckons real sailors don't pamper themselves; only sissies do. But isn't this confusing tradition with masochism or machismo? Most of the human race gets satisfaction from comfort and pleasure, not deprivation.

Simplicity is relative, anyway. A vessel capable of supporting a comfortable, self-sufficient lifestyle can be fairly simple, or at least each facet of the whole can be simple, and that's what counts. When basic features are thoughtfully arranged to work in harmony, a boat will afford pleasure reliably year after year—in Bora Bora, Tasmania, Puget Sound, or the Bahamas.

A BUSINESSLIKE APPROACH

You make your bed and sleep in it. No endeavor exemplifies that old saying quite like cruising. Once you cast off, the die is cast—your cruising comfort will equal your investment in it (money and elbow grease and expertise) before departure.

A businesslike approach is the only way to ensure a good return on any investment, including cruising. Try to keep an open mind, ready to take advantage of anything to further your cause—even if you didn't think of it yourself! Prepare for a rethink about boats, and about the sea. Sailors are an independent bunch, sometimes too stubborn for their own good. You can't afford to hang onto old values just because they are traditional; nor can you blindly accept modern practices.

When accepted convention and/or boatbuilding expediency conflict with comfort and safety, I'll try to help you make decisions based on something more concrete than myth. It won't help to get bogged down with theory and mathematical formulae either. Cruising in comfort is about human need: *people*, not numbers.

There are many ways to build boats. Just because I mention particular hardware and equipment doesn't imply that similar gear wouldn't work—unless something is especially praised or condemned. *Strategy*, not ill-considered consumerism, is the game. Happiness afloat is not really a bolt-on commodity, anyway; it's more basic. In fact it starts on the drawing board (or ends there, if you're not careful).

I'll leave the glamorizing and salesmanship to others, while we busy ourselves prying up damp rocks. When one faces pitfalls honestly, as we will here, they can be outfitted away. Turning a blind eye only promises misery.

THINK ABOUT YOUR NEEDS

Turning cruising aspirations into reality begins with a list of meticulously defined priorities—your priorities. A contented cruising life relies on features and systems that work *for* you and, when need be, *against* Mother Nature. Once you nail down your needs, you can conjure up the features and systems to meet those needs. As you read, climb aboard an imaginary boat and think about what I say as applied to your situation. Every cruising voyage is unique, and I don't presume you'll sail squarely in my wake. I'll tell you what I've learned as a boatbuilder, family cruising man, long-term liveaboard, and ocean sailor. It's your job to superimpose your needs to create a sailing lifestyle all your own. There are, however, some truths about cruising that don't invite interpretation if comfort and safety are to be achieved. I'll be hardnosed about them, for your sake.

By the time we part company, you'll have strategies mapped out to enable you to live like a king or queen on a sailboat anywhere you wish to travel. It won't necessarily cost you a king's ransom either—much of sailing comfort is fundamental. And incidentally, sound decisions often cost less than silly ones, particularly in the long run.

Although this book talks mostly about blue-water cruising, don't feel left out if you plan to sail closer to home. The principles of comfortable cruising apply in any waters.

1▶ The Foundations of Comfort

Shipboard features that answer human needs become more meaningful the longer the cruise. On a weekend sail, they're appreciated; on a lengthy voyage, they're a treasured necessity.

With this in mind, remember that hard cash and elbow grease can't erase foul play on the drawing board. Either you build the basics of comfort into your design, or your cruising days will be compromised—permanently.

Comfort is based on forethought and horsesense, not just dollars. What feels good is good, what works works. Cruising comfort depends on continuity, too: your needs probably won't change just because you move from a house to a boat. And there's another thing to remember about comfort—when you have it, you don't notice it much; when you don't, you do.

By and large, cruising sailors agree that cruising is *being* there, not *getting* there. An ocean passage is seen by many, including myself, as a ticket to the cruising grounds rather than a particularly desirable pastime in itself. Not that passagemaking is difficult or dangerous or dull. It's just that life on the hook has greater rewards. So features that enhance life while the boat is moored or anchored bear the sweetest fruit.

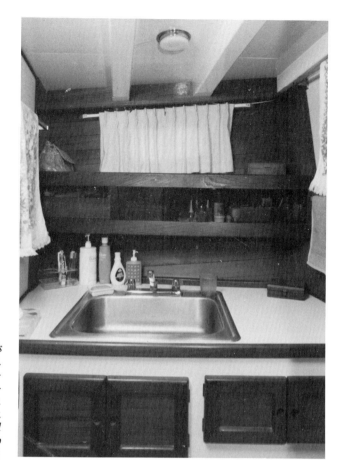

*Head compartment of author's
45-foot cutter* Dolphin Queen.
*Note towel racks, makeup cab-
inet, domestic-sized sink, stowage for toiletries under sink.
Not apparent is the shower,
multiple intensity lighting, and
forced air extraction. Photo
by John Powell.*

A HEAD IS A BATHROOM

Head compartments on sailboats are seldom worthy of being called bathrooms.
And they should be. Sure, for weekend sailors, an unpleasant head is but a
temporary inconvenience. But watch it! On extended voyages, little inconveniences all too often turn into big inconveniences.

A roomy head compartment offers welcome relief from the close quarters of
shipboard life. Ladies appreciate a sizable toilet area for primping, plucking, or
just plain privacy; men need a place to shave without barking their elbows; and
everybody aboard benefits from an out-of-the-way place to change clothes
without awkward contortions or audiences. Beyond that, a spacious head gives a
vessel an extra dimension at sea and at anchor, particularly in gloomy weather.
It's another place to be.

A roomy head provides stowage as well. Longer voyages are burdened with
sufficient toilet articles and related supplies to last the distance (soap, shampoo,

A small domestic sink under the side deck in Dolphin Queen's *aft stateroom takes the load off the main head compartment. Note folding writing desk, AC outlet, hot water radiator, and phone jack.*

towels, toilet tissue, cosmetics, medicines, etc.). It's logical to store these things in the head compartment, where they are used.

A large sink in the head is appreciated for washing hair and clothes. So is a medicine cabinet with a mirror door and glass shelving, a makeup cabinet, an illuminated makeup mirror, and bulk liquid dispensers for shampoo and hand soap.

Many sailboats over 40 feet come with two heads. While two bathrooms are popular and practical ashore, duplicating facilities aboard boats under 45 feet can waste precious space. A small counter or vanity with a sink and a mirror in the master stateroom is a workable solution. Part of the crew can wash up, shave, brush teeth, and apply makeup without tying up the main facilities. Then a single head does the job efficiently, leaving space for other important creature comforts, of which there are many.

A marine toilet should face either fore or aft. Don't bolt it down athwartships, or it will be tricky to stay aboard when the boat rolls in open water. Motion from rolling is more pronounced than motion from pitching.

Entry into the head compartment should be straightforward. Fancy, double-door entries are a nuisance. The worst setup temporarily converts (blocks?) a passageway into a bathroom or shower area with a door at each end. Your floating bathroom should be a slightly smaller version of one ashore: a handy, private area that's roomy, functional, bright, and cheerful.

A CIVILIZED SHOWER

This rudimentary facility of human hygiene should never be left ashore. Imagine sitting in the cockpit dumping buckets of cold salt water over yourself every morning of your voyage. Talk about masochism! And amazingly, people do it. Perhaps on-deck bathing is acceptable in remote, tropical lagoons, but sudsing up in front of God and everybody in cold, populous areas shocks bathers and spectators alike.

The idea that most ports of call have public hygiene facilities is a myth. If you do chance to visit a place with showers, odds are the "conveniences" won't be convenient. Maybe you'll have a marathon row in the dinghy against a strong headwind, then a long walk along a dusty road. When you finally reach the showers, you'll have company—lizards, cockroaches, and spiders. And by the time you get back to the boat, you'll be desperate for another shower. While showering ashore may be free, so is athlete's foot.

A custom fiberglass bathtub in the forepeak of a 58 footer, aft of the chainlocker. At sea, it's a stowage bin; at anchor, a pleasure, easily accessed from the forecabin.

Ideally, the boat should have a separate shower stall. However, this is not always possible on small vessels. Not to worry; a roomy head compartment makes a fine shower area, too. Just arrange a wraparound curtain that slides on an overhead track.

Ordinary detachable showerheads available in hardware stores work perfectly. Portability has advantages over fixed units: ladies can conveniently wash and rinse their hair in the head sink, and the toilet and its environs can be sluiced off quickly on cleaning day. A hand-held shower can also be led on deck through an opening port or dorade vent for rinsing off after swimming (organize a hose extension for this). This arrangement beats gravity-fed sunshower bags, which are troublesome to fill and stow and which eventually leak and grow algae.

Teak shower grids with self-draining pans underneath are traditional—and nonsensical. They hide dirt and hair that are otherwise noticed and immediately wiped up. Cleaning under grates at anchor is cumbersome; in a seaway, it's worse.

Surfacing an ordinary plywood floor and fitting it with a domestic bathtub drain(s) makes an effective water-catchment pan (a pan is necessary if a grate is used, anyway) without nooks and crannies to plague you on cleaning day. A white polyurethane paint job over a sanded and filled fiberglass laminate is sanitary and waterproof, and it reflects light for a brighter head compartment. A few strips of 3 M nonskid tape keeps a body from slipping.

BEDS, NOT BUNKS!

In your effort to build or locate a comfortable vessel to call home, give rapt attention to sleeping arrangements.

On too many sailboats, particularly racer/cruisers influenced by the IOR (International Offshore Rule), bunks are nothing more than glorified shelving. If you are a person of normal physical dimensions, some production cruising boats will also cramp your style. It pays to remember one thing about bunks: the longer you sleep in them, the smaller they get.

Recreational customers have been conditioned by salespeople to think it's a virtue if a boat sleeps a mob. They aren't fussy about comfort, so long as a boat floats while they own it and sails like a rocket. Consequently, people who live aboard often wind up with an overabundance of shelving but no beds.

Propaganda dished out by some well-known blue-water traditionalists advocating narrow "seaberths" for cruising can also result in sleepless nights, bedsores, and leg cramps. Any talk you've heard about seaberths should be taken with a grain of salt. Or take a sleeping pill—you'll need it!

Popular wisdom says we spend about a third of our lives in the sack. On a cruise, it's more like half, because a berth is more than a place to sleep; it's a *sanctuary*. There's no other place aboard that an individual can claim as personal territory. If a sailor wants privacy or solitude, he or she heads for their bunk. On a lumpy passage, a bunk is often the most comfortable place aboard, too. The offwatch can snuggle up with a good book rather than sit less comfortably in the saloon.

So the old seaberth argument is rubbish. Who wants to lounge on a slab? And narrow seaberths are not always comfortable at sea, anyway. When a yacht rolls heavily, it's helpful to assume the fetal position by wedging your body so it remains stationary in relation to the ship (knees drawn up and braced outboard, back pressed against the leecloth). Only a small child or a midget can manage this in a seaberth.

But here's the clincher: a berth may always be made smaller by shimming the occupant with pillows, sleeping bags, or spare bedding, whereas a small berth can never be made larger. You have to live with it—at sea and at anchor, where comfort counts most.

A single berth should be at least three feet wide at its head. Due to hull shape, berths are often narrower at the foot, which is no problem. It's your arms that need swinging room. A double berth must be twice as wide, although this is seldom arranged. Many berths advertised as doubles are reasonable only as singles.

In any case, comfort demands adequate berths. In hot, humid weather, when ambient temperatures are already borderline for a good night's rest, two bodies packed together turn a berth into a sauna. Even lone sleepers in tight single bunks roast from trapped body heat. What a shame to go cruising with a loved one and, after reaching paradise, wind up sleeping in undersized berths— separately.

Athwartships double berths (berths perpendicular to the boat's centerline, rather than fore-and-aft) are deservedly gaining popularity. They are built in spaces where a north/south bunk of the same dimensions wouldn't fit. As it turns out, an athwartships berth is quite comfortable offshore unless the vessel is rolling heavily. (I slept in one for three years, including a Pacific crossing. There were seaberths in the saloon, but I never needed one.) In port, it doesn't matter which way your head points. If you have a problem designing a master stateroom, try for a true double bed (queen-sized) as a first priority; the way it faces is secondary.

A berth's length depends on the individual, but it's smart to resist inflexible designs; taller folks will someday sleep in every berth aboard as guests or future owners. Berths should allow their occupants to stretch out all the way, with toes stretched out and arms comfortably folded over the head, if desired. Six feet six inches is a minimum; seven feet is better for taller folks. The industry considers a berth that's six feet two inches long to be generous, but it pays to remember that the sadists who design and build skimpy shelf-berths go home after work to sleep in king-sized beds.

Quarterberths are commonly as spacious as a coffin. Partial enclosure creates a steambath in tropical climates, and makes the berth difficult to make up. A good quarterberth (if there is such a thing) should have at least half its length exposed.

An athwartship queen-sized berth with foot partially under the side deck. Photo by John Powell.

A BERTH'S ENVIRONMENT

Since your berth is your private domain, the features surrounding it are important, too. Sitting headroom over the berth is mandatory, so you can sit or prop yourself up to read. You'll appreciate generous space over a berth when you make your bed, and the openness creates an airy, spacious atmosphere that's pleasing both physically and psychologically.

Ample sitting headroom over every berth aboard is unheard of on most production cruising boats. Vee-berths mock human need when they are placed high in the hull to create a semblance of width. (IOR-style boats are noted for sardine-like forecabins.) Forecabins are often placed too far forward, too, making it impossible to build in vee-berths of any size. Upper saloon berths are frequently located too high as well—it almost takes a forklift and pallet to get slotted into some of them. Beware of designs that squeeze 40 feet of features into 35-foot hulls. It never works.

A handy shelf for personal effects and a cup of coffee should be next to every berth. Bookshelves, drawers, and bin stowage for clothing and personal effects should also be allocated to each crew member.

If you can honestly call your sleeping cabin a bedroom, you're all set. If not, cruising could grow old.

CUSHIONS AND BEDDING

Upholstered cushions should be made from high-density foam. It'll seem overly stiff at first, but it breaks down in daily use and becomes more pliable. If you

A comfy berth on a 45 footer—6½ feet long, 3½ wide. Note bookshelves, opening ports, kerosene and electric lighting.

choose a density that feels comfortable right off the bat, your berth will be too soft in the long run. Pick five-inch foam if possible, four-inch as a bare minimum. Three-inch won't pack it; you'll be gouging the bunk board with your hips before your cruise is half over.

Forget sleeping bags for daily use. They are handy to have aboard for sleeping on the beach, but that's it. Sleeping bags are difficult to wash aboard ship, particularly in remote areas, because they take a Niagara Falls of fresh water to rinse and forever-and-a-day to dry. When you can't afford the water to clean them, which could be most of the time, they'll smell like goats.

Form-fitted sheets, blankets, and regular pillows, just like those that real human beings use ashore, are the perfect solution for sailing. Sheets are easy to wash and quick to dry, and fresh ones stow compactly.

Comforters are practical, too. In cool weather, they are snuggy-warm; in tropical climates, the quilt slips out, and the sheet envelope makes a good cover. Consider polyester rather than down comforters. They are more resistant to mildew and dry faster after washing.

LEECLOTHS

All fore-and-aft berths must be fitted with leecloths so the occupants won't be ejected in a seaway (it's hazardous to your health to go without!). A good leecloth is made of sailcloth or, better yet, of a strong free-breathing mesh called tramp netting. The bottom edge is snapped or permanently screwed to the inside of the bunk fiddle. Both upper corners are fitted with grommets, which are secured by lines to the overhead or an adjacent bulkhead (whichever achieves a 45-degree-angle fore-and-aft lead). Leecloths should be around 16 inches high, and four to four-and-a-half feet long. A gap is left at the head and foot for ventilation; besides, one's extremities need no support.

Wooden leeboards used to be standard cruising fare. They do look "shippy," but as you'll appreciate, a rigid timber partition is a miserable bedfellow at sea and, in harbor, an annoying obstruction when you want to sit on the edge of the bunk.

A GALLEY THAT'S A KITCHEN

Nothing boosts shipboard moral like good chow. To this end, a galley must be a practical, pleasant work area. The ship's cook deserves every convenience you can arrange—and then some. It's logical for the cook to have a hand in galley design and outfitting so the area is built according to an expert's needs.

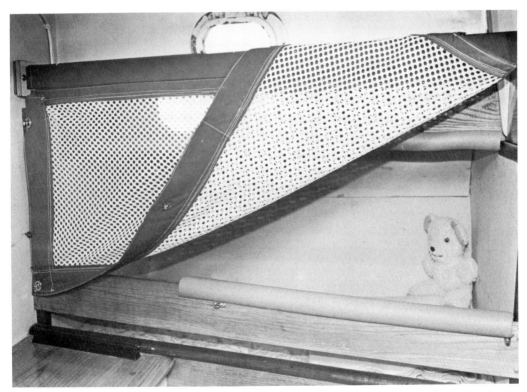

A playpen built for a newborn sailor by partitioning off half a forward berth. Tramp net screening and foam padding keep baby safe at sea or at anchor.

An upper saloon berth leecloth.

Dolphin Queen's galley. Note generous counter space; large cutting board, which stows in slot next to stove; double sinks; drawer and locker space; and outboard shelf for toaster oven or microwave. U-shaped design keeps the area free of traffic. Cutaway bulkhead joins the galley and saloon. Photo by John Powell.

Galleys shouldn't be at the companionway. This arrangement locates a vital shipboard facility right next to the weather deck in the midst of a high-traffic area—a sure way to build in harassment. Occasionally, the cook and inclement weather will clash, and the weather always wins! At the very least, a galley near the companionway should be offset outboard so it won't be invaded by pedestrians or soaked by rain squalls. But it's better off further forward, around amidships, where the boat's motion is easier and the environment more conducive to a cook's peace of mind.

Generous counter space for meal preparation is essential. Counters should be at least 18 inches deep, with one section at least three feet wide. Otherwise, activities such as baking, for which you need plenty of room for kneading and rolling bread or pastry dough, won't be popular. Counter space may be enhanced by placing the navigation area opposite. A chart table that does double duty as a bar and a galley extension in port makes intelligent use of a vessel's scant space. A navigation table that twiddles its thumbs while you're in port isn't pulling its weight.

Beyond these basics, go for appointments you enjoy (or take for granted) ashore, including a three- or four-burner stove with a thermostatically controlled oven and a broiler, and a stainless steel double sink (great at sea for securing hot

This Mariner LPG stove, a world-class appliance, has all the shoreside conveniences: self-lighting burners, thermostatically controlled oven, and, sorely missed aboard most cruising boats, an infrared grill.

foods while serving). Organize custom-designed nooks and crannies for cutting boards, appliances, glassware, cutlery, and such, so the area looks attractive and things are well secured at sea. Drawer and locker spaces in the galley (the more the merrier) should be positioned for easy access, regardless of stove position.

Some sailors advocate a traditional safety strap or belt for cooking. Your conscience will have to guide you on this. I feel the cook should be free to leap away from an overturned, boiling pot or flare-up on the stove. A safety bar in front of the stove provides good security without entrapment; it's handy to lean on or hang on, depending on the tack. Other safety rails placed where they naturally come to hand also help.

Your galley will see a lot of action; somebody will be cranking out snacks, drinks, and meals constantly. Be sure to choose a galley layout that allows at least two people to bang pots simultaneously (one mixing drinks and one manufacturing hors d'oeuvres, for example). Otherwise, you'll feel hemmed in all the time, particularly when you entertain guests. Cruising galleys require a larger percentage of a vessel's space than do recreational galleys. All the more reason to cut down on berths and heads.

THE SALOON IS THE LIVING ROOM

On vessels smaller than 30 or 35 feet, a spacious saloon is not always in the cards, particularly in light of other living or working areas that clamor for space. Nevertheless, the saloon is your below-decks social center, and it must do its job. The problem is, boat sizes vary, but people and their creature requirements don't.

Saloons function as living rooms, libraries, studies, sewing centers, dining rooms, offices, and hobby areas. Simply stated, they are the focal point of the accommodation. A good saloon drinks eight or ten, dines six—minimum—and does not sleep a soul.

That's right. Don't sleep anyone in the saloon on a regular basis; it has to remain public property at all hours. The saloon is where the on-watch roams at night on quick breaks and where insomniacs and night owls gather. If a warm body is always lying in state on a saloon berth, your boat will be a small world for her crew—too small! In adverse weather, saloon sleeping is a particular nuisance, for where else can the crew gather when confined below decks? Imagine what it would be like to have someone sleeping on your living room couch every night. Even your house would be a small world.

Saloons are lousy places to sleep, anyway, at sea or at anchor. There's activity at all hours: clanking cups and rattling hardware in the adjacent galley, radio communications, weather reports, navigational business, lockers and drawers opening and closing, lights snapping on and off. Whoever sleeps in the saloon will be last to bed and first to rise. And the daily conversion of a saloon berth from private to public property is tiresome. Lastly and most importantly, he or

A simple safety bar in front of a swinging stove prevents accidents and makes a good towel rack.

A spacious, cheerful saloon with home comforts. Formica surfaces brighten the area and accent wood trim. Photo by John Powell.

she who sleeps in a saloon is deprived of a fundamental right to personal territory.

With the foregoing in mind, a saloon table that converts into a double berth is no asset, not even for guests. If guest berths cannot be designed out of the saloon, try elevated pilot bunks.

Convertible tables also have design drawbacks. They tend to be flimsy, whereas in a seaway a table must be stout; it's often a bulwark for careening crew members. Convertible tables are not comfortable to sit at either. Since they have to fit between the dining settees when rigged for sleeping, they can't be built wide enough to overlap their settees three or four inches, as a table should. This forces you to lean forward while eating, perching less comfortably nearer the edge of your seat, and the back and thigh supports of a well-designed settee can't do their stuff.

THE ROLLS ROYCE OF SALOON TABLES

Husky fore-and-aft gimballed tables can be locked solidly at anchor or freed to self-level when the boat rolls or heels at sea. A steady, level surface for meal preparation and dining offshore is something special when everything else is in

This permanent table and U-shaped settee in a 45-foot offshore cruiser help her crew feel at home. The table support is a through-bolted tripod of varnished, laminated wood, both solid and attractive. The Naugahyde fitted cover is easy to clean, protects the table, and looks smart.

a state of perpetual motion. A gimballed table maintains its equilibrium thanks to a substantial counterweight underneath (often exceeding 200 pounds). Typically, gimballed tables are used with fore-and-aft settees, or one settee ouboard and movable chairs inboard. It's not a feature that suits dinette arrangements.

(Strictly speaking, although marine stoves and tables are said to be gimballed, they are really *swung*, because they pivot on a single axis. The term *gimbal* applies properly to the ship's compass and seagoing kerosene lamps, which self-level on both the athwartships and fore-and-aft planes.)

TABLE SPECIFICATIONS

Saloon tables should be at least 2½-by-4 feet for handwork, schoolwork, dining, and socializing. A smaller table will cramp your style.

For rigidity's sake, the table should be about one-and-one-half inches thick and, if not swung, solidly bolted to the ship at one end on a sturdy cleat and supported by a post near the other end. Tables mounted on single upright pedestals require substantial aluminum or stainless piping (at least four inches in diameter) with large, welded pads for a solid weight bearing. A good table can be jumped on anywhere without flexing.

FIDDLES ARE AWKWARD

Dispense with those traditional fiddles on table edges. They are a hindrance, particularly when dining in port (where you spend most of your time). Either fit removable fiddles or, better yet, use sticky plastic sheeting, available at ship's chandlery shops, to keep your plates and utensils from achieving escape velocity. The sticky sheets work wonders, while fiddles don't; things still manage to gain momentum and skip over them.

COMFORTABLE SETTEES

Settees in the saloon should be sofa-like in design: thick cushions with about a foot-and-a-half of front/back depth for good thigh support. Upholster the backrests, too, and rake them slightly to feel right to the loungee. Floor-to-seat distance must not prevent an adult's feet from resting flatly on the cabin sole. Test your sofa at home to get a feel for good settee design.

Curved settee ends that wrap around onto athwartship bulkheads let a person sit or recline comfortably, eliminating a hard corner.

No upholstery aboard (with the exception of water-resistant cockpit cushions) should be covered with vinyl. Vinyl, and similar nonbreathing materials, are hot and sticky in tropical climates and cold and clammy in cooler locales. A

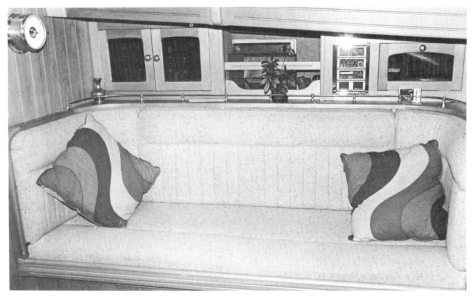

Sofa-like settees with wraparound upholstered ends give a feeling of luxury. Note the uncluttered look, with locker doors hiding shelf contents and built-in stereo system.

synthetic woven material such as nylon breathes, feeling neither sticky nor clammy. Nylon also resists mildew and when treated with Scotchguard does not easily stain.

All in all, the saloon is *the* place for your interior decorating talents to run riot, so make it as decadently comfortable as possible. Although it's traditional to retain a nautical flavor, this shouldn't take precedence over luxury. After all, it's your living room, not a historical museum.

AN ENTERTAINMENT CENTER

Some saloon layouts have two upper berths and one or two settee berths for guest accommodation. Are all these berths necessary? If not, think about converting the most convenient upper into an entertainment center. It's a perfect spot for a stereo system, slide or movie projector, guitar, autoharp, or what-have-you. And there'll be room left over for a full-length book rack behind the gear and next to the hull, and a second bookshelf right above.

COCKPIT LAYOUT

The cockpit is unique. It serves as a command center when the ship is underway and a socializing or lounging area when in harbor. For comfort's sake, think of it as an on-deck saloon. In favorable climates, it's where you'll be.

Cockpit sitting for six to eight people is a boon to cruising social life. You'll contemplate many a sunset and solve more than a few of the world's problems there. Coamings that double as backrests provide lounging-style comfort. Wide coaming tops are good for mounting winches and seating extra guests. Avoid a deep cockpit well; legs shouldn't hang in the breeze without foot support.

Lounging comfort is a good reason to locate the helm (steering wheel) out of the way. Then the entire cockpit area is free for people to move around and stretch out in. A pedestal steering setup, although popular, can be quite a

This saloon on a 47 footer has a semicircular settee with bolster cushions to provide an intimate and roomy conversation pit. Photo by Bill Montgomery.

Dolphin Queen's *saloon with a shelf behind the settee (in lieu of an upper berth) for the stereo system, slide projector, and speakers. Photo by John Powell.*

compromise on a cruising boat. It sits idle most of the time, right smack in the road. Think about mounting the wheel aft on a steering box or having two steering wheels forward, one to each side of the companionway, racing style. At sea, you'll be under autopilot or windvane anyway, and won't be using the wheel much. It goes without saying that the helm must be handy for maneuvering and steering when necessary; just try not to let it dominate life at anchor.

A single cockpit well is more convenient than a split, racing-style arrangement for lounging.

A small, removable cockpit table will see a lot of action at anchor.

COCKPIT LOCATION

A center cockpit sets the stage for headroom in an aft cabin under a raised deckhouse, sometimes a spacious stateroom. This also provides more room under the cockpit sole for a bigger engine room (since center cockpits are farther forward, the engine is located where the hull is deeper and wider). As long as a passageway exists alongside the engine room for travel between the aft stateroom and the main accommodation, the setup is great. Standing headroom in the passageway is enviable but not vital; stooping is 100-percent better than negotiating two hatchways and the weather deck to get back and forth. When you want another cup of coffee or a snack or a radio message, the hassle is madness. Furthermore, isolated aft cabins feel like prisons—you're totally sealed off from the rest of your home and your shipmates. Privacy is one thing; living like a hermit is taking it a bit far.

Aft cockpits offer different advantages. It's easier to see the entire sailplan for sail trimming and easier for the helmsperson to fend off or throw lines during docking and stern-to maneuvers with a shorthanded crew. A vessel that is not cut in half by a center cockpit feels bigger below decks because you can see more of it at once. (Center-cockpit vessels under 35 feet are likely to feel like two daysailers stuck together.)

Ideally, a vessel combines the best of both worlds with an aft cockpit *and* an aft stateroom, but this isn't feasible on most boats less than 40 to 45 feet. An aft stateroom is desirable for maximum separation between sleeping areas, and hence, maximum privacy. And the aft cockpit arrangement lets you enjoy greater operational efficiency. Pick your poison!

INVALUABLE HANGING LOCKERS

What could be more straightforward than hanging up your coat? Well, if you measured the total length of the closet space you have ashore in your house and then tried to make provisions aboard for half that, you'd end up sleeping on deck.

Tropical living won't tax hanging locker space, but cooler climates fill them to capacity. Parkas, winter jackets, heavy shirts, and long trousers come out of mothballs into daily service. Sailors learn to fold clothing they don't absolutely have to hang, yet hanging lockers may still bulge at the seams.

The number-one hanging locker is located at the companionway and should be self-draining to the bilge. This is where you hang wet gear before proceeding into the living areas (it's a good idea to fabricate a self-draining floor at the foot of the companionway stairs, too). Sailboats lacking generous wet lockers at the companionway haven't been designed by sailors. It's a feature you can't live without.

The wet locker should not be fitted with a door. When all hands are required urgently on deck, a door gets in the way. And wet gear dries faster without one.

Each sleeping cabin should have at least one hanging locker. It's probably wishful thinking to fit an extra in somewhere else for guests; the crew will claim squatter's rights before the first guest climbs aboard!

To design a hanging locker, take a normal clotheshanger (use only plastic ones—they won't rust and mark your clothes) and provide at least four inches of clearance at each end. Without good clearance, your clothing will chafe at the shoulders.

One hanging locker must extend right up to the overhead with no shelf or side deck on top. Otherwise, ladies have no place to hang long nightgowns, cocktail dresses, and winter coats. If you don't have a tall hanging locker aboard, I guarantee you'll want to give your eye teeth for one before cruise's end.

All lockers require first-rate ventilation, but hanging lockers are particularly in need, so fit only louvered doors. Without them, mildew will vandalize clothing and ruin shoes. More on ventilation later.

ROOM TO SWING THE CAT

A feeling of spaciousness, both actual and visually enhanced with decor, is important to your well-being aboard ship. For this reason, double sleeping cabins are preferable to minuscule singles. Little single cabins look cute and cozy on the drawing board, but they are often tomblike and stuffy in real life. Airy, roomy accommodation should receive priority over tiny cubicles—even at the expense of privacy.

A sensation of openness is extra-important in the saloon, where crowds gather. Galleys are commonly adjacent, and the more both areas create one great room, the better. Employ cutaway bulkheads to open up the galley/saloon cabin all you can. The boat will feel bigger and brighter, and the cook and bartender won't be shut off from people in the saloon.

The feeling of space may be improved by aligning passageways, rather than offsetting them. This lets you take in more of the accommodation at a glance. When a person in the forecabin can see all the way back to the cockpit (with the

The author's boat, with her navigation center and chart table opposite the galley for domestic use while in port. Standing at sea to plot positions is as comfortable as sitting; on the hook, a sit-down chart table wastes space. Photo by John Powell.

cabin door open), the boat seems larger. A good fore-and-aft view from the galley/saloon cabin increases apparent space, too. Being visually buried by immediate bulkheads is claustrophobic.

Natural wood paneling shrinks a space (psychologically), and traditional, paneled cabins can be coffin-like, particularly on dark days. By contrast, light-colored bulkheads have the opposite effect, making a space seem bigger than it is. And cooler, too, in hot climates. The same applies to upholstery. Light, cheery colors brighten and enlarge; dark, somber tones deaden and constrict.

A sizable mirror on a saloon bulkhead opens up the area remarkably.

Passageway cutouts in bulkheads and passageway dimensions should be generous. This enhances the feeling of spaciousness, makes it easy to stroll back and forth below decks, and is especially appreciated when you're moving gear and supplies around. Some builders, amateur and professional, fashion decorative submarine-type doorways, about four feet high with semicircular tops and bottoms. You know the ones. Although shippy-looking, they are more cumbersome to negotiate than regular doorways, and you will feel like a mole burrowing from cabin to cabin. Boats designed for living aboard should rely less on "cleverness" and tradition and more on function and practicality.

A door or bulkhead cutout should be at least 18 inches wide and reach from the floor to the overhead; stepping over sills and stooping are a constant inconvenience (sills are sometimes necessary for structural reasons, however). And such awkward areas are worse when rolling, pitching, and heeling at sea.

All walking areas below decks should have full headroom. Sleeping cabins in yachts occasionally fall short to increase floor area. Headroom can be compromised in a passageway between an aft cabin and the main accommodation on a center-cockpit yacht, as mentioned, and in the engine room. Otherwise, no.

A minimum cabin-sole-to-overhead distance to shoot for is 75 inches. This gives headroom to 99 percent of the human race. You can't very well build a boat for basketball players without sacrificing other features, unless the vessel's size presents no obstacles. Then seven feet of headroom, or more, is a superb way to achieve added spaciousness.

Fixtures that people regularly strike with their noggins must be relocated. Kerosene lamps are the most common culprits, and when lit and hot they can be dangerous. Placement of lamps, particularly on the saloon bulkheads near the table and near settees, requires some thought. So do bookshelves, electronic equipment, and electric light fixtures.

Sitting headroom is something to keep in mind, too. Settees should be positioned under side decks so people don't butt heads with the vessel as they sit and stand.

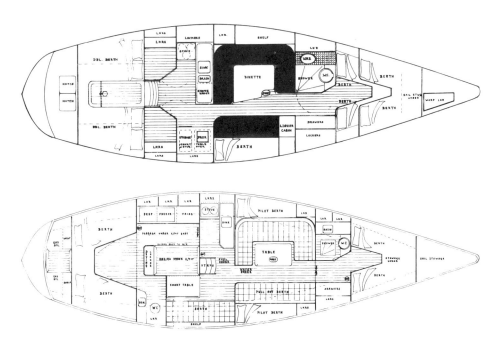

These two versions of a 46-foot medium-displacement cruiser make interesting study. The aft-cockpit design is suitable for racing and limited cruising; it sleeps a mob in close quarters. The center-cockpit layout, however, changes the whole complexion of the boat, with spacious private quarters for four and guest accommodation in the saloon. Note how the aft stateroom adds an extra dimension for living aboard. Courtesy of Salthouse Design Services, Ltd., Auckland.

A FOYER

Traditionally, offshore boats are believed unsafe if they have wide cabin soles below decks. It's said a body can be thrown from one side of the cabin to the other if the vessel lurches at sea. While there's some truth in this, particularly on tender boats, narrow floor spaces are confining. And inhibiting at anchor. With thoughtfully positioned grabrails, posts, fiddles, and handholds, a floor space five feet square—an impossibility on most vessels under 50 feet, anyway—won't let you out of reach of something solid to white-knuckle.

A small foyer area gives a boat a bigger feel, provides room for a crowd of guests to mill around while they get their bearings, lets two-way traffic pass without climbing over one another, and allows you to stand and chat over cocktails when you don't want to sit. A foyer also provides elbow room for serving drinks and food, and, when the mood strikes and the music's high, for dancing.

Compare a vessel lacking standing space, forcing you to sit whether you want to or not, with a boat that gives you the option of standing. You'll find the freedom to wander is worth fighting for. If the space is so large it bothers you at sea, cut it in half with a temporary, waist-high railing for passagemaking.

THE COMPANIONWAY STEPS

Steps for climbing in and out of the accommodation are often thoughtlessly designed and built. Even so, sailors seldom think to criticize them.

Offshore, Mother Nature sees to it that climbing stairs isn't what it was ashore, and in port you're often handicapped with an armload of supplies and gear. So, any way you look at it, steep stairs are dangerous. They must be slanted so that each successive step is clearly visible and positioned so that your foot lands on it naturally. As you ascend, ample tread offset keeps you from barking your shins. Good steps let you walk down safely with your back to them; poorly designed ones force you to turn around and climb down like a house painter.

Grab bars or posts should be placed for support while climbing or descending. Elongated cutouts atop each sideboard are handy to grasp while climbing, too. They'll help prevent accidents offshore and at anchor.

If you make companionway stairs of teak, oil the vertical pieces if you wish so they look beautiful, but leave the steps alone. Natural wood weathers quickly into a safe, nonskid surface—steps must *never* be slippery when wet. Smooth varnished or oiled steps are a menace.

Some builders screw brass or stainless strips or angles to step edges to reduce wear. DON'T! Wet metal, with a smear of oil your shoes picked up somewhere, is too slick for safety. And in case of an accident, a hard edge is merciless.

Ironically, the greatest risk on a well-prepared voyage may be a tricky companionway. If you're stuck with an obstacle course, don't hesitate to rip it out and build something safe.

REMEMBER THE RUDIMENTS

Ashore, basic creature comforts are almost considered a God-given right; afloat, there are no guarantees unless you adopt a determined attitude. It shouldn't be asking too much of a home, even a floating one, to let you walk freely, shower conveniently, dress, use the toilet, cook, eat, relax, and entertain. A home should bless its residents and guests with a good night's rest, too. Yet, although these things are basic to human comfort, designers often overlook them.

A grand staircase on a 54 footer and a roomy foyer area for milling around in. Note uniform step spacing, uniform step offset, grabrails and posts. No problem walking up and down these stairs.

Although treated with nonskid, these steps are irregular in size and awkward in a seaway. The engine gauges should be visible from the helm, not hidden below decks like this (unless duplicated on deck).

Cruising people who are thwarted in mundane, everyday activities soon learn discontent, and long-term frustration festers. This casts a pall over paradise, which leads to voyages being wound up early. Some folks learn the hard way that comfort is fundamental. Without it, cruising is no fun.

2▶ Electricity for the Cruising Yacht

A comfortable and safe cruising lifestyle relies on power—ample, dependable power. And you can have it! That old line about electricity and salt water not mixing is bilge water if your vessel's electrics meet tough marine standards. But there is a hitch: you must personally participate in the creation of your boat's electrical system. Every lifestyle has unique electrical needs.

SYSTEM RELIABILITY

Dependability and high performance are essential for all onboard cruising systems—especially the electrical network.

First, a system's output must have the brawn to cope with daily liveaboard service. Each component of a system should work at a relaxed pace for longevity's sake, and continuous duty demands must be backed by continuous duty capability.

Second, all components of a system must be designed and installed to function in the marine environment. Components must be of equal quality, too; a system is only as good as its weakest link. Rugged hardware for commercial marine service stands up best offshore; gimmicks stamped out for Sunday recreation don't. Search for straightforward equipment and strive for logical installations. The setups that provide faithful service may look simple, but they often take the most expertise to design and build.

Third, any system must be accessible for preventive and corrective maintenance. Offshore, this can make the difference between a problem quickly resolved or a prolonged breakdown, perhaps for the duration of a passage. Buried, hard-to-reach components are production expediencies that cause sailors' headaches.

Easy maintenance also relates to equipment design. Can you take something apart without special tools? Is the equipment designed for maintenance? Do spares slip in quickly without fuss? Is a component designed to be maintained *in situ,* or does it first require laborious removal? Is the equipment sold worldwide so parts and spares are available overseas? Again, commercial-grade hardware has the edge.

Part One—The 12-Volt DC System

The 12-volt system is the fundamental electrical network. It starts your engine and powers the ship's lighting circuits, radios, navigational electronics, stereos, exhaust blowers, fans, a host of pumps, and much more. The 12-volt system also energizes special equipment to create household AC (alternating current).

AUTOMOTIVE STARTING BATTERIES

Lead acid batteries store electrical energy created by the vessel's charging equipment, and 12-volt accessories tap the batteries, drawing power on demand. Batteries also act as a buffer between the charging equipment and accessories to smooth out voltage irregularities. They are rated by their storage capacity measured in amperes per hour.

Traditionally, pleasure boats reserve one battery bank for engine starting. The theory is, if the house banks are inadvertently flattened, there is still energy available to start the engine for propulsion and recharging. A fresh bank of batteries ensures quick get-aways in emergencies, too. Hand starting, although an enviable backup, can be too slow to save the day.

Nevertheless, starting batteries should be wired for switching to the house circuits for emergency power. If the ship's banks are accidentally discharged, the starting bank can keep the boat alive temporarily until charging is convenient or practical.

Automobile-type batteries are used when a bank is reserved strictly for starting. The plates and plate separators are designed to expose the maximum amount of active material to the electrolyte (acid solution) for a fast chemical reaction and, hence, the momentary bursts of energy starter motors require. Top-quality automotive batteries like the Sears Diehard work well aboard ship for this purpose.

Ask your engine manufacturer for guidelines on starting-bank capacity. Then throw in a substantial fudge factor (say another 50 percent) to compensate for aging, as batteries gradually lose their capacity to store and deliver energy. Reserve cranking power hedges your bets for brisk starts with a partially discharged bank, too, particularly during cold weather, when starting loads are high. Generous starting capacity also ensures cranking endurance for bleeding fuel-injection systems.

DEEP-CYCLE HOUSE BATTERIES

While living aboard at anchor, house banks are slowly depleted as the ship's accessories nibble away at them. When the batteries have delivered about half their rated amps, they are recharged, and the cycle repeats itself: deep discharge, quick recharge, and so on, day after day, week after week. This allows long interludes of electrical convenience, punctuated by brief charge-ups.

In normal service, starting batteries deliver but a fraction of their rated capacity. They are high-energy sprinters, not marathon runners. If they are cycled deeply, channel-type separators and low-density plates designed for speedy chemical reactions permit deterioration; the active material washes off the plates (sheds) and settles uselessly at the bottom of the battery case. Shedding occurs with each deep discharge, and storage capacity diminishes—permanently. After 50 deep cycles, or fewer, an automotive battery is finished.

Special batteries are required for deep discharge service. They use high-density plates and interlocking fiberglass separators to inhibit shedding. Examples are industrial batteries used in electric forklifts and golf carts and top-of-the-line deep-cycle recreational vehicle batteries.

Tubular cell batteries are in a class by themselves, true commercial performers outlasting ordinary deep-cycle batteries by years.

CRUISING WITHOUT A STARTING BANK?

Most deep-cycle cruising banks have plenty of punch to start an engine, but it usually takes more bank capacity to power a long-range yacht's accessories for extended intervals between charging. Thus, multiple house banks could override the need for a bank reserved specifically for starting. If, after considering the options, you don't agree, then by all means stick to a standby starting-bank system. Much depends on your house-bank capability—that is, their number and storage capacity.

Three equal banks—all of them deep-cycle—provide robust electrical capability

A cell of tubular plates (left) and a complete unit. Six of these two-volt cells in series make up a 12-volt, 210-amp/hour "battery" (amp/ hour capacity remains the same when batteries or cells are wired in series; amp/hours are cumulative when batteries or cells are wired in parallel). Tubular batteries last ten years or more in cruising conditions. The price of longevity is increased initial cost, larger physical dimensions per amp/hour, and more weight per amp/hour.

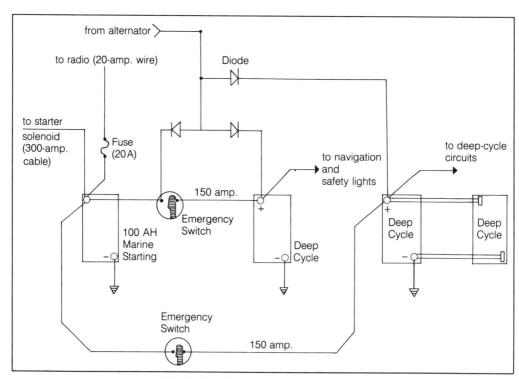

A safe and simple multiple bank option using a single large alternator. Additional alternators may be included at any bank without modifying the circuit. Diodes automatically isolate banks from each other. Note standby starting battery and deep-cycle battery (or bank) reserved for navigation and safety circuits. An additional larger deep-cycle bank serves other ship's circuits. Two manual switches bring deep-cycle banks on line separately or together for emergency starting. Courtesy of Ocean Energy Systems, Ltd.

at anchor. When no single bank is kept fully charged, sure starts must rely on forethought and judgment. First, each bank must have the beef to start the engine at half charge. Second, every bank must be wired for switching to the house circuit individually and in parallel, and each must be wired for switching to the starting circuit individually and in parallel. Third, you have to manage your electrical resources with a discharge program that reserves energy for starting. The three banks are never exhausted simultaneously (full discharge is hard on batteries, anyway). In principle, you can have power for good living and starting security without separate starting batteries. But you have to be vigilant.

By using deep-cycle banks exclusively, each bank works for a living; there is no wasted storage or discharge potential. And all banks can be grouped to apply your total electrical force to a single task, like pulling the anchor, vacuuming up a mess, or showing a movie, without the need to start an engine for electrical production.

Caution: a standby starting bank is advisable for all engines without hand starting. In the final analysis, sure starts must be failsafe.

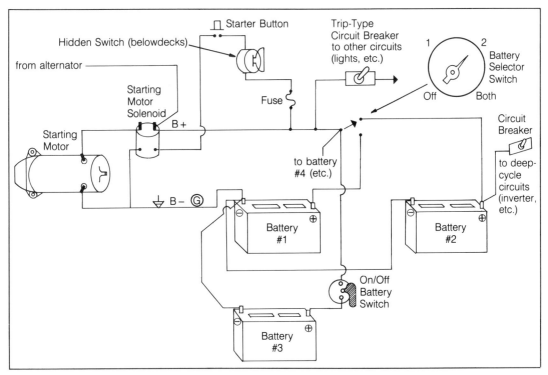

Optional multiple bank system charged by a single large alternator. Banks one and two supply ship's distribution and starting separately or together. Bank three can be brought on line, too, or isolated as a standby bank for any purpose (electric anchor windlass, emergency power for lights and radios, inverter use, etc.). Bank three would have its own alternator, not shown. Courtesy of Ocean Energy Systems, Ltd.

HOW MUCH BATTERY CAPACITY?

To arrive at total capacity, first compute projected daily consumption in amp/ hours by multiplying the current draw in amps by daily operating time in hours and/or fractions thereof for each accessory. Use the formula *amps equals watts divided by volts (amps=watts/volts)* for appliances rated in watts. The grand total is amps consumed per day. Cold-weather consumption must be upped considerably. For tropical cruising, things like 12-volt fans and 12-volt refrigeration work longer hours in hot weather (more on this in Chapter 5). Once you have an idea of your daily consumption, double it! It's not feasible, for example, to draw 80 amps of power from an 80-amp/hour battery. If you want 80 amps of useful power, you need, as a minimum, a fully charged 160-amp/hour bank to supply it—in theory.

In practice, though, you need more. Throw in an extra 20-percent capacity for expected battery deterioration. An 80-amp-per-day lifestyle now requires 200 amp/hours of storage. Well, not quite. Add another 20-percent capacity, because batteries are rarely charged up completely at anchor, and you won't have the maximum rated amperage on hand. So our 80-amp lifestyle now needs 240 amps of storage. But wait! This is a minimum for *each* battery bank, not overall capacity. Freedom on the hook is hampered by restrictive charging schedules, and several banks, each powering the ship for 24 hours, give you the flexibility to pick and choose charging times. A generous two- or preferably three-day power supply has the brawn to weather occasional lulls from natural charging systems, too.

Batteries are expensive, and it's tempting to be too conservative when computing capacity. It's also tempting to hang on to them until the bitter end to get your money's worth. You may get away with this for weekend sailing, but cruising far afield with old batteries or insufficient capacity is a different story—a hopeless battle of need versus supply.

To ensure snappy electrical performance on an extended voyage, don't cast off with batteries that will reach their third birthday before you get back. Three years (less if you treat them badly), no matter what the battery salesmen say, is the absolute limit for batteries in continuous deep-cycling service at anchor (long-life tubular cell batteries excepted). You'll see why shortly.

BATTERY BOXES

Batteries are heavy and have to be strapped down or positively confined in strong, leakproof boxes against the possibility of a knockdown or rollover. Box covers, if used, must breathe. In addition, the battery compartment must be well ventilated so hydrogen gas created during the charging cycle can dissipate. Otherwise, trapped gas sparked by operating machinery or electrics may ignite.

Never fit batteries low in the bilges (batteries in special watertight, remote-vented boxes excepted). Although placing them higher raises the vessel's center of gravity slightly, it's a necessary precaution in case of flooding—seawater kills batteries dead. In an emergency, dead batteries could be catastrophic: no radiotelephones, no electric bilge pumps, no lighting, no SatNav, no radar, and perhaps no hope.

Don't build boxes that fit your batteries like a glove. Allow an inch or so of clearance all around and use shims to take up the slack. That leaves you the option of later fitting a larger size for added capacity. Overseas replacements don't usually squeeze into tight North American boxes, either.

CHARGING AT ANCHOR WITH THE ENGINE

Engine charging is disruptive, and it's human nature to rush it. As a result, batteries on cruising boats are often abused with accelerated charging rates. To reduce charging times, many sailors manually increase field voltage (and hence generator or alternator output) during the initial part of the charging cycle compared to the gentle rates controlled by preset automatic regulators.

Mechanical regulators with accessible relays may be tweaked for faster charging by cranking in more spring tension on the voltage relay; the charge is tapered manually by easing tension. Or, voltage relay contacts can be bridged with a tiny jumper wire and alligator clips, spurring the charging machine into full gallop. These schemes are crude, if not downright murder.

This 12-volt alternator installation is businesslike. Note dual vee-belt drive and husky output cable, essential for efficiency.

It's better to employ a single-pole, triple-throw field-control switch with a rheostat for initial manual charging, a regulator for automatic taper charging, or an "off" position (field cutout). Rheostats are preferable to cruder current-boosting methods; they allow infinite adjustment at the twist of a dial.

By and large, sailors who force-feed their batteries do so out of desperation, because they have greatly underestimated the storage and charging capacity they need. Such shortsightedness results in a vicious circle: inadequacy soon becomes a terminal liability as the batteries continue to deteriorate from maltreatment. And unfortunately, replacement batteries are only a stopgap measure; they too are doomed from day one unless the system is upgraded.

Destructive charge rates brought about by inadequate storage and charging capacity are offshoots of bad preparation or bad management. However, cruising circumstances shorten battery life if the banks cannot be brought to full charge (equalization) periodically. This is not feasible at anchor with diesel-powered charging alone. Equalization from a prolonged trickle of amps is impractical in terms of engine hours versus amps stored. Only a well-rounded alternate energy package, as discussed shortly, will power your lifestyle and pamper your batteries.

Although hardly a concern to boats at anchor (but potentially so with shore power), deep-cycle batteries lose storage capacity when they are kept fully charged without occasional workouts, too.

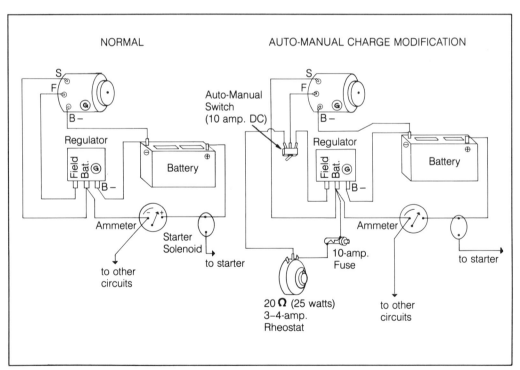

Manual and self-regulating field-control schematic. Courtesy of Ocean Energy Systems.

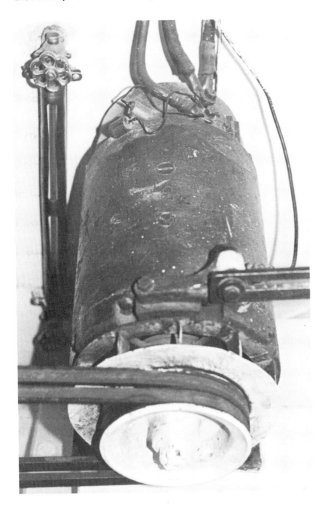

This old Delco generator was developed during World War II for landing craft. Output is about 60 amps continuous at 13.8 volts. That these machines are still in use today says something about their reliability.

GENERATING EQUIPMENT—ENGINE DRIVEN

Most marine diesels are equipped with a standard alternator, which keeps the starting bank topped up or charges one of the deep-cycle banks if there's no starting bank *per se*. But one standard alternator won't power decent living. The cruising life revolves around several engine-driven charging systems for two reasons: backups safeguard against power blackouts, and backups working together as a team greatly increase production.

Therefore, in addition to the standard engine alternator, auxiliary alternators serve each additional bank. This doubles or triples electrical output for every engine hour, which doubles or triples the stored energy available to your accessories (assuming the battery capacity is available to absorb output).

If one of the alternators walks off the job, the bank it served can be paralleled with another bank and functioning alternator, and the vessel remains a going concern. The dead alternator can be dealt with at leisure; there's no need for panic stations with backup systems. In this regard, three banks are preferable to two of the same overall capacity.

Marine alternators are designed and built for the environment, and good ones are rated for continuous duty (make sure yours are). Big deep-cycle house banks work charging devices hard. Most automotive alternators are not designed for continuous, high-output service. They replace the few amps used for starting, then loaf the rest of the time (heavy-duty units in police cars and ambulances excepted). Consequently, automotive alternators pressed into cruising service may overheat, particularly in the tropics. Overheating burns out bearings and destroys windings.

So choose husky alternators that perform effortlessly, rather than forcing lesser ones to labor at full tilt. This can make the difference between eventual failure and lifelong service. As a rule of thumb for cruising, maximum alternator output in amps should be one-third the rated amp/hour capacity of its bank. Thus, a 240-amp/hour bank is charged by a 75-amp alternator.

Install identical alternators all round. And tuck another safely away as a spare. Then each machine can be quickly replaced, even at sea. Think about exchanging the standard alternator on the engine for a bigger one matching the others, particularly if it too charges a deep-cycle bank. It's always preferable to

Perhaps the most sophisticated and efficient windmill available for yachts worldwide (12-volt, 100-watt, five-foot model shown). It features permanent magnets, three-phase AC output (rectified to DC), tapered roller bearings, hollow aerodynamic blades, constant speed governor, and watertight electrics. Designed service life is 25 years. Manufactured by Ocean Energy Systems, 20 Wynyard Street, Devonport, Auckland, New Zealand; distributed in North America by Whitefish Marine Inc., 4611 11th N.W., Seattle WA 98107.

upgrade one component rather than bring a whole network down to the lowest common denominator. And common equipment reduces outlays for spares.

Whether or not you decide on field controls that let you select both manual and automatic charging, it's smart to have field-cutout switches to positively disable each alternator. Otherwise, the combined load of multiple alternators may work against your starter motor, making engine starting sluggish or impossible. The reason: vee-belt step-up ratios for full output and cool running at fast idle (to charge on the hook) cause alternators to put out at engine-cranking speeds, too. Field cutouts also relieve an engine of alternator loads for propulsion in emergency maneuvering. This is vital when every horse counts!

It's a good practice to warm up the engine for a few minutes before kicking in all the alternators. A 60-amp alternator takes approximately one horsepower to spin at full output; three horsepower will gang up on a cold engine. After warmup, the extra load of multiple alternators is welcomed at anchor. The engine's combustion chambers run hotter, and the injectors stay cleaner.

Alternators have overshadowed generators in automotive applications, because they produce electricity at low engine speeds. They are also lighter, more compact, and have superior cooling for tropical service. But commercial and military versions of Delco generators, to name one brand, also perform at low rpm's. If you find one of these treasures in a surplus yard, it could be your friend for life. Generators have the advantage of being easily jury-rigged if a regulator goes on strike and there are no electronics to worry about.

SUPPLEMENTARY CHARGING DEVICES

Efficient charging by diesel power is an important facet of a flexible 12-volt system, but it's only the beginning. When a vessel is anchored or under sail, it's not thrifty or pleasing to the ears to fire up the engine if you have other sources of energy—particularly those supplied gratis by Mother Nature. Harvesting energy from nature gives the opportunity for a high standard of living—anywhere.

THE WINDMILL ALTERNATOR

More and more boats are seen in anchorages with curious propellers—windmill alternators—spinning in the breeze. These machines are hoisted aloft in the rigging, out of harm's way. A tail plane weathercocks them into the eye of the wind. And, nearly silently, they spin out amps day and night.

Windmill alternators must be sizable to be major contributors to shipboard power. The little ones with two-to-three-foot propellers trickle out an amp or two in normal wind conditions—hardly worthwhile to those who count on the benefit of electric living. In a gale, toy windmills whir out four or five amps, but you can't very well wait for gales to run the stereo.

Windmills six to eight feet in diameter are something else. They'll supply power to meet most electrical needs in ordinary wind velocities (8 to 12 knots). In tradewind locales where the wind blows 15 to 20 knots consistently, an anchored yacht with a good windmill will have a generous supply of silent power on tap for music, lights, pressure water, radio communications, conversion to AC, ice-cold beverages, even ice cubes.

Efficient, state-of-the-art windmills are built around a custom alternator with a rotating field of permanent magnets bedded in epoxy. This field spins around the *outside* of the stator windings (the opposite of normal alternators). A windmill's alternator is larger in diameter than engine-driven types, output being equal, increasing the speed of the rotor in relation to the fixed stator for operation at reduced rpm's. This is important. Engine-driven charging equipment can be spun at any rpm by manipulating vee-belt pulley ratios. Not so with windmills. Blade design and wind velocity dictate rpm's, and the alternator must be built specially to work under variable wind conditions. Also, rpm step-ups on windmills (via vee-belts) kill efficiency by introducing extra friction. For decent windmill performance, friction must be kept to a minimum. The best windmill alternators use tapered roller bearings immersed in an oil bath for low friction and long service life.

The permanent magnetic field, as opposed to the electromagnetic fields of engine-driven alternators and generators, contributes greatly to economy. If the wind dies down below charging velocity, windmills with electrically excited fields discharge batteries. Permanent magnetic fields do not. A well-designed windmill gives but never takes.

A state-of-the-art windmill can increase battery life. It's liable to be the only charging system you have with the guts, prolonged output, and energy-free, quiet operation to equalize your house banks fully at anchor.

SOLAR CELLS

Solar cells convert sunlight into amps for battery charging. The panels have advantages—no moving parts and no maintenance. They are bolted permanently in place to function at sea and at anchor. A rectangular panel approximately one by two feet will trickle out about three-quarters of an amp per hour in brilliant sunlight. Cost is high, dollar for amp—up to eight times more than a good windmill, depending on local wind and cloud behavior—but this is partially offset by convenient, hassle-free service.

Despite modest output, solar panels can be a charging aid well worth having aboard. They probably won't supply enough power on their own to meet your needs, but that's not the point. A few panels in parallel add to net daily electrical production. And every amp counts.

Don't count on full output from sunrise to sunset, because performance varies with sun angle. And unfortunately, when a shadow falls across a few cells (from the ship's rigging, for instance), the panel's output falls markedly. For best

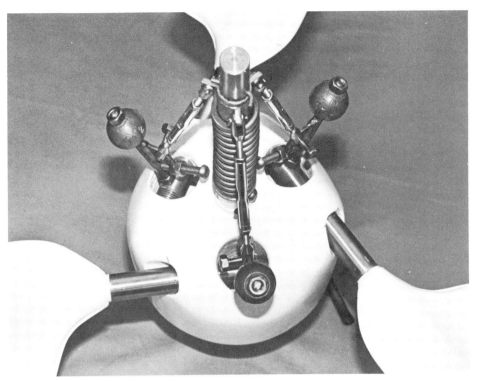

The guts of Ocean Energy's 100-watt windcharger showing the spring-loaded centrifugal governor and variable-pitch mechanism. The alternator is made of epoxy/fiberglass, stainless steel, and bronze to withstand the marine environment. These machines are designed to begin charging at low wind speeds (six knots) and produce significantly in average wind conditions. Peak advertised output of more rudimentary windmills measured at higher wind speeds is meaningless to the liveaboard.

results, solar panels should be positioned in areas freely exposed to the sky. Even so, if you honestly want five amps from panels, you had better buy at least ten amps' worth. Manufacturers' advertised outputs are not based on average conditions.

WATER-DRIVEN CHARGING DEVICES

A sailing vessel moving smartly through the water has the potential to create huge amounts of electrical energy. This is accomplished via water-powered propellers spinning alternators.

One type available over the counter resembles an old-fashioned taffrail log. The alternator sits on the stern rail and trails a line and a propeller. Many manufacturers of wind chargers offer this option. They have one main disadvantage: a rat's nest when the spinning line and propeller snare a fishing line. Rigging and unrigging them can be a bit fussy, too, particularly when changing from the windmill mode to watercharger mode at sea. All the same, they work.

Another type looks similar to a small electric outboard motor and clamps to a stern bracket. The propeller drives a powerhead alternator. Output is generally less than taffrail types due to smaller proportions. But something going into the batteries is better than nothing. They have the advantage of easy deployment, and they don't interfere with trolling.

When choosing a wind- or watercharger, remember: they must deliver the goods in average conditions. Theoretical peak output at high wind or hull speeds is meaningless.

FREEWHEELING SHIP'S PROPELLER

More substantial water-driven charging systems are custom made to work off the vessel's drive train. A large pulley is fitted to the propeller shaft, and an alternator is belted directly from it. The propeller shaft is allowed to freewheel as the yacht sails.

Output from a vessel's freewheeling alternator under sail can be astounding—more than enough to run 12-volt refrigeration, lights, electronics, and an electric autopilot. But don't count your amps before they're hatched; there are tricks to freewheeling success.

Boats under 40 feet in length do not always generate as much power under sail in average conditions as is first hoped. There are two reasons for this. One, longer waterlines tend to give more boat speed, and speed through the water is critical. Generally, five knots is the threshold at which freewheeling begins to generate. And two, smaller boats tend to have smaller propellers, and propeller size and configuration are major factors in success. For low-rpm applications like water-charging, three-bladed props tend to create more torque than two-bladers of the same diameter (similarly, three-bladed props are more efficient for motoring and maneuvering). As a rule, propulsion propellers under 18 inches in diameter are likely to be borderline performers.

On the other hand, props over 22 to 24 inches in diameter and boat speeds in excess of six knots generate more amps than you would believe: anywhere from 15 to an incredible 40 amps per hour, depending on the installation.

Freewheeling ship's propellers wear out cutless bearings more quickly because the shaft turns constantly at sea rather than staying braked. Pack a few spares aboard. Also, investigate the effects of freewheeling on your reduction gear's thrust bearing. I freewheeled a Borg Warner Velvet Drive transmission from Seattle to Auckland without a hitch. Periodic startups (a five-minute run three times every 24 hours) helped keep the thrust bearing lubricated. Despite continuous, day-in-day-out use, it always ran cool.

Velvet Drive transmissions have planetary reduction gears that absorb considerable power while freewheeling. You'll need to average at least five-and-a-half knots and have at least a 20-inch, three-blade prop to generate five amps

A 15-inch driving pulley gives this setup a seven-to-one step-up ratio. With a 20 x 16 three-blade propeller and drag from a Velvet Drive transmission, output is zero amps at five knots, five amps at 5.5 knots, ten amps at six knots, and nearly 15 amps at seven knots. Alternator is junkyard Mazda. No field control necessary.

and up. Otherwise, look around for a hydraulic transmission without planetary gears or think about a manual transmission.

Freewheeling propellers turn slowly, peaking at around 400 rpm's. Figure on 150 to 200 rpm's as an average. You need a pulley ratio of about seven to one to twist the alternator fast enough for electrical output at sailing speeds (most small alternators begin to charge at 1,050 to 1,200 rpm's). If your pulley ratio is lower, the system won't work. Beware of a pulley ratio that's too high, though. The ratio's upper limit is dictated by prop-shaft revolutions when motoring at full power. The alternator must not exceed its maximum speed (check with your manufacturer, but commonly between 8,000 and 12,000 rpm's).

Automotive alternators are fine for freewheeling. Output seldom, if ever, tests the alternator's capability, and overheating is no concern.

METHODS TO INCREASE FREEWHEELING EFFICIENCY

The most effective way to increase freewheeling performance is a dog clutch (also known as a sailing clutch) with a separate thrust bearing. This gadget disconnects the propeller shaft from the engine's transmission. Considering that reduction-gear drag exceeds alternator drag, this really improves output. A dog clutch lets smaller vessels with smaller props have working freewheeling setups, too. And larger boats fitted with them generate power at slower boat speeds. The extra output at higher speeds (it could double!) can be converted to 110 volts AC (once the batteries are up) for watermaking, heating water, vacuuming, and such.

Freewheeling efficiency can also be improved by replacing the common vee-belt setup with a flat, notched belt drive. Belt friction is thereby reduced by ten to 15 percent. A flat belt also bends more freely around its pulley than a vee-belt does. This means you can use a smaller alternator pulley, and hence, a smaller pulley on a prop shaft in tight quarters.

Efficiency goes downhill when step-up ratios are achieved in two jumps with an intermediate lay shaft. Another vee-belt and two extra bearings rob power.

Variable-pitch propellers offer a chance for more efficiency, because they can be adusted for maximum freewheeling torque under varying charging loads and boat speeds. Fixed propellers designed for driving or pushing are at a disadvantage when spun by water flow. A fixed prop designed for both freewheeling and powering will improve freewheeling at the expense of powering. Sometimes you just can't have your cake and eat it too.

A SEPARATE FREEWHEELING INSTALLATION

A final freewheeling scheme makes use of an offset propeller shaft with its own stern bearing, low-friction stuffing box, and thrust bearing. It is not used for propulsion. Commonly, systems designed specifically to do one particular job are the most effective. In this case, the propeller can be shaped exclusively for freewheeling, and no power-robbing freeloaders like reduction gears and large-diameter shafts (more bearing friction) detract from performance. Also, sufficient output is possible with smaller propellers (diameters of 14 to 18 inches). Drag from the extra prop is minimized under power or sail by using a two-bladed wheel, which, in an efficient application like this, works. Better yet, use a variable-pitch prop that can be feathered when watercharging isn't required.

Brakes are necessary to halt prop-shaft rotation and shut down watercharging on all systems except those directly coupled to a manually clutched transmission. Hydraulic sailing brakes that automatically apply friction upon engine shutdown are convenient (used with hydraulic transmissions only). For freewheeling, fit an in-line ball valve to keep the brake pressurized in the open position after engine shutdown (the valve is shut while the engine is running). To stop shaft rotation with the engine at rest, simply open the valve.

WINDMILL AND WATERCHARGING REGULATION

Most powerful windmill and water-driven charging systems require voltage regulation so they won't overcharge the batteries in high-output situations. Upper-limit cutouts give minimum protection, terminating the charge when battery voltage reaches a preset value. These are manually reset. More elementary systems are switched on *and* off manually. Very low output chargers hooked to large battery banks may require no regulation whatsoever—overcharging is impossible (usually when average output is less than five percent of bank capacity).

High-tech windmills and taffrail waterchargers generate three-phase AC that's rectified to DC. One regulation scheme employs electrical braking. When the batteries are up, a direct short is induced by the regulator, and the machine slows to a crawl, still under load since the short circuit is isolated from the batteries by a diode. Windmills with electrical braking should be fitted with a toggle switch to stop rotation manually as well. This is a handy feature for rigging and dismantling, although manually operated swing tails stop rotation by forcing the blades edge-on into the wind.

More commonly, automatic regulation of windmills and waterchargers with permanent magnetic fields is done by switching their output to a dummy load (fixed resistance), because electrical braking is not always forceful enough to control overspeeding in all conditions. The dummy load is simply a heater coil mounted on the regulator or, more usefully, immersed in a hot water tank. Output current is switched automatically back and forth from the batteries to the fixed resistance as required. Thus, the machine remains under load continuously so it won't overspeed and suffer damage.

Waterchargers with electrically excited fields (mainly those with automotive alternators) should be manually regulated by a rheostat or a simple on/off switch. Automatic regulation causes prop-shaft revs to fluctuate unpredictably during light charging loads at high boat speeds, resulting in overspeeding and excessive shaft vibration. This wears bearings needlessly. It's better to bring the batteries up with a reasonable load on the alternator, brake the shaft when battery voltage reaches the limit, and switch off the field voltage. Field voltage to the alternator should be supplied from the alternator side of the ammeter. Then net charge into the batteries shows on the instrument. Remember: slow boat speeds will discharge batteries if the field current is inadvertently left on.

ELECTRICAL DISTRIBUTION

Manufacturing sufficient electrical current and storing it for later use is a step toward cruising in style. But it all counts for nothing without first-rate distribution. Too many cruising yachts—otherwise nice boats—make a mockery of the electrical art; some out of Taiwan have cornered the market on electrical chaos.

SOLDER ALL JOINTS

A great opponent of electrical reliability on cruising boats are those dreadful, automotive crimp connectors. They are so commonplace nowadays that you can't be blamed for thinking they're okay for marine applications—just about every boatyard uses them. Yet, the first step toward a lasting and efficient

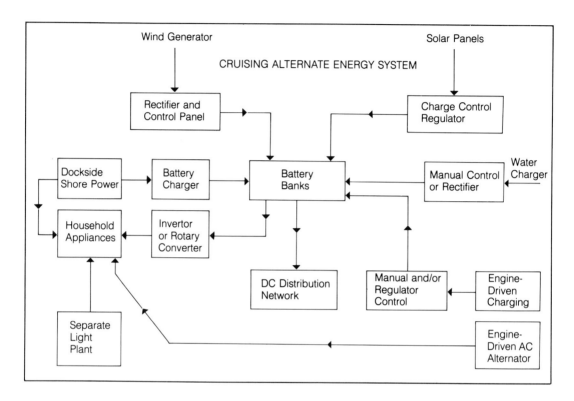

CRUISING ALTERNATE ENERGY SYSTEM

This sanitary distribution panel features digital amperage and voltage readouts, both DC and AC, and hour meters for engine, refrigeration (to compute daily running times), and generator. Breakers are logically grouped: lighting, pumps, blowers, electronics, and AC power. Also incorporated is an alarm section. Photo by Bill Montgomery.

electrical network is the elimination of weak links. And crimped connectors are weak links.

All wiring must be soldered! This includes the joints at the masthead, the spreader lights, nav lights, every wire-to-terminal connection below decks, battery cables, the works!

Marine electricians, professional or amateur, who crimp connections on an ocean-going yacht without soldering them lay the groundwork for future misery. Corrosion is an ever-present enemy aboard ship, and electrical systems built to automotive standards are living on borrowed time.

Wire-to-wire joints are best avoided, too. Continuous runs of wire are more reliable than joined scraps. Unfortunately, boatyards frequently join shorter lengths of wire with crimp connectors in the most outlandish places. A favorite spot for a crimped joint is inside a bow or stern pulpit to connect a nav light. This is dynamite! When hidden corrosion blacks out a nav light, as it can, there is no quick remedy. The connection has to be fished out and redone.

Wire-to-wire joints, when unavoidable, should be firmly twisted together mechanically, soldered, and protected with heat-shrink tubing. Heat-shrink tubing does a good job of sealing out moisture and is a less bulky insulator than the plastic-covered crimped connectors. This simplifies stringing wiring through tight spots during construction and simplifies retrieval, if it ever comes to that.

SUPPORT WIRE SECURELY

There are no applications aboard ship for agricultural electrician's tape. It eventually loses its grip. If it was used to cover a bare joint, there is the possibility of a short circuit. If the tape secured a wire or a wire bundle, the wiring won't be secure forever.

Instead, use plastic quick-ties to discipline and organize wiring. They are available with a lug for a screw or bolt to fasten a wire or wire bundle permanently to the ship. Tie your wire bundles every six inches with quick-ties and fasten them to the vessel every foot or so. Single wires are best supported with plastic clamps (always use nonconductors to support wiring so chafe won't cause fireworks).

The practice of routing electrical wiring through PVC tubing is gaining popularity in production ships. It looks neat, but *please don't do it!* Tracing faults and adding new circuitry is all but impossible. Keep in mind the rules of good system design. One of them is easy accessibility to every component, including wiring.

PROTECT COMPONENTS FROM THE ENVIRONMENT

To combat corrosion, position electrical components in protected areas free from salt spray and moisture. Pay particular attention to fuse panels, switch panels, and distribution panels. These nerve centers belong under side decks away from hatches and opening ports. Cockpit instrument panels must be protected by sealed Lexan windows.

Sometimes it's necessary for switches to be placed in the weather where you can reach them from the helm. If so, watertight switches and switch boxes are available for the job (you'll find them where commercial fishermen shop). Don't be tempted to mount a cheap hardware-store toggle switch near an exposed area. It won't survive.

BEWARE OF THE VOLTAGE DROP

A foe of electrical efficiency is what's known as the voltage drop. Corrosion at unsoldered wire-to-terminal joints or metal-to-metal contacts at junction blocks causes voltage drops that worsen with time. A corroded connection eventually fails completely. Automotive crimp connectors create more than their fair share of voltage drops on boats that sail oceans.

Poor engineering can cause built-in voltage drops, too. The more current an electrical accessory or appliance draws, the larger the wiring to that device needs to be to carry the load. And the farther an accessory is from a distribution panel, the larger a conductor's diameter must be as well. This is vital in high-amperage situations like 12-volt refrigeration, high-wattage radiotelephones, 12-volt bilge pumps, big exhaust blowers, and search lights.

When wiring size is inadequate, some of the energy meant for an accessory is wastefully radiated as heat directly from the conductor, and the accessory is on short rations. Some electronics are voltage sensitive, so that a voltage drop is harmful. In extreme cases, a voltage drop causes overheating and permanent damage (some 12-volt refrigeration inverters are particularly fussy).

To test for voltage drops, first turn on the accessory in question. If the accessory has a variable setting, turn it to full output (in the case of a radiotelephone, you would set the instrument to "transmit"). Then measure the voltage at the battery terminals with a voltmeter. Record the reading and compare it with voltage measured at the accessory. A variation of a quarter-volt or more is bad news. It's prudent to correct a variation over a tenth of a volt.

Undersized alternator-output wiring, commonplace on pleasure boats, causes a voltage drop between the output terminal and the battery bank, and some of the energy that should be charging your batteries never gets there. Check this out while the alternator works hard against a discharged bank by measuring voltage at the output terminal and at the battery. It should be the same.

Wiring that's warm to the touch is terribly inefficient. Hot wiring is *dangerously* small for the job. Considering the small additional cost and long-term benefits of appropriate wire sizes, it's a pity most boats are wired so inadequately. All it takes is a little understanding to do it right.

AWG WIRE SIZES FOR CRUISING 12-VOLT SYSTEMS

(3 percent voltage drop)

Maximum Current in Amps	Feet from power source to accessory and return										
	20	30	40	50	60	70	80	90	100	110	120
5	14	12	12	10	10	8	8	8	8	8	6
10	12	10	8	8	6	6	6	5	5	5	4
15	10	8	6	6	5	5	4	4	3	3	2
20	8	6	6	5	4	3	2	2	2	2	1
25	8	6	5	4	3	3	2	1	1	1	0

Adapted, by permission, from *Your Boat's Electrical System*, Conrad Miller and E.S. Maloney, page 58, copyright 1981, The Hearst Corporation.

12-VOLT WIRING TIPS

Avoid running wiring through the bilges. Pumps and other electrical appliances below the cabin sole should have their wiring fed down directly from a higher level. The most convenient location for wiring is at the hull/deck joint. Then individual circuits may logically branch off on their appointed rounds. The trouble is, a tight hull/deck joint is imperative; otherwise, there'll be trouble.

Mechanical joints such as terminals bolted to junction blocks, gangplugs, jacks, and battery-cable lugs must be kept bright and conductive with a protective film of Teflon grease. It prevents corrosion by displacing moisture, so smear on plenty.

Don't design tricky circuits. For example, vessels have been wired so the current from an alternator to a battery bank is interrupted if a master switch is put wrong while charging. If the alternator still feeds the ship's distribution network during the interruption, a voltage spike zaps whatever accessories were turned on, and the alternator's diodes may commit suicide in sympathy. When the engine is running, or when it's at rest, no switch, however it's set or thrown, should have an adverse effect on equipment. Wiring and switching must be idiot-proof. Even if you think you'll remember a strange switching arrangement, one day in the heat of the moment you'll surely forget—and blow it!

One way of avoiding trouble is hard-wiring the alternators directly to the battery banks they serve, bypassing the selector switches altogether. Since you will have one alternator for each bank, there is no need to switch the output from bank to bank as recreational systems do for charging multiple banks with a single alternator. Hard-wired alternators always charge their assigned banks, regardless of battery-switch position. With large alternators, this takes quite a load off a master switch, too, eliminating one more component in a high-amperage circuit (always desirable). Also, the alternator's output lead is shorter when it doesn't detour to a switch; short runs are most efficient.

Loose mast wiring spells trouble. Sooner or later it beats itself to death. Secure it *outside* a length of PVC piping with quick-ties and fasten the piping to the inside of the mast with sheet-metal screws. Since there are no wires in the pipe, the screws can't cause short circuits. And this way, wiring doesn't hang in the tube without support. Provide an extra set of wires at the spreaders and at the masthead that can be fished out someday for additional accessories.

Protect each and every accessory with either a circuit breaker or a fuse. *No exceptions!* And color code your wiring so future alterations, additions, and trouble-shooting will be straightforward.

MONITORING THE 12-VOLT SYSTEM

A system with alternate energy sources, several banks of batteries, soldered joints, efficient wiring and distribution, and moisture protection goes a long way to ensure an electrically enhanced cruise. But you have to know what all your amps are doing, or you can still end up in the dark.

Each charging device should have its own ammeter to measure output. Most automotive ammeters are too insensitive; it's best to use commercial-quality instruments showing one-amp increments. (Smith's top-of-the-line gauges, made in U.K. and standard on Lister engines, are nice.) Sensitive gauges are particularly important in low-amperage circuits of auxiliary charging systems so you can adjust the equipment for optimum output.

Wire your alternator ammeters to indicate true current flow by placing the instruments *between* each charging source and its battery bank. Another ammeter is placed between the primary discharge circuitry and the battery selector switches. Then input and output readings are kept separate, showing exactly how much the charging units are producing and exactly how much the ship is consuming. Most recreational builders connect the charge and discharge circuits to a single ammeter that reads zero when charge and discharge current are equal, regardless of amperage.

Tying input and output current into a single ammeter does show net charge to the battery or battery bank in the circuit (or net discharge as the case may be). At first, this seems of real value, but it's not. What's important is the *state* of charge. Is the bank fully charged, or nearly so, or is it just about flat?

A delicate discharge ammeter helps you assess the condition of your boat's distribution network. With the master switch on and every single accessory switched off, you theoretically should have a zero discharge reading. Watch the ammeter as you cycle the master switch off and on. If the ammeter deflects toward the discharge side as you engage the master switch, there is a load (resistance) somewhere. Start isolating circuits by pulling fuses or throwing breakers until you find the culprit. This helps locate corroded switches, leaky junction blocks, and/or malfunctioning appliances. Sometimes an alternator's regulator circuitry draws a fraction of an amp when the system is at rest. If you discover yours does, switch the rheostat/automatic switch to the central (off) position or switch off your field cutout. This should chop the current to the regulator.

An accurate discharge ammeter also tells on greedy accessories, giving you the option of replacing them with more efficient ones.

Determining state of charge requires another instrument—the voltmeter. All battery banks should be wired to a voltmeter via switch(es) that select each bank individually. Even if you have three banks, use just one voltmeter. Individual instruments may vary, and accurate comparison between banks will be hit or miss (multiple voltmeters are okay if they can be user-calibrated to read identically).

Choose a voltmeter with an expanded scale between 11 and 15 volts. Values outside this range are beyond a 12-volt system's normal operation and of no concern. A sensitive instrument is important. Try to find one that indicates to the tenth-volt, even if this requires a bit of interpolation.

While the batteries are charged, the voltage gradually climbs. When the automatic voltage regulator is in action, there is nothing to do but watch. However, if you are in the manual mode, and the reading reaches 14 to 14.1 volts, you have to make a decision. If engine time is a factor, you have the option to stop. This gives you about an 80-percent charge. If you want to bring the batteries up further, carry on charging but keep backing off the rheostat (or switch to automatic), thereby reducing the alternator output so the voltage is held in check. If the charge rate (amperage) is already tapered well down by either manual or automatic regulation, the batteries are probably 90 percent up (at 14 to 14.1 volts). True float voltage (100-percent charge) is a few points higher, but you won't generally waste engine hours to achieve it unless the vessel happens to be under power.

It's important to monitor voltage and battery behavior together. Manual charging isn't too destructive to the batteries' lifespan so long as it's done with care. Avoid excessive gassing and watch for heat buildup—if you cook a battery by overcharging it, you've consigned it to an early grave. Remember: you can't afford to let a manually excited alternator run overtime *once*. Use a loud kitchen timer, caution, and your voltmeter.

Use your nose, too! While experimenting, uncover your batteries and get to know them personally. If you smell acid in the air, they are being charged too vigorously—back off on the voltage! Acid fumes result from excessive gassing. Electrolyte pooling around the filler caps may be another sign that you are overdoing it, unless the batteries are filled too high. Leakage is caused by heavy gassing, too.

When charging terminates, voltage falls back to 12.5 to 13, depending on temperature and the specific gravity of the electrolyte. Then the reading gradually declines with discharge until the battery bank has nothing left to give (approximately 11.5 volts indicates rock bottom). If you value your batteries' health, though, never permit full discharge. When accessories such as fans operate lethargically and lights grow dim, the voltage is much too low.

To get a seat-of-the-pants feeling for a safe low-voltage threshold before recharging or termination of discharge (i.e., switching the vessel to a fresh bank), check cold-engine starting performance at progressively lower levels. Naturally, this concerns only deep-cycle banks, not a starting bank, if applicable, which cannot be cycled. Once you find the bottom line for brisk starts, record it. Do this with each bank individually; paralleling them to test for quick starts is cheating, because it's your ace in the hole for emergencies. Next, determine the voltage at half charge as indicated by a hydrometer, corrected for ambient temperature. Your battery manufacturer will supply you with a table of specific gravities relative to states of charge. Now, whichever voltage level is highest and therefore safest (the one for quick starts or the one at half charge, according to the hydrometer) is a workable low-voltage limit. As your batteries age, this level will need revision.

Combining intelligence from ammeters and a voltmeter helps trouble-shooting. For instance, a depleted bank that soars to maximum voltage as soon as charging begins is on its last legs (unless too many amps are being forced on too little battery capacity). Batteries should control voltage for a gradual rise. If a bank hits bottom quickly after chargeup, there is something amiss with the batteries or a big resistance in the circuit somewhere. A no-load situation over a week or two when the boat's idle and all switches are off should not cause an appreciable drop in voltage, either. If so, the batteries or wiring need a checkup.

LOOK FOR A SANITARY INSTALLATION

Whether you have a trained eye or not, it's easy to recognize a well-wired boat. *Look for compulsive neatness.* Wiring arranged in an orderly and logical fashion, with great attention to detail, is a sure sign the electrician had skill and incentive.

Messy, tangled runs of wire wound hither and yon should promote deep suspicion. The same goes for haphazard placement of important panels and equipment. Almost without fail, disorder means trouble.

THROW AWAY THE KEY

Most modern marine diesel engines come complete with a panel, which should have gauges rather than idiot lights to monitor the engine's vital signs, such as oil

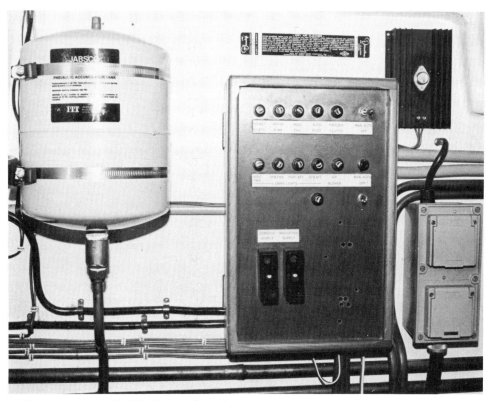

Meticulous attention to detail is the sign of a craftsman.

pressure and coolant temperature. Many manufacturers incorporate a key-start switch on the panel. Since your diesel engine uses compression ignition, not electric ignition, the key serves no useful purpose. Do yourself a favor: deep-six the key and replace it with a push button. Install oil pressure switches to replace the "on" function of the key switch, which energizes your charging circuits and engine alarm systems.

A key switch usually corrodes and causes grief sooner or later, but more to the point, keys of any kind aboard ship are a damn nuisance. Combination locks at hatchways and push-button starting will simplify your life. In an emergency, you want the engine running *now*, not after a frantic search for a misplaced key. Wire a toggle switch cutout in a hidden spot below decks to disable the starting circuit for security when you're ashore.

SPARES AND TOOLS TO MAINTAIN A 12-VOLT SYSTEM

A good system won't act up more than once in a blue moon, but you better have comprehensive spares and tools aboard just in case. Take along a multimeter so you can check voltage and resistance in a suspect circuit or accessory. For electrical work en route, either repairs or additions, you'll need solder, nonacid electrical flux, a soldering gun, a butane soldering torch, a selection of wire terminal ends matching what's used aboard, a few extra junction blocks, a selection of wire in various sizes and colors, a wire crimper/stripper tool, a pair of heavy side cutters, a small vise, a variety of quick-ties and wire bundle clamps, and an assortment of heat-shrink tubing.

Spares not specifically mentioned elsewhere include a selection of fuses (or breakers), toggle switches, windlass foot switch, a battery master switch, an oil-pressure switch, a replacement voltmeter and ammeter, voltage regulator(s), backup fan motors (cabin, radiator heater, air-cooled refrigeration condenser, etc.), squirrel-cage blower motors, pump motors, alternator parts like bearings and slip rings, and light bulbs or spare fixtures for everything (compass, nav lights, strobes, flashlight, dome lights, instrument lights, etc.).

On a voyage to remote areas, the foregoing may only be the tip of the iceberg, depending on how your boat is equipped. You can see how important spares become, electrical and otherwise. When all toggle switches, for example, are identical throughout the vessel, it's simple to organize backups. The same goes for fans, blowers, basic categories of light fittings, pumps, etc. If you intend to build a boat, remember equipment continuity. And as you purchase hardware and equipment, buy backups, replacements, and/or spares right on the spot. Otherwise you'll have to retrace your steps later, when the trail is cold. Some things you'll overlook; others will be out of stock.

Part Two—110-Volt Alternating Current

A flexible 12-volt system adds so much to the cruising life that doing without it is like turning the clock back a hundred years.

A 110-volt AC electrical network, once considered the domain of goldplaters, has also become an ordinary part of cruising comfort. Shipboard AC enhances your standard of living by powering luxuries and conveniences you had ashore. The same is true of 230-volt, 50-Hz shipboard power in countries where applicable. The rules of installation are similar.

SHORE POWER

It's beneficial to provide a shorepower system during construction whether or not you intend actually to produce 110-volt AC current aboard. You will appreciate the efficiency and safety of convenient outlets throughout the boat for lights, power tools, heaters, and fans, eliminating a snakepit of tangled extension cords. And it's easier to install 110 volt AC before cabinetwork gets in the way.

When the boat is launched and you live aboard at the dock, you will appreciate the AC network every day and forget the slight initial cost.

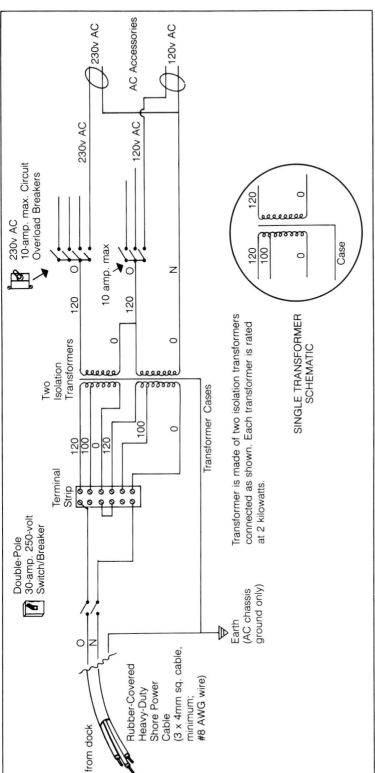

This shorepower circuit is designed for international travel with two, 2-kw (2,000-watt) isolation transformers. By rearranging wires on the terminal strip, a variety of input and output voltages and amperages are achieved at 50 or 60Hz. Each transformer has two taps to fine-tune output. Incoming voltages may be in the 120v or 240v ranges; output is 120v and/or 240v, depending on whether the transformers are wired in series, in parallel, or used separately. Both incoming lines are isolated so appliances such as a good automotive battery charger may be used safely. The AC grounding network services AC equipment only—never connect it to the 12v DC grounding or bonding system! Note the double-pole input breaker/switch, a vital component for chopping both incoming lines so the system is safe for switching terminal leads or working on electrical equipment regardless of reverse polarity or corrosion at the dockside receptacle. Tar-potted transformer windings stand up best to corrosive cruising conditions. (Ocean Energy Systems, Ltd.)

DO'S AND DON'TS OF AC WIRING

AC circuits are similar enough in houses and boats to lead the amateur electrician astray; although the differences are subtle, the repercussions can be serious.

The first discrepancy is the wire itself. Ashore, single-strand copper wire is used. Aboard ship, due to vibration from the power plant, single-strand wire can fatigue and break. Only multiple-strand wire has the flexibility to endure.

Next, because of the corrosive marine environment, the quality of the components must be upgraded. Most domestic fittings used in housing make poor sailors. Modern domestic outlets, for example, are plated steel, which rusts when exposed to salt air. Outlets designed with a push-in self-locking hole for single-strand conductors are not suitable for marine applications, either. Like 12-volt wiring, 110-volt AC wiring must be soldered to terminal ends bolted to the components.

Circuit protection aboard also must be of a higher grade. Use a Lexan breaker panel or plastic breaker box, not the domestic painted steel units. And marine circuit breakers resist moisture; domestic breakers do not.

Each circuit must be safeguarded by a breaker. Certainly, most dockside receptacles are protected from overload, but reliability is questionable. And they use a single large-value breaker, around 20 to 30 amps—too big to protect each circuit aboard ship adequately. Generally, 110-volt AC shipboard outlets use ten-to-15-amp breakers (230-volt AC outlets, half as much); other circuits are protected with a breaker rated slightly above the expected load. Only fast tripping prevents damaged appliances, smoldering wiring, or personal injury.

The boat's main circuit breaker should be double pole to isolate both the phase and neutral circuits; household breakers are single pole. Since current leakage due to corrosion is not uncommon in dockside power receptacles, it's important to break both incoming lines to stop stray current when the boat's unattended.

Ashore, the ground (earth) wire is attached directly to Mother Earth, but this is not done aboard. A marine AC system is fully floating. In other words, the ground wire does not connect electrically to the boat's structure, her nonelectrical equipment, nor to the negative (also called ground) circuit of the 12-volt system. To do otherwise invites damage to underwater metallic components by electrolysis. There's also a possibility of ruining your neighbor's day in the bargain.

In addition to circuit breakers, ground fault interrupters (called earth leakage breakers in some countries) should be considered. These are special circuit breakers designed to trip when a small resistance is sensed between the live and ground circuits. Salt water is an excellent conductor and consequently a hazardous environment for faulty, high-voltage electrics. A ground fault interrupter protects you against dangerous shocks from bad wiring or defective appliances and is imperative in potentially lethal 230-volt AC systems (or an isolation transformer).

If you are building your own boat, the AC system is one area where you should seek professional consultation to double-check your conclusions. It might only take an hour with a qualified expert to check your system, ensuring the safety of you and your boat.

THE STEP-DOWN TRANSFORMER

In many countries, 110-volt AC is not supplied. New Zealand, Australia, and Europe, for example, have 230-volt (sometimes called 240-volt) AC current supplied at 50 Hz (cycles per second), unlike the North American 60 Hz. Appliances with 60-Hz electric motors run about 20 percent slower on 50 Hz, yet most operate satisfactorily. However, a transformer is necessary to step 230-volt overseas voltages down to 110 volts.

At first glance, a transformer that knocks 230 volts down to 110 to 120 volts would seem right. Note quite! Ideally, the voltage should be lowered a bit more, to 100 to 105 volts. Otherwise appliances with electric motors (electric typewriters, sewing machines, drill motors, etc.) designed to operate at 60 Hz and running slower on 50 Hz could overheat.

The best transformers for cruising have a series of output terminals to choose from for fine-tuning output voltage. This inexpensive feature is important in less developed countries and island nations, where domestic voltage is wildly inconsistent. Regardless of incoming voltage, output can be set just the way you want it.

With this in mind, it's better to organize a transformer that meets your specifications beforehand and build it into the boat permanently. Choose one with plenty of capacity, say at least 3,000 watts (3 kw), so you can heat water and use the microwave, or operate the toaster oven and charge batteries at the same time. Often, the limitation on shorepower usage won't be your equipment. Most of the waterfronts of the world seldom have outlets capable of more than two kilowatts (2,000 watts) before something ashore trips, smokes, or melts.

STEP-UP TRANSFORMERS

Sailors from 230-volt AC countries take the opposite approach with a step-up transformer when visiting 110-volt AC areas. Then their 230-volt stuff works on North American voltages. Actually, transformers are often identical; how you hook them up determines whether they step up or step down.

Technically, stepping down is preferable, giving cruising folks with 110-volt AC systems the advantage, as amperage on incoming shorepower lines is halved. Conversely, stepping up from 110 volts to 230 volts doubles the incoming load, which requires heavier input wiring. And obviously, 110 is going to be a lot safer around salt water than 230.

AN AC VOLTMETER

Since shoreside sources for domestic power (either 110-120 volts or 230 volts) can be inconsistent, as mentioned, you need to know what's coming aboard. An AC voltmeter wired to the incoming AC line tells you this. A second voltmeter is handy for monitoring transforming output so you know what your goodies are actually getting and, in the case of variable output transformers, which output terminals to select.

SHOREPOWER BITS AND PIECES

Pack aboard some short lengths of 30-amp cable (identical to your existing shorepower cord) to make adaptor pigtails. On each, wire a standard marina-type outlet that fits your shorepower cord. At the other end, wire plugs purchased in your travels that fit the overseas receptacles. After visiting a few countries, you'll have an inventory of pigtails, allowing you to plug in anywhere.

Stow several three-conductor extension leads, one of them 50 to 75 feet long and at least number 8 AWG, to increase the length of your existing shorepower cord for plugging into distant receptacles. Take along a light-duty extension cord (12 to 14 AWG) that reaches the masthead from an onboard power source so repairs or modifications requiring power tools or soldering irons can be carried out anywhere aboard.

MANUFACTURING YOUR OWN 110 VOLTS AC

Equipping a boat to make use of shore power when berthed near an electrical receptacle is part of the game. After all, dockside power is there for the taking. And it's convenient. However, much of cruising is spent on the hook amid the real attractions, and comfort there is the name of the game.

The pleasures of AC really come into their own out in the boondocks. Particularly in the galley. It adds spice to life when you can pull a few modern conveniences out of the hat—things like an electric mixer, a food processor, a toaster oven, a blender, an electric coffee grinder (why not?), and maybe a microwave oven. Remember: what's ordinary ashore is extraordinary afloat. AC power is handy for maintenance, too. Electric-drill motors, soldering guns, sanders, and saws all have their day.

Best of all—and a shame to do without—is a domestic vacuum cleaner (most 12-volt ones have emphysema). Hoover's Porta Power, a compact, one-horsepower marvel, works wonders for cleaning lockers, bins, shelves, and carpets.

Further uses for AC power are: electric scuba compressors (eliminate the gas engine), slide and movie projectors (it's fun to show pictures as you take them, rather than waiting months to see how they came out), an electric typewriter (why go back to the Stone Age for cruising?), and an electric sewing machine.

POWER INVERTERS

Inverters draw from the 12-volt system and output AC power. They are a valuable cruising aid, compact and simple to install. They're available in sizes to fit all budgets and all power requirements, from mini 10-watt small fry all the way up to 2,000-watt (two-kilowatt) workhorses and beyond.

A 500-watt inverter covers a lot of bases aboard a yacht by running power tools, most kitchen appliances, typewriters, and sewing machines. A 1,000-watt inverter makes you feel like you never left the dock. Verify the wattage of the appliances you plan to sail with and choose an inverter to handle the largest load you can't get along without.

Inverters vary in quality, but even cheap ones can be quite effective. Most of them deliver square-wave AC output, and some of your appliances may run a

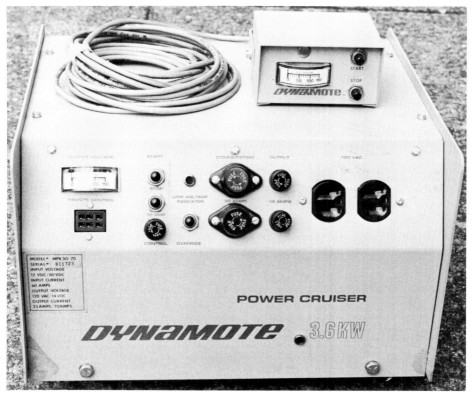

Dynamic inverters provide AC power from the DC output of a standard 12-volt alternator while the engine is running. Unit pictured delivers a maximum of 3.5 kilowatts. Static inverters, although similar in appearance, operate directly off the batteries whether the engine is operating or not. Photo by Jon Skoog.

little slower than they did ashore. Normally, this doesn't matter a bit. More sophisticated inverters, however, output a modified frequency closely resembling domestic sine-wave AC, and they'll run anything.

Also available are marine inverters that produce AC from DC and rectify and transform AC shore power to DC for battery charging. This combines two functions in one unit to save space.

Small inverters under 1,000 watts are seldom wired into the shorepower circuitry; appliances are plugged in directly. So, shorepower wiring or not, you can have AC power aboard.

ROTARY CONVERTERS

Another machine tapping the ship's battery banks for AC power generation is the rotary converter (also called motor generator). It's a compact unit containing a 12-volt motor coupled to an AC alternator (either 110v, 60 Hz, or 230v, 50 Hz), outputting real sine-wave AC like domestic electricity in a house.

A good example is Honeywell's Rediline motor generator, popular with cruising sailors and marketed worldwide. The Rediline operates on the demand principle: As a load is sensed in the circuit, it automatically kicks in. When an appliance is shut down, the converter shuts off too, conserving 12-volt power.

Honeywell's Rediline motor generator supplies AC power from the batteries on demand. This is the 1.8-kilowatt (1,800 watt), 12-volt-to-110-volt AC model. Note input fuses.

WHAT COMES OUT, MUST GO IN

Healthy AC outputs, from either an inverter or a rotary converter, require equally healthy DC inputs. For instance, a 100-watt, 110-volt AC sewing machine draws about ten amps at 12.5 volts DC, assuming a 20-percent conversion loss. This won't overburden an engineered 12-volt base designed to cope with AC conversion, and diversified charging systems will quickly replace consumption. But you can't tack an AC machine onto an anemic 12-volt system and expect anything but flat batteries.

Many cruising people find an inverter or rotary converter raises their standard of living so much that no other method of manufacturing AC current is necessary. Often a convenience appliance like a vacuum cleaner or a blender is in operation for such a short time that, although loads on the 12-volt system may be high, the duration of the load is shortlived, and total amperage consumed is modest. (A 20-minute cleaning job with a one-horsepower vacuum cleaner at 20-percent loss in conversion efficiency equals 25 amps at 12.5 volts DC. A one-horsepower blender zapping a piña colada for 30 seconds consumes only 0.5 amps at 12.5 v!)

Timing the use of inverters or rotary converters lessens strain on batteries. Chores may be scheduled to take advantage of periods when 12-volt power is in good supply (a fair breeze turning a windmill, for example, or a good turn of speed offshore with a water-driven charging system or while motoring in a calm).

The advantages of 12-volt-powered AC systems are quiet operation, low cost (compare to the following AC schemes), and easy installation. AC power is available at the flick of a switch without involving the vessel's power plant or an auxiliary generator set.

ENGINE-DRIVEN AC ALTERNATORS

If your AC requirements exceed what a 12-volt-based system will deliver, an alternator belted off the propulsion engine is the answer. The addition of an AC alternator is fairly straightforward on boats already wired for shore power. The alternator shares the same network; input choice is managed via a triple-pole, triple-throw selector switch (off, generator, or shore power).

Two general types of AC alternators are on the market. The simplest relies on constant engine speed to regulate output (since rotational speed governs Hz); another is self-regulated by a variable-ratio belt drive, which maintains steady alternator rpm's over a range of engine speeds (examples are the Auto-Gen and Vari-Gen). Belt-driven alternators for cruising usually output 3,000 watts (3 kw) and up. They'll handle things like AC refrigeration, AC scuba compressors, microwaves, washing machines and driers, and so forth.

Alternators belted off the propulsion engine without variable ratio drives should be geared for AC generation both on the hook and underway. A fast-idle, slow-cruise setting (commonly around 1,200 revs) is a good compromise.

A no-nonsense direct-drive AC alternator installation. Output is a maximum of 3.5 kilowatts (3,500 watts) at 230 volts, 50 Hz.

THE HERTZ METER

Your engine's tachometer indicates the approximate rpm for controlling AC frequency, but you need a meter displaying cycles per second for precise regulation. Many alternators have built-in safety circuits, which kill field current when the machine spins too fast or too slow—a desirable feature. This protects against overheating and possible damage from running under load at incorrect rpm's.

A hertz meter also monitors the frequency output of separate light plants to make sure diesel governors are set properly.

SEPARATE AC LIGHT PLANTS

Few cruising boats under 50 feet in length can accommodate an auxiliary power plant specifically for generating electrical power. Alternators belted off the

Vari-Gen's variable-ratio, 110-volt, 60 Hz AC alternator. Output, approximately 4.5 kilowatts (4,500 watts).

propulsion engine are much simpler, cheaper, and take up much less space. For most cruising families, a separate setup adds too much additional complication, too—another starting system, cooling system, fuel system, and exhaust system, plus maintenance of another diesel engine. However, a marine light plant generates enough pleasure to meet any standard of living, and it is very much at home on a bigger boat. There comes a point when operating large propulsion engines to spin tiny (in relation to engine size) alternators is too inefficient. A separate AC electrical plant makes sense when several thousand watts of power, or more, are required for long periods each day. The sky's the limit: diesel generator sets are manufactured from 3 kw all the way up to monsters that can light up entire cities.

If your cruising life centers around an auxiliary generator, make certain the exhaust system is whisper quiet. The same rules of courtesy apply to propulsion engines used for battery charging or AC production. With today's waterlift exhausts and secondary rubber mufflers (like Elastomuffle), there's no reason to disturb an anchorage—or yourself.

MODIFYING ACCESSORIES

An amp saved is an amp earned. Greedy AC appliances should be replaced by ones with smaller appetites whenever possible. This saves energy and money, and you may find a less elaborate and less powerful AC system does the job. A blender, for example, which draws 1 kw (1,000 watts) can be retired in favor of a new machine that draws only 500 watts. Or install a microwave oven of 750 watts input instead of 1,500. In both cases, your lifestyle stays relatively intact.

Also, an appliance can be modified to consume less power. For instance, a slide projector's 500-watt bulb can be exchanged for a 200-watt bulb, and 12-volt electrical consumption from an inverter or rotary converter is cut by 25 amps or more per hour—an incredible energy savings! Powerful projection bulbs are unnecessary for close-quarters viewing below decks, anyway. Even 100 watts is sufficient.

Converting part of an appliance to 12 volts also saves power. I modified a Bell & Howell slide cube projector by fitting a duplicate quartz reflector-type bulb of 100 watts, 12 volts (USHIO Halogen JCM), which fits right into the existing bulb socket. The socket wiring was isolated from the projector's AC circuitry and plugged into the boat's 12-volt system directly. When the projector was used at anchor, only a few watts of AC from a smaller, more efficient inverter powered the fan and slide changer. Since the conversion of 12 volts DC to 110-120 volts AC is less than 100-percent efficient—actually approximately 60 to 90 percent, depending on the inverter or rotary converter—direct 12-volt consumption saves energy.

Sometimes an appliance may be made more energy efficient by eliminating a feature you can live without. For example, removing the light bulb from a 110-volt AC sewing machine saves considerable power, particularly when it runs off a 12-volt-based AC source.

Another energy-saving scheme works with appliances with several power settings. For instance, an AC soldering gun with two trigger positions—150 watts and 300 watts—works fine on the lower setting. It just takes a few more seconds to heat up.

Although personal computers can be plugged directly into an onboard power source outputting sine-wave AC, many of them are basically DC machines in the first place (AC is converted to DC by an internal power supply). If you wish to have a personal computer aboard, talk to a technician familiar with your equipment. It may be simple to modify it to run directly off 12 volts. This saves considerable energy by avoiding the conversion of DC to AC and then back to DC again.

BATTERY CHARGERS

It's wasteful to fire up the engine to charge batteries at the dock when shore power can be exploited. True marine-type chargers, commonly called converters or rectifiers, isolate both incoming AC lines from the 12-volt system with a double-wound transformer. Automotive chargers isolate only one AC line and therefore are discouraged by most bureaucracies responsible for marine standards because of potential AC leakage into the 12-volt system due to reversed polarity or dockside wiring problems.

Nevertheless, a commercial-grade automobile battery charger may be used aboard ship with an isolation transformer, or perhaps without if you watch polarity (the phase line must be isolated), if you have first-class AC and DC wiring, and if you have an electrolysis monitoring system. It's a tempting option in light of a marine charger's high price tag per amp and general lack of features important to the liveaboard.

Your cruising battery charger should have both manual and automatic voltage regulation so you can control charge rates as shipboard life dictates. Additionally, the charger should have an ammeter indicating output and an adjustable timer for operation over a specified period with positive shut-down. The more control you have over charge rates and incoming shorepower loads, the better. Unfortunately, few marine chargers give you this control.

Living aboard ship at the dock places heavy demands on battery chargers. It's easy to err by choosing a charger that's too small. Anything less than 50 amps output is likely to prove inadequate for handling big cruising banks. Ideally, charging is done with dispatch and terminated so the other AC appliances have a chance at the shorepower supply (more on this in the next chapter).

A charger should live in a bone-dry place close to—but not with!—the batteries. Short cables are best. Make sure there's no voltage drop between the charger and the batteries at maximum output. Otherwise, the charger will be fooled into thinking battery voltage is up when it's not, and your banks will never be fully charged. This has plagued many sailors, and it's been their own fault for hooking chargers up with inefficient wiring.

For tropical service, choose a charger with forced air cooling (a fan). At the very least, install the charger where there's generous natural ventilation. Considerable heat dissipates from transformer windings and diode heat sinks.

At anchor, a powerful AC battery charger provides another useful backup charging system on vessels equipped with AC alternators.

Part Three—Ship's Lighting

Kerosene illumination is ineffective and inconvenient except for atmosphere. Moreover, in the tropics, kerosene lamps raise cabin temperatures uncomfortably, and highly refined smokeless and odorless fuel is not always obtainable in remote areas. Electric light is the only way to go. After all, it's the 20th century.

RUNNING LIGHTS

The 1976 Colregs (International Regulations for the Prevention of Collisions at Sea) specified ship-lighting requirements, but these regulations should be seen by offshore yachtsmen as substandard. Your colored lights should be visible at least four miles away, and your white lights, at least six.

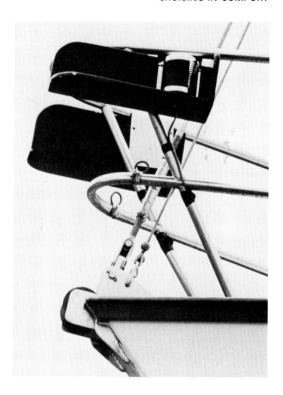

Port and starboard running lights mounted so they don't shine on sails. Note shielding to eliminate ambiguity, although this is not usually critical with good vertical filament light fixtures.

Vertical filament bulbs in fixtures with edge-glued, sectored lenses are a great improvement over useless first-generation navigation lights. Now, for the first time, you've a chance of being seen at sea. Shipping lanes are meaningless anymore. There is traffic everywhere, so it's unhealthy, not to mention unsociable and selfish, to sail a blacked-out ship. A cruising boat must show her nav lights all night long, every night. In this age, an electrical system that can't power a few amps' worth of running lights is irresponsible.

Red and green port and starboard lights should be mounted high on the bow or bow pulpit so they won't ruin night vision by reflecting on sails. In addition, carry a combination masthead tricolor, which conserves power by using one bulb for three functions (a good idea even if your boat is too large to carry it legally). Lights behind flush-fitting, colored Plexiglas lenses in the hull are unacceptable; they offer no sector demarcation, and others cannot judge your course accurately.

The steaming light (now unromantically called the bow light) is used when a vessel is motoring under power. It lives high on the front of the mast. On double-headed rigs, it should be mounted above the inner forestay. Then it won't shine on a staysail while you're motorsailing.

The stern light is near the helmsperson, particularly on aft cockpit vessels, and it needs special attention so it illuminates nothing aboard. Make sure it's brilliant and very high off the water so freighters overhauling you can see it miles away.

To repeat: no navigation light should illuminate decks or fittings. If they do, fabricate shields to shroud them. Otherwise, running the ship at night will be a game of blindman's bluff. Regardless of boat size, choose big lights that do a seaboat justice—a 30-footer needs to be seen just as badly as a 60-footer!

ANCHOR LIGHTS

Position the anchor light at the masthead for unimpeded, 360-degree visibility. Use a number 90 bulb, drawing about one-half amp per hour, a pittance to a good 12-volt system. Then you'll feel inclined to run it continuously after dark in every anchorage. Vessels without masthead anchor lights are vulnerable to collision, particularly where there's commercial activity at night. Kerosene lanterns hung in the foretriangle are hidden by the rig at certain angles. They tend to be dim at best, and they blow out or run out of fuel when you need them most. And kerosene riding lights are a hassle to rig and light.

MASTHEAD STROBES

A masthead strobe light for cruising is not optional. There are times when it's indispensable. Some strobes for pleasure boats overheat and fail in continuous duty. Guest's 250,000-candlepower fixture, although not as powerful as others (such as Perko's), is more reliable, perhaps because less output means less internal heat buildup. Aircraft strobe lights, although expensive, are ideally suited for cruising, because they are very powerful and function continuously in severe service.

Strobe lights penetrate fog like no other light. Powerful ones actually reflect off moisture high in the atmosphere and can be seen over the horizon. Technically, strobes are supposed to be emergency lights. However, in thick weather, anything that advertises your position and helps others see you has merit—emergency or not. Some offshore cruising people operate them all night, every night. They treasure their skins above all else.

SPREADER LIGHTS

Spreader lights serve two purposes, and it's convenient to have a set for each contingency. Bright, four-inch, sealed-beam units light the decks to assist boarding parties in an anchorage and help with activities like retying the dinghy and adjusting an awning.

However, bright spreader lights will blind you on a dark night offshore. Smaller fixtures with bayonet-type sockets fitted with number 90 bulbs (as a starting point) provide soft illumination for working the ship. Not one boat in a thousand has two sets of spreader lights, but make sure yours is one that does. As a bare minimum, install a rheostat to dim sealed-beam units.

A COCKPIT LIGHT

For an inexpensive feature you'll love in port, mount a small dome light with an integral switch on a piece of quarter-inch plywood. Drill a couple of holes in the plywood base so it can be lashed under the boom, directly over the cockpit. A length of wire and a plug fitting the searchlight socket at the companionway finishes the project. With a tiny bulb, it directs a muted glow over your cockpit for boarding, after-hours socials, or as a night light (in addition to the anchor light) when you go ashore. It's great for cockpit dining, lighting a tabletop better than kerosene lamps. And you can flick your little cockpit light on and off at will. Best of all, it draws next to no power.

THE SEARCHLIGHT

A hand-operated quartz-halogen searchlight is a standard cruising tool. You'll use it to check your position in an anchorage in relation to shoreside landmarks. At sea, it lights up sails to broadcast your position to a ship that's too close for comfort. And it's useful to retrieve something lost over the side. A searchlight even provides entertainment by illuminating fish and other organisms in the water alongside the vessel.

To rig a searchlight, you'll need a socket on the foredeck and a long cord to reach the stern and amidships from the companionway socket.

FLASHLIGHTS

One flashlight should live at the companionway so you can grab it from the cockpit or from below decks for tasks like checking the engine room or helping someone climb aboard. Mount another in the galley for lighting the oven, checking the souffle, and topping up kerosene or alcohol pressure tanks. A third hand light is convenient near the forecabin for use in the head and forward stowage areas.

Convenience aside, it seems the more desperately you need a flashlight, the deader the batteries. But with three or four hand lights aboard, you'll surely be able to find one that works!

Diving lights are the best flashlights for cruising. They are fully waterproof so the innards won't corrode. And ones with three batteries (D cell) and large reflectors are brighter than common household types. Diving lights also float!

BELOW-DECKS LIGHTING

Every berth and every settee should have a swivel reading lamp at each end. A light at the berth's foot may not be used for reading, but it's handy for area lighting. Offset your reading lights so they'll shine on the page of a book, not the back of a head. And place them outboard so they won't interfere with getting in and out of a bunk.

Swivel lights with translucent shades do a better job of lighting a cabin, yet opaque shades may be preferable in double cabins where shielding protects another's right to sleep.

Most bunk and cabin lights come with standard bulbs that will practically burn the pages out of a book. Lower wattage bulbs are less harmful to night vision at sea and use less energy. So again, little number 90 bayonet bulbs are about right. At sea, you may find smaller ones plenty bright.

Make sure to carry a selection of bayonet bulbs of various wattages to tailor illumination to different circumstances.

MULTIPLE INTENSITY LIGHTING

The head, galley, and saloon are three areas that benefit from two or three levels of illumination.

Level one serves the on-watch at night when they need to use the head, pour another cup of coffee, or check a chart or a reference book of the stars. These activities require muted lighting, a rarity on production boats. Although red lighting is traditionally advocated as least destructive to night vision and is therefore used frequently in navigation areas on yachts, in practical terms the scheme has drawbacks. To be effective, every light you use must be red. Lighting a cigarette, flicking on a flashlight, or using a white dome light means that you'll have to stabilize your night vision all over again. Furthermore, reference books and some charts have colored features that are camouflaged by red light.

Normal, low-intensity lighting is a more practical alternative. Perko's No. 140 12-volt light is one inexpensive way to achieve night lights throughout the yacht. This tiny fixture has two mounting holes (no switch) and can be mounted anywhere. Just make sure your night lights are under something: a cabinet, locker, shelf, side deck, or whatever. Low-level lighting must be indirect so you are not blinded by the fixture's filament.

A Perko 140 light at the companionway is handy to have on all night. Power drain is infinitesimal. A dim glow around the steps lights the way without distracting the helmsperson. Others at the chart table, galley, and in the head are godsends offshore. Toggle switches may be positioned where convenient, and the lights themselves mounted where they are most effective. Once you have them, you'll love them. And they cost peanuts.

MIDDLE-OF-THE-ROAD INTERIOR LIGHTING

The next level of illumination is provided by dome lights with bayonet sockets. Most of the time, you'll use six-watt number 90 bulbs in them, at least at sea. In

Deadlights are effective illumination aids, and they don't drain the batteries. They are particularly help-
ful over the galley, saloon, and in the head compartment.

port, you may decide to put in larger, 25-watt bulbs for brighter light in key
locations (saloon and galley, most likely).

Dome lights are universal cruising lights. Install them in the engine room, the
chainlocker, the saloon, hanging lockers, lazarette, galley, head, sleeping-cabin
overheads, passageways, wet locker, you name it. It's good policy to put them
anywhere you feel there is a slight chance of needing them, including most areas
where you normally poke around with a flashlight. A light fixture draws
nothing when it's off; salting the boat with them simply adds convenience.

HIGH-INTENSITY LIGHTING

Many shipboard activities rely on brilliant lighting. Sewing, maintenance on
delicate equipment, arts and crafts, schoolwork, and cooking while in port are a
few examples.

The best alternative for high-level illumination is fluorescent lighting, giving
the most light for the least energy with a minimum of shadow. Fluorescent
fixtures over the saloon table, in the head, over galley counters, in the engine
room, and in some passageways can be morale boosters at times, too. Brilliant
interior lighting at anchor or dockside makes the vessel seem larger, helping to
create a festive, cheerful mood, especially when the crew is confined to quarters
during bad weather.

Use double-tube units only. Single-tube fluorescents are more likely to
interfere with radio receivers and flashing depth sounders. However, double-
tube lights do impress some AC ripple into the 12-volt system. This is easily
remedied with 25-volt, 5,000-microfarad capacitors wired in the boat's circuitry

at each junction where fluorescent-light wiring ties in to peripheral wiring. Make certain to observe polarity when installing the capacitors, and interference will be history.

McClean Electronics' Travelight is a 12-volt, double-tube fluorescent that's reliable for cruising. Stock up on spare tubes and stow a complete spare fixture just in case the tiny inverter dies (they last years). Select tubes with a color temperature similar to incandescent light, rather than the usual cold, bluish light of traditional fluorescents.

Quartz-halogen is another source of bright cabin light. Although more economical to operate than normal incandescent tungsten bulbs in terms of output versus amps, quartz-halogen bulbs radiate considerable heat, noticeable in the tropics. They are also costly to replace and have a fairly short life. However, quartz illumination is a good alternative for those who don't like the feel of fluorescent light.

RHEOSTAT CONTROL

The spreader lights are not the only lights that benefit from rheostat control. The compass light should be adjustable for ambient lighting conditions so the card is clearly visible without causing eye strain. The same is true of the cockpit engine-instrument lighting and lights at the chart table. On the social side, if you liked variable intensity lighting over your dining-room table ashore, for a few dollars you can have it aboard in the saloon. It's cozier when lighting is adjusted to match the spirit of an occasion.

A DESK LAMP

With so many lights below decks, it's not always appreciated that fixed bulkhead and overhead fixtures are somewhat inflexible. In fact, however, sewing, school-work, arts and crafts, typing, intricate repairs—any close work—will be enhanced by a portable light source that can be directed exactly where you want it.

A common, garden-variety gooseneck desk lamp with a weighted base solves this problem. Convert it to 12 volts by exchanging the AC bulb for a 12-volt, 25-watt bulb or by jury-rigging a bayonet socket in place of the original 110-volt screw socket; wire a 12-volt plug to it, and install a 12-volt outlet where the lamp is to be used. Your 12-volt desk lamp will see a lot of use.

A TROUBLE LIGHT

You can convert a domestic mechanic's trouble light to 12 volts simply by exchanging the medium screw bulb for a 12-volt one and fitting a searchlight plug instead of the 110-volt AC plug. Then you have a bright portable light for maintenance, checking plumbing, looking for leaks, you name it. It can be used to light the decks in harbor, too.

Part Four—Tying It All Together

Metallic underwater components—skin fittings, rudder bearings, propellers, and propeller shafts—are vulnerable to deterioration unless protected. A faulty electrical system can cause a form of metallic disintegration called electrolysis.

Underwater fittings are also potential victims of external electrical activity, such as electrical problems on a neighboring boat, a faulty dockside electrical receptacle, steel dock components without protective anodes, or nearby marine construction activities (welding can be bad news!). Another phenomenon, galvanic corrosion (the chemical reaction between dissimilar metals in an electrolytic solution such as seawater), can destroy skin fittings, too.

Although galvanic and electrolytic processes are two different things, a bonding system will help protect your boat against each. First, ensure that all metallic underwater fittings are of high-quality bronze or stainless steel. Through-hull valves should not contain steel or brass parts. Rudderposts, bearings, propellers, and propeller shafting must be made of acceptable marine materials. This isn't usually a problem when the source of the components is a recognized marine outfit, as opposed to some obscure salvage yard where material composition cannot be verified.

An effective bonding system connects all metallic underwater fittings together electrically to a single common point, normally an engine stud. The negative battery cables bolt to this same point, too. This eliminates the possibility of a voltage potential between two or more grounding points due to corrosion or differing inbuilt resistances.

A good bonding network follows the basic rules of offshore electrics. This includes soldered joints, and bright, corrosion-proof connections to components. A skin fitting is bonded by drilling and tapping a small hole in its flange and fastening the bonding wire with a soldered terminal and bolt. Grease the contact against corrosion. Voltage drops in your bonding circuit will reduce bonding protection. Use a substantial copper strip or single-strand wire (4 to 6 AWG) down the vessel's centerline as a bonding trunkline, with individual circuits branching out to each fitting.

A sacrificial zinc block or cap (perhaps several) is attached to the boat underwater and wired to the bonding network at the common point. Should an electrical potential cause current flow between hull fittings and the ocean, the zinc anode, being lower on the galvanic totem pole, is eaten away first, saving your expensive goodies from harm.

A variety of methods achieve good bonding. Sometimes a zinc cap is simply part of, or attached to, a propeller nut. Since the propeller and its shaft offer the largest metallic surface area and are the most expensive components to replace, direct protection makes sense. An electrical path from the propeller zinc to the common grounding point is important so that the other bonding components can share the protection. Obviously, the propeller shaft connects to the engine, and it may seem the job is done. Often, however, this is not the case. Flexible propeller-shaft couplers or corrosion between the flanges may thwart conductivity. So may oil-coated reduction-gear bearings.

To be certain, rig a carbon brush against the prop shaft. Either a gravity swing arm or a spring-loaded arm applies pressure for firm electrical contact. The brush is wired to the common bonding point, tying it all together. The brush also eliminates a potential source of radio static from a turning shaft.

One zinc anode, especially a small one on the prop, may be too shortlived. To increase both the level and the length of protection, install another, more substantial zinc block on the hull and electrically connect it to the common point, too. Thick, uncored GRP hulls can be drilled and tapped for stainless threaded studs. The studs, embedded in epoxy, protrude inside the hull for wiring to the common bonding point and stick outside the hull for bolting on the zinc. It's cheap insurance.

Zincs lose their effectiveness during long periods of immersion as nonconductive oxide builds up. To prolong their life, wire-brush them periodically to expose bare metal. Stow a half-dozen spare zinc anodes for a long voyage. Otherwise, you may not find duplicates overseas, and you'll be stuck with custom fabrication.

Steel and aluminum vessels need special attention to ensure galvanic and electrolytic protection. Bronze skin fittings must be isolated with insulated bushings or pads to avoid the dangerous situation of electrically mated dissimilar metals. With that insulation, a metallic hull itself can act as the sacrificial anode. When possible, the skin fittings are made of the same material as the hull, or else nonmetallic through-hulls are used. Further, it's prudent to install an impressed current electrolysis control system, which monitors and neutralizes electrolysis.

If your vessel is constructed from steel or aluminum, consultation during construction with a marine engineer who specializes in electrolytic and galvanic protection will be a wise move. Protection really starts on the drawing board and is implemented as the boat is built. It's not something that can be tacked on as an afterthought. For technical marine advice, go to commercial sources. They deal with the sea as professionals, not sportsmen.

LIGHTNING PROTECTION

The danger of being struck by lightning is negligible ashore or at sea. However, if you ever experience a severe electrical storm aboard, you'll be thankful for preparations to safeguard the vessel. The psychological boost to morale from lightning protection is priceless, too. Electrical disturbances can be quite spectacular—and scary.

Lightning protection relies on an effective electrical path from the masthead to the sea. If an efficient conductive route exists, the discharge will dissipate harmlessly into the ocean.

An aluminum mast and wire rigging conduct lightning but stop a bit short of passing the current into the ocean in most cases. For example, a strike may run down the upper shrouds to the chainplates, which normally terminate a few feet above the waterline. Lightning will bridge this gap, perhaps damaging the hull. Sometimes a boat may seem to have built-in protection, such as a forestay connecting to a bobstay that contacts the sea. But this won't necessarily ensure safety, for lightning likes to travel to the sea in a straight line, essentially vertically, and it can bypass an electrical path that lies at a tangent to its destination. So don't try to sidetrack lightning with sharp bends or horizontal runs.

A properly grounded aluminum mast is a good lightning arrester; the mast itself is a huge, natural electrical conductor. To complete the circuit in a keel-stepped mast, rig a cable from it vertically to an immersed grounding plate. All components must be beefy, with clean, bright electrical joints solidly bolted together. Corroded joints defeat the purpose. Lightning will bridge an inefficiency, which can fuse (melt together) metal components and start a fire.

Masts stepped on deck should be wired vertically by a heavy cable to a stainless steel compression post underneath, and the bottom of the post wired vertically to the grounding plate (run the cable straight from mast to plate if the post is made of timber).

Lightning rods are more at home on barns than yachts. In theory, a masthead rod is tied into a vertical conductor leading to a grounding plate underwater. Two awkward problems with lightning rods complicate the issue. First, they are bound to affect VHF radio performance (VHF radios have masthead antennas on cruising boats, and it's a poor practice to mount an antenna parallel to another conductor). And second, a massive discharge of lightning may bypass a lightning rod in favor of a larger and more "attractive" mass of metal—the aluminum mast and all that rigging.

The bonding network is part of the lightning-protection system, too. It's linked to the groundplate and wired to every large metallic object aboard (tanks, engine-room equipment, etc.) so any significant mass of metal that could attract a side flash during a strike is earthed.

If you are caught out in an electrical disturbance, disconnect all radio antennas (receivers and transmitters). Otherwise, should you receive a strike, the antennas would lead the charge to your electronics with potentially devastating results. During an electrical storm, stay away from potential conductors, such as rigging, metallic compression posts, metal handrails, and electronics, that might attract a discharge. Even if you have carefully grounded all these items, you could still get your fingers burned.

Many cruising boats carry a heavy set of battery jumper cables for electrical emergencies. Clamped on the upper shrouds and trailing in the ocean, they'll offer lightning one more path to the sea.

Part Five—Electronics

Installing whatever electronics you need to support your cruise is simplified with a sound 12-volt base and good bonding. When a vessel is wired to tough marine standards, there is little to do but fit and tune the equipment. On the other hand, a poorly wired boat makes life difficult. You may need new distribution panels, upgraded wiring, revised bonding—maybe even new selector switches, battery cables, and junctions. Electronics are only as good as their power source and, in some cases, their grounds.

Before choosing electronics, investigate what offshore fishermen use (when applicable). There is no better recommendation than praise from the commercial sector. Remember: recreational gear is influenced by economics, often at the expense of trustworthy, long-term performance.

THE VHF/FM RADIOTELEPHONE

The VHF, as the VHF/FM radiotelephone is casually known, has become a standard cruising tool worldwide. It's used to borrow a cup of sugar from a neighboring yacht, for continuous weather reports, and for contacting a harbormaster when approaching a foreign port. A VHF links you with ships at

A neat navigatorium with built-in SatNav, VHF, single sideband, a bookshelf, and a well-done distribution panel. Note gooseneck chart light.

sea—any sea—and puts you in touch with commercial telephone services ashore for phone calls to any corner of the world. For these reasons and more, choose a VHF with all the national and international channels, totalling about 55 transmit and more than 100 receive frequencies. All-channel sets cost little more than radios with limited frequencies.

Models with an optional remote station are particularly suited to cruising. Then you can talk and listen from the cockpit *and* the saloon. This gives you convenient communications at anchor and at sea.

A telephone-type handset in lieu of the usual microphone is a good feature, giving you the option of listening via the normal loudspeaker or the earpiece. This way, communications won't disturb sleeping crew members.

A VHF is easy for the handyman to install. Naturally, the gear must be positioned in a dry, protected place. Wiring is sized to prevent the slightest voltage drop for best performance, so be careful about tying into existing circuits. A set rated at 25 watts output (maximum by law) draws about four amps from the batteries when transmitting and about one-half amp on receive, so battery drain is minimal. Which is just as well, for you'll probably keep the set switched on 24 hours a day at sea and all your waking hours when you're aboard in port. They aren't much use turned off.

Since very high frequency (VHF) radio waves are line of sight, meaning they don't curve with the earth's surface, the higher the antenna, the longer the range. The most efficient antenna for cruising is a masthead whip (about 42 inches long), because it offers the least windage and the greatest elevation. Expect a yacht-to-yacht range of 30 miles, yacht-to-ship of 40, and yacht-to-shore up to 70 miles (due to the higher elevation of shoreside antennas).

The coaxial cable leading from the antenna to the radio should be the larger RG-8/U size for transmission efficiency. Don't use the smaller RG-58A/U coax. Pack the connections with Teflon grease. The coax joint at the antenna is particularly vulnerable to corrosion, so make sure it's sealed tight. Rest assured that salt spray will reach the masthead; in gale-force conditions, aircraft at 1,000 feet get smothered with it.

SINGLE-SIDEBAND RADIOTELEPHONES

Reliable communications over great distances (hundreds to thousands of miles) are the domain of single-sideband radios (SSB). There are two choices: marine SSB and amateur "ham" transceivers.

Marine SSB operates on medium- to high-frequency wavelengths. Frequency selection for long-distance communications varies with the time of day or night for maximum propagation. Similar to the less efficient and obsolete double-sideband marine sets that SSB replaced, fixed frequencies are allocated for ship-to-ship, ship-to-shore, and marine telephone (calls can be expensive). Marine SSB radios are costly and, as such, are favored more by the commercial marine sector—i.e., offshore fishing and charter work—and less by the cruising fraternity.

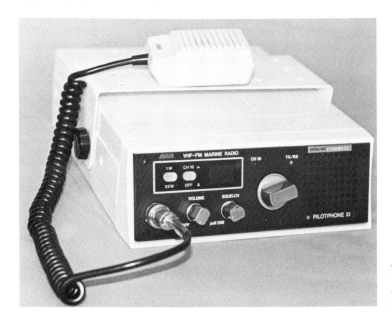

An all-channel VHF radiotelephone is a standard cruising tool.

SSB radiotelephone installations are complex; only licensed technicians approved by government bodies are supposed to oversee installations and tune them. Special groundplates, antenna loading couplers, one or more elaborate (compared to VHF) antennas, and high power consumption are a few of the hurdles to overcome. All a far cry from a simple, inexpensive VHF setup. However, SSB does the job when long-range communication for business or pleasure is sought without investing months of study in a radio license.

Ham radio, another long-range SSB performer, is found aboard cruising sailboats all over the world. Although it's considerably less expensive than marine SSB equipment, the purchaser is faced with stringent licensing. Winning a license to broadcast involves mastering Morse code and radio theory.

Amateur radio has taken to the sea like a duck to water, and the Japanese have jumped on the bandwagon with a variety of 12-volt transceivers for mobile applications. Installations are similar to marine SSB, but they are do-it-yourself affairs; advice is freely available from fellow enthusiasts. Offshore, hams use a stern-mounted, loaded whip antenna. At anchor, more efficient dipole antennas are temporarily strung in the rig.

There are cruising amateur radio networks worldwide, some that plot cruising sailors' wanderings by computer to help you keep track of friends and aid search and rescue. Shore-based private stations number in the thousands worldwide. Somebody, somewhere, will always hear your call. Shore-based hams often have phone patch equipment for handling courtesy calls from your boat, but this is illegal in some countries outside the U.S.

Cruising has inflicted two problems on amateur radio. First, there are the folks who don't pay their dues by working for a license and set about operating pirate stations aboard yachts. Sooner or later they get blackballed, but meantime, they help clutter the airwaves. Second, some cruising people get their licenses, not

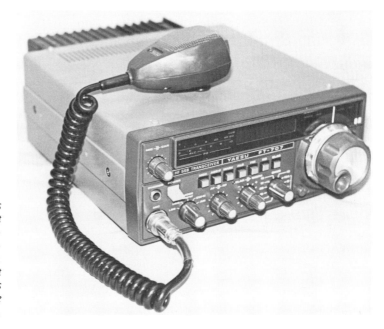

*"Ham" transceivers
like this compact
Yaesu provide world-
wide communica-
tions aboard ship.
Cost is modest, but
earning an operator's
license takes some
doing.*

because they are really interested in ham radio as such, but because they like the safety of long-distance radio or they want to gossip with friends and relatives while cruising, using their radios like glorified CBs. This state of affairs tends to irritate more serious members.

In some ways, ham radio takes the romance out of sailing. Learning intimate details about the next port of call over the air before landfall—where to buy bread, who's in port, who sells cheap wine, who jumped ship when—is hot stuff for some. Others like to discover these things for themselves, firsthand.

Safety is another story. Long-range communications via ham radio have saved lives and property, no question. Yet if help is not near at hand in an emergency, all the talk in the world won't save the day. It's naive to think of amateur radio as a security blanket, although many sailors do. Cruising security, specifically in distant waters, is based on immediate things like a crack crew and a stout ship, not a sympathetic ear hundreds or thousands of miles away.

DEPTH SOUNDERS

Install two of them: one with a range of around 200 feet for anchoring and another with a range of at least 100 fathoms (600 feet) for working continental shelves to aid navigation. Two instruments provide vital backup capability in case one goes haywire. Cruising without a working depth indicator doesn't bear thinking about. Both instruments should be located for viewing from the helm and shaded from direct sunlight.

Digital-readout depth sounders are popular, although rotating flasher types (LED, not old-fashioned neon) might suit you better. While negotiating a strange anchorage, the relative position of the flasher on a circular scale is all you need to know. You've committed the instrument's face to memory like an analog wristwatch. Although certainly a matter of preference, numbers nervously jumping up and down on a digital display can be disconcerting.

Transducers are mounted on fairing blocks so they point straight down for maximum signal bounce. While it's okay on a recreational boat to mount a transducer inside a fiberglass hull in a water- or mineral-oil-filled chamber, the hull thickness of a beefy cruising boat reduces performance too much, so don't. Locate the transducers forward. This gives you a few moments' warning when inching your way in shallow water. An aft-mounted transducer may only confirm what you already know—you just ran aground! Mount the transducer away from the keel so the cone-shaped signal has a clear shot at the seabed without interference.

At least one of your depth sounders should feel at home on a commercial fishing boat. Choose a model with a wide-angle transducer for reliable signal return when the boat is rolling or heeling. High output is necessary to compensate for wide-angle transmission and to give consistent readings at maximum range, regardless of seabed type or sea state. Inexpensive recreational sounders are unlikely to have the power to bounce signals off soft bottoms at extreme range. And they usually have narrower signals, which don't function well at sea.

SAILING INSTRUMENTS

Thanks to the racing fraternity, the cruising sailor has a range of sailing instruments to choose from that help run the ship. Of particular benefit are boat speed, distance log, apparent wind direction, and apparent wind strength. Resistance from seat-of-the-pants sailors notwithstanding, there's no doubt that sailing instruments help improve dead reckoning accuracy, offshore safety, and peace of mind. Nothing beats raw, unbiased data—the more the merrier—on which to base decisions.

Avoid instruments with mechanical drive senders. Electronic paddlewheels are more reliable and need less maintenance. Position the paddlewheel speed/log sensor where a momentary inrush of seawater will flow freely into the bilges or shower pan so you can remove it for cleaning. A resettable trip log is handy for noon-to-noon dead reckoning and short passages. Make sure the instrument(s) has variable intensity lighting, both for the digital readout and mechanical pointers. Mount the sensors in clear air or water, as the case may be, heading parallel to the boat's centerline.

Sailing instruments draw a fraction of an amp, and any vessel can have them without special electrical preparation. Take pains to calibrate each feature accurately to your boat. Of special concern is the speed and distance log, which

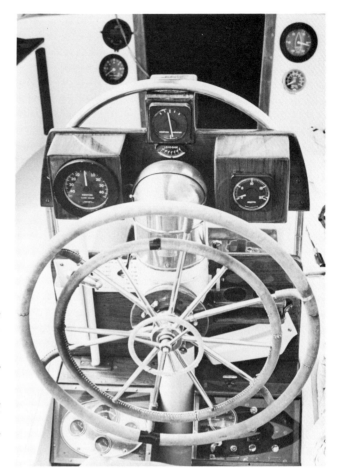

This offshore cruising yacht is an ex-racer, hence the extra instrumentation. Nevertheless, sailing instruments benefit cruising folks, too. Featured here are: rudder-angle indicator, apparent wind angle, knotmeter, inclinometer, apparent wind speed, and engine instruments, to name a few. Real data are always preferable to seat-of-the-pants guesswork.

must be calibrated initially by running the vessel two ways over a measured nautical mile.

RADAR

Radar has come of age for cruising yachts with gear that's easy to install, compact, and lightweight, drawing just a few amps on 12 volts. The equipment is divided into two main units: an above-decks rotating antenna enclosed in a plastic dome to prevent entanglement with running rigging, and a console with controls and a screen readout positioned below decks near the helm.

Like VHF radiotelephones, radar waves are line of sight. Most small sets suitable for sailboats have a range of approximately 16 miles. For maximum performance, the antenna dome must be positioned high off the water, either mounted on a post at the stern or, preferably, higher up the mast. Mizzenmasts on ketches and yawls are made to order for mounting radar antennas; they can

A common radar-antenna set-up for cruising. The pylon is a good place for a stern light and man-overboard pole bracket, too. Performance with low-power sets (16 miles or less) is satisfactory. Scanners for longer range radar should be mounted higher on the mast.

also be placed on the front of a single mast somewhere above the lower spreaders or alongside the mast over a spreader.

Radar is an important navigational tool, in many ways of greater practical value to offshore people than satellite navigation. On an extended cruise to strange ports of call, radar offers the security of accurate position finding relative to nearby landmasses, and it enables the user to locate other vessels and exposed reefs that are difficult to spot with the naked eye. In other words, radar takes some of the worry out of being close.

To get the most out of radar, enroll in a course. It requires more practice and familiarity than any other electronic aid with the exception of a weather facsimile receiver.

LORAN-C

North American coastal sailors can take advantage of Loran-C, an all-weather, electronic position-finding system. It uses synchronized pairs of shoreside transmitters to compute position lines by the time-difference principle. Several position lines are had by pairing up different signals in a chain, giving a fix. Accuracy is right on, and the process is almost instantaneous. Loran-C receivers are similar in size to VHF radios and consume only a few amps of 12-volt power. Minimal operator knowledge is required—one of technology's gifts to cruising.

To use Loran-C, you'll need an on-deck whip antenna resembling that of a CB radio. The receiver may be located anywhere below decks that's convenient unless it has a course-keeping feature—then it should be visible to the helmsperson. Models with microprocessors automatically calculate great circle waypoints and intermediate rhumbline courses, course and speed made good, and time to the next destination. Some alert you when you near a preselected position.

SATELLITE NAVIGATION

Loran-C has a limited offshore range and is not an asset on an overseas voyage to remote regions of the South Pacific, for instance, where there is no coverage. Satellite navigation, however, receives and interprets signals from orbiting satellites, not shore stations, and consequently offers worldwide position finding to approximately one-half mile, uncorrected.

Like Loran-C, SatNav computes great circle waypoints, course and speed made good, and so forth. It even interfaces directly with an autopilot to steer a boat electronically. Readouts are in longitude and latitude for simple plotting. Unlike Loran-C, SatNav does not give continuously updated fixes, because satellite transits (when they pass over your position) are sporadic. Dead reckoning from manually keyed-in data or updates from onboard electronic sensors (course, speed, etc.) fill the void between fixes.

SatNav receivers draw a few amps of 12-volt power, a small price considering the benefits. The receiver may be mounted anywhere below decks that's convenient. A dome-shaped antenna looking like a pregnant Frisbee is mounted above decks, typically on a stern pylon or backstay or at the masthead.

WEATHER FACSIMILE RECEIVERS

Weather facsimile plotters, casually called Weatherfax, are compact units, looking a little like a portable typewriter without keys and combining radio receivers and printers. The system has eight zones worldwide and is of great merit when cruising remote areas where weather reports are unheard of or no more accurate than holding up a wet finger.

Several times each day, a weather map is produced, showing barometric isobars, estimated wind speed and direction at different altitudes over your area, and a synopsis of ocean swells. At sea, this information can help you steer around bad weather. At anchor, it gives the cruising crew data on which to base departure decisions.

A typical SatNav antenna installation on a backstay.

A weather facsimile receiver and plotter on a cruising boat. Choose electronics used by commercial fishermen. Furuno equipment is marketed worldwide and has a good offshore track record.

Interpreting the information to advantage takes a bit of study. And you should print a facsimile every day the weather is of concern to assess trends. If you decide to use this technology—and it's a beauty—it'll pay to befriend someone at your local weather office to help you learn the ropes.

There are two printing systems to choose from: dry and wet. Although a bit more expensive, the dry-paper system has better resolution and a longer shelf life.

Electrical consumption is about one-half amp on standby and two-and-a-half amps while plotting.

Antennas are about 18 feet in length, and an insulated backstay is about the only alternative on a sailboat. It can be shared with an SSB radiotelephone by using manual or automatic switching gear, which disconnects the Weatherfax receiver during radio transmissions.

BURGLAR ALARMS

When you live aboard, many domestic and marine intruder alarm sensors are impractical. In hot weather you'll have all your hatches open, so traditional magnetic make-and-break switches at these points, practical on unattended vessels, are worthless. Ultrasonic and infrared setups below decks are of no value either; by the time the alarm is tripped, the unwelcome guest is already in with you. All sensors must trip when an intruder is still on deck, preferably at the moment of boarding.

A pressure-sensitive mat in the cockpit combined with monofilament fishing-line trip wires attached to pull switches is one on-deck system to consider. Better yet are pressure-sensitive switches placed between deck beams under areas of unsupported decking and/or under the decks at stanchion bases where minute flexing from weight or strain occurs. Strain sensors attached to lifelines would be of value, too, as it's almost impossible to climb aboard a yacht without using the lifelines.

Wire your sensors to a relay and timer to activate an audio alarm for a period of time before automatically resetting. These components are available at most automotive parts stores. A big eight-inch, 12-volt bell or whoop-whoop horn is fine for the audio part of the alarm—either one will wake the dead—but wire the spreader lights as well. Suspicious types on deck at night get rattled by bright lights. You'll need a diode in the circuit between the bell and spreader lights, or the bell will sound every time the spreader lights are turned on. (A diode allows current to flow in one direction only—i.e., from bell to lights, but not lights to bell.)

NOISE SUPPRESSION

Aside from the previously mentioned fluorescent lights and rotating propeller shafts, other kinds of shipboard equipment can create electrical noise that can interfere with your electronics. Examples are alternators and generators (heard on radios as a whine), mechanical voltage regulators (irregular buzzing sound), electronic tachometers, and accessories with electric motors. Any noticeable electrical interference to electronics must be rectified.

Alternators and generators can normally be quieted by bolting a 0.5 microfarad capacitor to the machine's case (negative ground) and attaching the capacitor's single lead to the positive-charging (output) terminal.

Noisy mechanical voltage regulators are best exchanged for quieter, more reliable electronic regulators that have no arcing contacts.

Electric motors may often be electrically silenced with little 0.001 microfarad ceramic disk capacitors connected directly across the input wiring as close to the motor as possible.

A well-found cruising yacht is spared the greatest noisemaker of all, a gasoline engine with its high-tension spark ignition. If you're having trouble sorting out the noise, count your blessings—it could be worse.

A LIFESTYLE OF YOUR CHOICE

When taken in bite-sized chunks, marine electrics *are* digestible. Current is created, stored, and led to the things it runs. Just remember: you must be able to *create more than you'll ever need to store,* and you must be able to *store more than you'll ever need to run your accessories.*

Offshore sailors are often too nonchalant about electrics for their own good, relying on their builders to carry the ball. Trouble is, builders can't be expected to understand cruising electrical systems, either, especially since a given boat's setup must be tailored to the owner's cruising lifestyle.

The first thing to settle on is an overall concept that will support your way of life. What do you want your electrics to do for you? Once you know this, you can flesh out the details, one step at a time. It's important to work your way through the design of a system backwards: needs first, strategies to meet needs second, hardware to put strategies into action third. Too many sailors ask an existing system to support their lifestyle, and it won't.

And finally, aboard boats, it's false economy to stretch a dollar too far, electrically or otherwise. Implement whatever first-rate features your budget allows and draw the line there. Then you'll receive lasting pleasure from what you have.

3▶ Plumbing to Live Aboard

Like electrics, workable plumbing networks are the product of forethought and sensible engineering to suit liveaboard conditions. Again, simplicity, accessibility, and ease of maintenance are foremost for continued reliability. Although plumbing systems are less complicated and costly to implement than electrics, they have a great impact on cruising comfort.

HANDPUMPS ARE HISTORY

The days of traditional handpumps for sailboat sinks are over, so far as liveaboard convenience is concerned. Handpumps take up too much counter space and are ridiculously inconvenient when you need two hands for a job. Manual pumps are still useful as backups to the pressure freshwater system in key areas like the galley, despite the reliability of a well-designed pressure water system powered from a dependable 12-volt base. However, all manual pumps at sinks should be foot operated, leaving both hands free for washing. A swing spigot without a pumping mechanism takes up less counter space. Chances are,

82

your backup manual pumps will rarely see action. But considering Murphy's Law, you'll surely need one if you don't have it!

FRESHWATER CAPACITY

Habitual water rationing due to limited tankage detracts too much from a contented existence. Ideally, a long-range yacht should pack 100 U.S. gallons of water per person, 75 gallons per person being a bare minimum without a watermaker. Traditionally, water capacity was geared to sustain life aboard ship on long ocean passages, but this is no longer a satisfactory yardstick. The demands at anchor, in the name of decent family life, are much higher. At sea, showers are not a daily ritual, because the vessel's motion sometimes makes them a bother. Meals are often simpler and less frequently served at sea, meaning less hardware to wash less often. Hobbies and sporting activities, which consume considerable fresh water at anchor, are suspended. So a boat catering to comfort on the hook carries a surplus of fresh water for ocean passages—by default.

At anchor, particularly in the tropics, activities that consume fresh water are many. An economical shower will use about two gallons per person; washing up in the galley consumes another two gallons per person each day; and things like shaving, brushing teeth, washing hands, flushing salt from diving gear, sluicing off after a swim, and rinsing underwater cameras gobble at least another gallon per person. This can add up to five gallons per crew member a day.

Galley handpumps, either salt or freshwater backups, once obligatory, have been superseded by foot pumps. Note single lever mixer valve with swing spigot—household fixtures and sinks are the only way to go.

In theory, then, tankage for 100 gallons per person will last the crew 20 days. In reality, the time the boat spends on passages (during which consumption drops) and slight regimentation aboard in harbor when necessary extend this to one month or more. Dishes can be washed and rinsed in salt water, for example, and crew comfort continues largely unaffected. (It's desirable, however, to rinse dishes in fresh water so they dry thoroughly; saltwater rinsing also rusts metal pots, pans, and utensils.)

During dry spells, when water catchment isn't feasible, or in anchorages where the water source is unhealthy, tankage for a month of comfortable living is imperative.

FRESHWATER TANKS

GRP (glass-reinforced plastic or fiberglass) and stainless steel are the two most common tank materials. Both are fine, but GRP tanks can be more easily botched by poor craftsmanship. Laminating water tanks is a meticulous job. Thoroughly saturated, chopped strand matt is preferable to woven roving, which, when not thoroughly saturated, creates a wicking action and may leak. GRP leaks can be difficult to trace, because the water may travel quite a distance within the laminate before surfacing outside the tank.

Internal sealing of a GRP tank is done with several coats of resin followed by two coats of high-quality sanitary gelcoat. Every last pinhole in the laminate must be filled. A surfacing agent is mixed in the final coat for tack-free curing. The tank is left to air for a few weeks with the inspection covers removed. Electric lights suspended in the tank create heat and speed curing. When allowed to cure properly, the first few tankfuls of water taste of resin; thereafter there's no taste at all. Green tanks prematurely filled can, however, leave a bad taste in the mouth for ages.

Glassing tank tops in place is a common practice—and far from foolproof. It's best to treat a GRP tank like the hull of a boat, and the tank's top like a deck. Since hull/deck joints bonded with GRP often leak, conscientious builders fasten the two components together mechanically with bolts after applying a generous coat of two-part Thiokol to the mating surfaces. Tanks built this way don't leak a drop.

Water is heavy—a full 100-gallon tank weighs almost half a ton—so tank mounting (if tanks are not integral) must be beefy. Tanks positioned above the waterline can raise a vessel's center of gravity. Well-designed cruising boats carry their water, or most of it, below the cabin sole. Large water tanks should not be positioned near the vessel's ends, or trim will change with different tank levels, and the boat's moment of polar inertia will be higher when the end tanks are full. Excessive weight at the bow or stern hampers a vessel's ability to lift quickly in a seaway whether beating or running before it, and more green water or spray comes aboard in rough weather.

Tankage under bunk settees is the result of inadequate cruising design. Settees offer the driest, most convenient stowage aboard for foodstuffs and such. Tank storage only wastes valuable space.

INSPECTION PORTS

Water tanks must be cleaned periodically to remove scum buildup on inside surfaces. Also, dirt and sand collect in tanks and, if allowed to accumulate, clog strainers and wear out water-tap washers. Worse, a sealed tank without access for maintenance sets the stage for a future nightmare if there's ever a leaky fitting or a structural fault.

Screw-in plastic inspection covers with "O"-ring seals are ready-made for tank access but are not strong enough to stand on. Tanks located under the cabin sole must have the access ports recessed and protected with stiff covers made of plywood, GRP, or noncorrosive metal. Dabs of Vaseline on the threads and the O ring lubricate the contacting surfaces and reduce the chance of leaks.

Plastic ports should not be responsible for containing water at depth under pressure; they are not designed to do so. Access through tank sides is achieved with strong GRP or stainless steel bolt-on cover plates with rubber gaskets.

Every inch of a water tank's interior must be within reach for scrubbing or repair. This requirement dictates the number and placement of inspection ports. If tank baffles are fitted (to reduce sloshing and increase a tank's strength), then an inspection port should be installed in each bay.

DIVIDE THE SUPPLY

Three or four smaller water tanks have important advantages over one or two larger tanks. Structurally speaking, smaller tanks are easier to build and install, because they carry less weight. Also, internal sloshing in a smaller tank is less forceful. Larger tanks need heavier construction and stronger mounts, increasing cost. Big tanks are built in permanently—they'll never come out through a hatch—whereas smaller tanks, if not integral, can be removed. Multiple tanks can be your salvation when shipping water from a dubious source. An empty tank or two can be topped up and a tank or two of water from a previous supply held in reserve in case the new water turns your stomach. And if there is ever a problem with a leaky tank or part of the plumbing network, at least some of your precious fresh water will be safe.

A series of smaller tanks helps husband the water supply as you switch from tank to tank, giving you an indication of water consumption and reserve. For more precise monitoring, fit each tank with a sight gauge. Instrument gauges are crude indicators and dipsticks are almost useless, particularly at sea.

WATER-TANK FILLS AND VENTS

Tank fills are most efficient when plumbed nearly vertically—avoid horizontal sections. Every bend or elbow in the fill line restricts the passage of water, so avoid them, too, if you can. Tank-fill plumbing and deckplates should be at least one-and-one-half inches in diameter, or large hoses and funnels won't fit. Raincatcher awnings in tropical downpours overload small tank-fill systems, and rainwater wastefully overflows out the deck scuppers. Fills that freely take water without choking or backing up are appreciated when watering with jerry-jugs, too. Manually pouring water down puny spouts is tedious.

Water-tank vents should be located inside the vessel. Don't be tempted to do otherwise. Below-decks vents are less prone to clogging by insects, and the possibility of salt contamination in heavy going offshore is eliminated.

Vent placement requires ingenuity. There's only one sane way to determine when a tank is completely filled—by a sudden gusher on deck. Otherwise, watering is a two-person chore: one filling and another below decks watching a vent in readiness to shout, "It's full!" To streamline the chore of shipping water, each water-tank vent should be positioned and aimed where overflow would do no harm. Ideally, vents live in places that already have self-draining features. An inverted U-shaped snout positioned in the corner of a sink works well. A vent that dribbles into the shower pan works great, too (rig an inverted U in the line just before the vent to keep soapy water out of the freshwater supply).

Vent plumbing must be essentially vertical, leading high above the center (measured athwartships) of a tank's top so water won't spill from the tank when the boat heels or rolls. Sometimes it's necessary to install a siphon break at the apex if the vent line continues down to a low-drainage area. Fittings and hoses should be at least a half-inch in diameter to evacuate air quickly from a tank for fast filling.

THE PRESSURE WATER PUMP

The heart of the cruising pressure water system is the 12-volt pump. Positive-displacement diaphragm pumps have a good track record for cruising, the most well-known being PAR units. PAR diaphragm pressure water pumps will chug away every day for about a year before the check valves wear out. Replacing them is a simple chore. The rest of the pump components last years.

Electrical consumption of any pressure pump is peanuts when measured over a 24-hour period. The PAR diaphragm pump, for example, draws eight to ten amps while pumping; total running time to supply a crew of four generously is around ten minutes a day. This equals a battery drain of about two amps every 24 hours—hardly significant.

To ensure continued service, carry a complete spare pressure pump aboard, identical to the original, with terminal eyes already soldered to the wiring for quick exchange. Then a faulty pump can be switched in minutes, the pump fixed in a quiet anchorage when you're in the mood to tinker, and the repaired pump placed in the spares locker to await its turn at bat.

Tuck away a rebuild kit and several additional sets of check valves or impellers, whichever your pump uses. If you have PAR pumps, also stow a spare quarter-inch allen screw, the one that secures the diaphragm connecting rod to the rotating cam. This bolt has been known to fail, and a spare, costing only a few cents, can save the day.

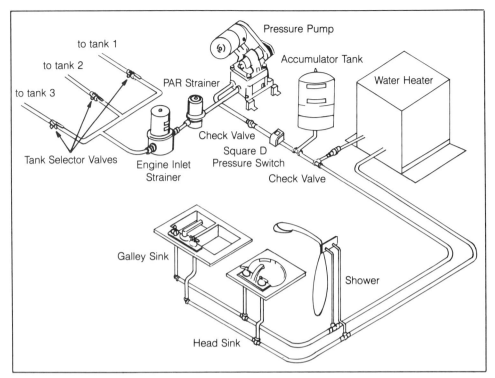

Typical pressure water system.

THE PRESSURE SWITCH

Do not use PAR's standard pressure switch. Obtain a Square-D domestic pressure switch, the model with 20 psi (pounds per square inch) kick-in and 40 psi cutout rating. It's adjustable, containing two sets of contact points designed for AC circuitry—you'll use one set for 12-volt DC operation and have a spare set in the bargain. Adjust the pressure switch so the pump kicks in at five psi and shuts off at 25 psi. Higher pressure settings waste water, increase the chance of leaks in the plumbing system, and shorten the life of the pump by overloading it. The broad kick-in/kick-out range is important to reduce pump cycling.

Tee your Square-D pressure switch into the pressure side of the plumbing system (between the pump and first faucet in the system). Do not attempt to install it on the pump; simply leave the standard PAR pressure switch in place to block the hole and forget it. If you use another brand of pump, make sure the standard pressure switch is heavy duty and fully adjustable. Sealed, preset switches won't let you tune your system for liveaboard service.

PLUMBING THE PUMP

It's handy to locate all the tank-selector valves centrally in one place. Arrange them in order or label them so anyone can figure out which tank is selected by which valve. Include the tank's capacity on each label for reference. Ninety-degree ball valves with Teflon seals are handier than ponderous screw-type valves. It's inconvenient and unnecessary to install water-tank shutoff valves at the tanks; head pressure is minimal, and water leaks easy to control. (With fuel, however, a shutoff at the tank is imperative.) The valves may be plumbed to the tank and to the pump with tasteless, sanitary, clear plastic tubing and stainless steel hose clamps. Don't plumb the pump with rigid piping; it must be free to jump and vibrate while it runs.

Protect the pump from dirt, debris, and sand with a strainer. PAR's strainer is fine as far as it goes, but a large engine intake strainer plumbed in front of the small PAR unit will increase the volume of refuse catchment. It's surprising how much grit and junk freshwater sources contain. Two-stage straining ensures longer pump life and greater reliability.

A check valve at the pump's outlet blocks pressurized water from straining the pump's check valves and diaphragm while the pump is at rest. PAR's inline check valve works fine. (The pressure switch mentioned above is installed downstream of the check valve, toward the taps.)

THE ACCUMULATOR TANK

A vital component of a good pressure water system is the header or accumulator tank. It contains nothing but air when the system is not pressurized. But as pumping begins, water flows into the header tank, compressing the air. After the pressure switch shuts down the pump, a quantity of water under air pressure is held in the tank to be used at the taps on demand. Meanwhile, the pump is not needed until the stored water is used up and the pressure falls low enough to activate the switch.

The header tank eliminates the annoying on/off clicking and buzzing from rapid cycling, increasing the life of the pump and pressure switch. And the accumulator tank acts as a surge cushion when the pump operates, smoothing out jerky pressure jumps that otherwise rattle and vibrate components.

Sears Roebuck and Company markets header tanks for domestic wells. Their smallest, an epoxy-lined, five-gallon tank, is perfect for the cruising yacht, providing about two gallons of pressurized water between cycles (full header tanks contain about half pressurized air and half water when the pressure switch is set up properly).

The pump should be fitted with a manual cutoff switch to disable the pressure switch, halting automatic cycling. Then you can use the accumulator as a reservoir holding a measured amount of water for showers; once the water stops flowing, the shower is over. It's a good way to conserve water aboard, as good as any manual shower arrangement, and absolutely fair to everyone. The override switch can be shut off at night, too, so a cycling pump won't annoy sleepers. The header tank holds plenty of pressurized water until sunrise. Another benefit of a header tank comes into play when the pump or the electrical supply is temporarily inactivated for maintenance: a quantity of pressure water remains on tap.

A header or accumulator tank is necessary in any pressure fresh-water system to reduce pump cy-cling and system surge. Note puri-fying filter. This water system was done with copper, but PVC and CPVC are just as good and are cheaper and easier to work with.

SINKS AND TAPS

So-called marine sinks are more costly than domestic versions. Marine sinks also tend to be smaller and unnecessarily deep and, although traditional, are more awkward to use. Marine sinks usually have tiny outlets and miniature straining baskets, whereas domestic models have large refuse baskets and outlets that drain more efficiently.

However, the primary advantage of domestic hardware is tap design. Household faucets use O-ring seals, not old-fashioned rubber washers. O-ring cartridge faucets last years without leaking. Shutoff positions are just that—positions. You don't have to bear down on them to stop a dribble.

O-ring cartridge faucets are available in single-lever units that combine hot and cold water or as individual faucets. Pack away spare cartridges, and you're set for life. Just watch out for quality. Some domestic tap handles are constructed of chrome-plated plastic. After a few years aboard ship, the plating begins to peel, and the handles look shabby. Take along spare plated plastic handles or stick to chrome-plated brass. Don't forget spare baskets for each sink, either. They like to jump out of your hand when you shake them out over the side. Davy Jones has hundreds of them.

Shoreside sink installations have a secondary set of valves underneath the counter to shut off city water for faucet maintenance. They are not necessary aboard ship.

PLUMBING THE PRESSURE SYSTEM

Tubing and hose clamps used to plumb the tanks to the selector valves and on to the pump inlet are not suitable for the pressure side of the water system unless they are reinforced with synthetic webbing.

Although there are many varieties of marine tubing and fittings for pressure systems, the best alternative is also the simplest and perhaps the cheapest: domestic half-inch PVC and CPVC (for hot water) rigid piping. PVC household plumbing is easy to work with, never corrodes or deteriorates, and is available anywhere worldwide. Glue-on tees, elbows, and threaded fittings route straight runs of piping neatly through the boat to components. You can cheat a little by bending the pipe slightly to fit with the careful application of heat from a propane torch, although it's better to make liberal use of elbows. The end result is workmanlike, totally leakproof, and lasts forever.

Pressurized plumbing must be clamped down securely at regular intervals. This prevents vibration from the boat's power plant and flexing from rapid pressure variations when the pump runs or taps are being snapped on and off. Clamps should not strain or distort the plumbing; fit bonded pads for mounting.

PVC and CPVC piping have the advantage of being easily modified later if another sink or tap is needed. Cutting and gluing in additional piping to the vessel's existing pressure system is no problem.

Use a length of reinforced high-pressure hose at the water-pump outlet tying into the PVC network to maintain pump flexibility. Adaptor fittings are available over the counter in plumbing supply centers for hose-to-PVC-pipe connections.

HOT WATER HEATERS

You've probably experienced an interruption in the hot water supply at home because of a power failure, multiple loads run through the washing machine, or copious consumption by another member of the household. The chill of a cold shower is not soon forgotten. Considering this, purposely setting out on a voyage without a hot water system is a curious exercise in self-denial.

A hot water system is a natural extension to an existing pressure water setup. Even a modest water heater of five gallons' capacity improves the quality of life remarkably on a cruise. In cold weather, life's downright grim without it.

Marine hot water heaters differ from domestic units in that they have heat exchangers for converting waste engine heat to hot water (in addition to the standard electrical element for use with shore power or a shipboard AC alternator). Heat exchangers can be tied into a marine heating system, too. This widens your options for hot water at anchor.

For world cruising, the standard element supplied with most water heaters—usually 1,500 watts or more—must be replaced with a less hungry one, around 750 watts. Otherwise, your water-heater element hogs all the shore power; worse, there may be insufficient current in some places to operate the water heater at all. Never count on more than 1,000 watts from a shoreside source. When more power is available, a high-drain heater still dominates your life by monopolizing shore power so you can't use other appliances concurrently.

To control and monitor water-heater operation, install a cutout switch and a pilot light in the galley. This lets you switch off the element momentarily while using a galley appliance, vacuum cleaner, hair dryer, whatever. The pilot light acts as a telltale: when it goes off, you know the hot shower you've been waiting for is ready.

A water heater is teed to the pressure water system, and its outlet supplies all the hot water faucets aboard. It sounds simple, and it is, but there can be exciting teething problems if you don't follow a few simple rules.

The first trick is fitting a check valve at the inlet port to the water heater. This prevents hot water from backfeeding into the cold side of the plumbing network. Use a PAR check valve for hose-type plumbing or a domestic check valve designed to connect with PVC pipe, whichever suits.

As water heats, pressure in the hot water tank increases. The check valve won't allow expansion to equalize back into the header tank. By law, water heaters come with a pressure-relief valve to bleed off excessive pressure, but these are set to domestic household conditions (150 to 180 psi), not liveaboard reality, even when tanks are sold for marine use. The standard pressure-relief valve must be replaced, or your plumbing will be strained needlessly, and there'll be a wasteful high-pressure gout of water each time a tap is first cracked after the water-heater cycle. An adjustable pressure-relief valve solves the problem. Since the pressure pump is regulated to a maximum of 25 psi, it serves no purpose to subject your hot water plumbing to pressures over 50 psi during periods of hot water expansion. Just crank in the differential between maximum pump pressure and pop off pressure that prevents the relief valve from bleeding from pump pressure alone.

Every time the hot water tank cycles and cold water is heated, there'll be a slight dribble as the pressure-relief valve does its duty. This is of no consequence; the tiny quantity of water lost isn't enough to worry about. Rig a hose from the

This 15-gallon water heater is hung from the engine room overhead in a 45 footer. Energy is supplied by an AC element or a diesel-fired cabin heater.

relief valve to the bilge (or a receptacle so the water can be salvaged) to keep waste water from dripping over equipment near the water heater. Make certain the hose is at least three-quarters of an inch inside diameter—pressure relief must never be restricted. A thermostat malfunction or partially dry water heater from an empty water tank can cause massive expansion.

Some countries with very high domestic water pressures have water heaters with a pressure-reducing valve at the inlet port. If you install one of these heaters, the pressure-reduction valve must be removed, or you are in for trouble. A low-pressure shipboard system may not overcome a pressure-reduction valve, and inflow can be restricted or blocked entirely, causing abnormally high temperatures, steam, and possible element failure.

MONITORING THE FRESHWATER SYSTEM

Pressure gauges teed into the pressure water system are seldom seen on yachts—and they're extremely useful! All it takes is an inexpensive automobile oil-pressure gauge plumbed with one-eighth-inch plastic tubing.

A pressure gauge indicates whether the pressure switch is operating satisfactorily and lets you calibrate initial settings. The gauge tells how much water is in the header tank at any given time (you will become adept at judging this). And a gauge reveals the water heater's relief-valve pop-off pressure and allows you to adjust it correctly. Abnormal operation of the pressure switch or the relief valve shows up at a glance.

The gauge must be plumbed into the hot water side of the pressure system. Anywhere that's convenient will do; the pressure is equal everywhere. If the gauge is fitted to the cold water part of the system, the performance of the hot water network will remain a mystery, because the hot water tank's inlet check valve isolates the two. You'll notice that hot water pressure is always equal to or greater than cold water pressure.

FRESHWATER CONSERVATION

Freshwater consumption is of particular concern when cruising remote locales. You can't always be certain when you'll have the opportunity to replenish your stores.

Showering with a header tank disciplines usage, as explained earlier. Education also minimizes waste. A pressure system can be surprisingly stingy once the crew is tuned into conservation. Pressure taps can be cracked for a fine trickle. You can wash both hands at once very economically—by comparison, hand pumps are clumsy and wasteful. Even foot pumps offer less control. Naturally, shoreside habits like letting the water run while brushing teeth are banned on boats.

The manual switch that disables the pressure pump helps acclimate an inexperienced crew to the facts of life. When the supply of pressure water stored in the accumulator tank is exhausted, you can hold a conference about the amount of water used, how long it lasted, and where it went. A few meetings of your water-conservation committee before departure will save tanks of water on the voyage.

The crew, children and adults alike, quickly master the arts of miserly consumption. Then only your landlubberly guests bear watching. Generally, a boat with generous tankage provides plenty of water without strict rationing—at least that's the theory—but there's never enough to throw away.

SINK DRAINS

The ideal drainage scheme for routing waste water overboard runs against the grain to those who believe in the elimination of every through-hull fitting possible. A sink drains fastest with the least likelihood of blockage when the most direct route to the sea is taken. This means through-hulls for all.

Some vessels are built with collector boxes over a single hull aperture below the waterline. Waste lines are connected to this box. Although this certainly dispenses with many through-hull fittings, collector boxes set the stage for a plumber's nightmare, because they encourage a multitude of long horizontal drain lines winding hither and yon through lockers and bilges. This overcomplicates what could be a simple system and compromises dependability. Long horizontal runs are most susceptible to blockages from soap and grease buildup. At best, drainage isn't up to par.

A few extra skin fittings on a cruising boat will not, in any measurable way, affect the vessel's performance. This is one area where racing philosophy butts heads with cruising common sense. A collector box is no safer than individual seacocks and through-hulls for each drain line—indeed, just the opposite is true in instances where drain lines are not valved at the box. If seacocks are fitted to each drain line at the collector box, it's the same as having an equal number of valves spread around the boat. After all, what's inside the box but the sea? Collector boxes are a haven for marine growth and difficult to keep clean inside. An inspection port on the box—a potential source of leakage—can only be used during haulout. At least individual through-hulls can be cleaned out at anchor by a person with a mask and snorkel.

A good bronze or fiberglass-reinforced plastic through-hull fitting with a compatible valve won't let you down unless it's damaged by freezing water or, as in the case of the metallic fitting, weakened by electrolysis or galvanic corrosion. Preventive maintenance, periodic inspection, and proper bonding ensure this won't happen.

Select high-quality valves and skin fittings and plumb them with high-pressure, reinforced neoprene hose, using two stainless steel hose clamps per end. Make sure the hose clamps have stainless steel worm gears—automotive stainless hose clamps usually don't. Install your sink, aim the outlet hose downward at a steep angle, and locate the skin fitting as best you can, keeping in mind the criteria for through-hull placement that follow.

For efficient drainage, don't skimp on hose or through-hull size. Inside diameter should be at least one-and-a-quarter inches for short runs, and one-and-a-half inches for runs over four feet.

LOCATING THROUGH-HULL FITTINGS

Every through-hull aboard must be convenient to reach quickly. Generally, inaccessible seacocks are never used, defeating their purpose. Not only is a

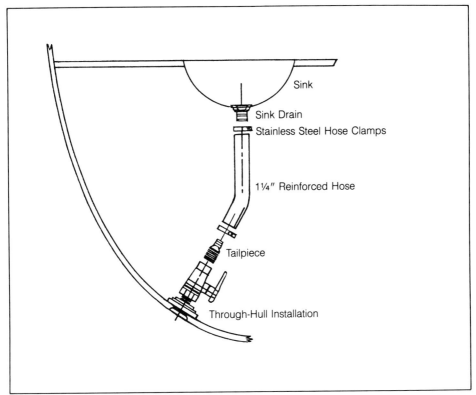

Direct discharge sink drains are most efficient. Outboard sinks less than two feet above the waterline may flood at sea, a problem that can be avoided on the drawing board.

margin of safety lost when a boat is vacated with wide-open seacocks, but infrequently cycled seacocks tend to seize up.

Easy access is particularly important in an emergency when you must shut off the sea fast. You can't waste time ripping up floorboards and throwing gear aside to find a valve.

Plastic screw-in inspection ports make inexpensive through-hull access covers. Install them above every valve under the cabin sole. Make sure all seacocks can be reached easily through the inspection ports by planning their location during construction. If possible, all seacocks should be less than a foot under the floorboards.

Seacocks inside lockers or hidden behind bulkheads are easier to reach with inspection ports, too. Label them all with name tags and familiarize the crew with each seacock's function.

Every below-the-waterline outlet should be placed on one side of the hull, if possible, and all inlets should live on the opposite side. Then seawater ingested for engine cooling, head flushing, dishwashing, and food preparation is less likely to contain contaminants from sink drains and head outlets. Longer cruising keels provide a good barrier between inlets and outlets.

Marelon flush through-hull fitting, threaded for a valve. Also available in mushroom head and configured for direct hose connection. Although similar in appearance to inferior plastic fittings, Marelon will not shear off with impact, crack in freezing conditions, or become brittle with age. Either buy Marelon or stick to bronze. R.C. Marine also makes vented loops for head outlets, Y-valves, and cockpit drains of Marelon. Photo by R.C. Marine.

SUMP TANKS

A direct shot to the ocean is the most efficient way to discharge waste, but it's not always a practical solution. Sinks positioned near a vessel's centerline must be elevated about a foot above the waterline to resist flooding in a seaway. Outboard sinks, adjacent to topsides, must be higher (perhaps several feet) above the waterline, or rolling and heeling under sail will flood them.

Sinks in flush-decked, heavy-displacement boats are special problems. The level of accommodation is lower in relation to the waterline, and even centerline sink drains can't always be plumbed directly to a seacock. And of course, a gravity shower drain is impossible on a sailboat. These drainage problems are solved with a sump tank, a catchment basin evacuated by an electric pump.

The sump tank doesn't need to be large in capacity—three to five gallons is enough. All drains feeding the sump tank angle downhill along their entire length. Horizontal runs or very long runs are best avoided. Think of the sump tank as you would a seacock and apply the same thinking about waste-line size and downward gradient.

An effective sump tank is placed low in the boat for maximum drainage efficiency. It should be centered between the fixtures it serves to discourage long, level waste lines. Shower drains need special care. Don't connect two showers to one sump tank, or one shower pan may flood the other in a seaway. Shower drain lines and fittings should be at least one-and-a-half inches inside diameter, no matter how short they are. At sea, a single, centrally positioned shower drain is inefficient; water piles up in the leeward side of the pan while heeling. When a boat rolls, water sloshes back and forth vigorously, skipping past the drain. To end this nuisance, install a drain in each lower outboard corner of the pan. Run each drain line into the sump separately. Dual shower drains do a better job in port, too. And you have twice the catchment area for hair.

Sump tanks need a see-through, watertight inspection port on top; O-ring pop-out covers do the job perfectly. Periodic cleanout is necessary or accumulated grease, soap residue, and hair put the system out of action.

Drains to sump tanks should have water traps just as sink drains in houses do (water traps are not necessary on drains exiting directly to the sea). PVC traps are preferable to chrome-plated brass ones, which will corrode. Without traps, foul odors from bacterial growth in the sump tank invade the vessel's accommodation through drain lines. Bacteria grow in cycles when temperature and salinity of the residual waste water in the tank is just right.

Since water traps block the flow of air displaced as the sump tank fills, drainage will be sluggish unless the tank is vented. Position the vent on deck to dissipate bacterial odor out of doors. Otherwise, your guests will ask a lot of embarrassing questions.

SUMP-TANK PUMP-OUT

Centrifugal bilge pumps are not suitable for sump-tank pump-out, because they don't pass debris reliably. PAR's one-inch, positive-displacement, diaphragm-type bilge pump is a good choice. It pumps out refuse that sneaks past the galley sink basket. Locate the sump outlet at the tank's low point. The discharge line from the pump outlet must rise a few feet above the waterline with a siphon break valve at the apex before exiting the hull lower down via a skin fitting. Without a vented loop above the waterline, the tank will flood when the boat heels or rolls under sail.

A sump tank is really a bilge in miniature. Centrally position a float switch inside the tank for automatic operation. Provide a manual override switch, too, in case the float switch becomes jammed with grease or refuse. This lets you pump out the sump tank manually until you have time to clean it out (not a nice job at sea). The manual switch also serves to empty the tank for preventive maintenance.

The PAR diaphragm bilge pump is similar in design to the pressure water pump, and the spare parts inventory follows suit: a complete standby pump with soldered eyes on its wiring, a rebuild kit, and a few extra sets of check valves. Pack away a spare float switch or two as well.

There are other ways to drain below-the-waterline sinks. Some vessels have valved drain lines and a manual diaphragm bilge pump for each fixture. After each use, the sink is pumped out by hand. For long-term liveaboard service, this is quite a hassle. Individual valves and pumps could cost more than one automatic sump-tank system, too, particularly if many sinks are involved.

Under no circumstances may shower, sink, or refrigerator drains lead to the bilges. The consequences are offensive, unsanitary, and unsafe if debris and deposits restrict bilge pump operation. Enforced pump-out of bilges in port carries engine oil overboard along with waste water—very antisocial.

GATE VALVES, BALL VALVES, OR SEACOCKS

Seacock is a sort of blanket term, casually referring to underwater through-hull valves. But technically, it's a specific design resembling a giant petcock. A seacock's housing has a tapered bore, and a rotating inner plug is lapped to fit it precisely. Ports in the outer casing align with a passage through the rotating plug when the seacock is open, allowing fluid to travel through the fitting.

The bore and rotating plug have considerable contact area, and this is the weakness of a traditional seacock. When the lubricant is finally washed out, the valve becomes harder to operate and eventually sticks fast. Corrosion can roughen mating surfaces, too, locking the seacock up tight. There are through-hull valves for cruising, which make better sense.

Bronze ball valves with Teflon seals have advantages over traditional seacocks: internal mated surfaces are minimized, and metal-to-metal contact is eliminated by the nonmetallic seal. Ball valves operate by 90-degree action, like the old seacock—except ball valves need less muscle to manipulate and less maintenance.

High-quality, all-bronze gate valves do the job, too, with reservations, but are best avoided. They must be manufactured entirely of bronze, not a mixture of brass and bronze components (this is true of any bronze valve contacting salt water). The problem with gate valves (and some ball valves) is that they are used in shoreside applications where all-bronze construction isn't a concern. Gate valves are prone to marine growth on their machined mating surfaces when left open for long periods in liveaboard use. Then they refuse to seal tight. Gate-valve failures on vessels operating in salt water are not unknown. Cheap valves combined with inadequate galvanic and electrolytic protection make for disaster. These liabilities aside, gate valves have screw action, and for convenience every last valve aboard should have 90-degree action. It's also obvious at a glance whether a 90-degree valve is open or closed, but you can't tell by looking at a screw-type one.

Fiberglass-reinforced plastic ball valves are something to think about. They offer the convenience of a bronze ball valve without the disadvantage of metallic construction, so any fears of deterioration from galvanic or electrolytic action are laid to rest. Reinforced plastic valves are fitted to thousands of boats all over the world, and they are proving reliable. Yet bronze is strong stuff, and a metal surface is undoubtedly more resistant than plastic to damage from scraping and poking on cleaning day. Since each material has its advantages, choice may be based on application: nonmetallic valves for metal hulls and bronze ones for vessels made of GRP or timber.

This ball valve has 90-degree action, total immunity to corrosion and electrolysis, and resistance to marine growth. Both valve and through-hull are made of Marelon, a fiberglass-reinforced type of nylon. The material is temperature stable and stands up to vibration, solvents, and impact. Ball and seat composition are specially formulated for long life. Note mounting lugs (optional). No normal plastic fitting, this is the one product that rivals bronze for strength. A must for metal hulls; a sensible option for wood and GRP vessels. Approved by the Underwriters Laboratories. Manufactured by R.C. Marine Products, Parkway Drive, Mairangi Bay, Auckland; marketed in North America by Forespar, 2672 Dow Avenue, Tustin, CA 92680. Photo by R.C. Marine.

R.C. Marine's Marelon ball valve and neat stainless steel bulkhead bracket with hose nipples. A row of these is perfect for water-tank selection, etc. Photo by R.C. Marine.

THE MARINE HEAD AND ITS PLUMBING

Toilets on recreational craft can be inexpensive fixtures; they are used intermittently in leisure time. But a marine toilet aboard a cruising yacht is subject to continual, daily operation. Quality, then, is a priority. Only the best units will serve the crew year after year.

One robust head on the U.S. market is Wilcox Crittenden's Skipper. It has a large under-bowl piston requiring a minimum of strokes to discharge sewage. The operating lever is long, applying great power to the piston with little effort. Its castings of solid bronze are tougher than the more delicate plastic molding on less pricey toilets. And it has a sizable base for sturdy mounting.

The Skipper flushes readily. The inlet valve is a spring-loaded, foot-operated pedal, and the user doesn't have to bend over to operate a lever or twist a valve by hand. A foot-operated inlet valve also leaves one hand free for the ship at sea.

If you choose the Skipper, it has one weak link you must prepare for: the internal lever arm connecting the pump handle to the piston can fracture. Make sure you have spares aboard; a lever arm is not included in the standard spares package.

Regardless of the head you choose, rebuild kits must be stowed aboard for yearly overhaul. In addition, pack away four or five extra joker valves, those black rubber nonreturn gismos that live in the outlet elbow. Joker valves perish quickly and should be replaced every three months or thereabouts to keep a head working in top form in continuous duty.

Any head built of bronze castings, such as the Skipper, will benefit from custom treatment before installation. When the fixture is new, right out of the box, disassemble it completely. Take all the external bronze bits in for a quality chrome-plating job. Then reassemble the head and bolt it in place. The chrome-plating exercise serves two purposes: first, you gain familiarity with the innards of an important piece of equipment by taking it apart yourself, and second, the head will be more attractive and the finish more durable over the years (bronze soon corrodes, bleeds green through the standard white paint job, and looks seedy). A chromed toilet is also easier to clean. Make sure the inside of the piston bore is sealed off against plating; chrome in there will peel and chew up piston leathers.

Blake's Lavac head takes a different approach and is worth a look. It flushes by vacuum. As waste is pumped out via a reliable diaphragm handpump instead of the more troublesome conventional piston-type head pumps, an O-ring-sealed seat lid creates a partial vacuum in the bowl, sucking flushing seawater in through the inlet plumbing automatically. The design is simplicity itself, with a fraction of the moving parts of ordinary heads.

HEAD DISCHARGE

Holding tanks and sewage-treatment devices that comply with U.S. law will seldom, if ever, be an asset overseas because of the scarcity of pump-out facilities.

Wilcox Crittenden's Skipper. Note chrome-plated bronze parts, teak seat and lid, beefy mounting base, and pedal operated inlet.

If you are planning a voyage outside American waters, don't get too carried away with bulky and expensive holding or treatment equipment. Just install the bare minimum to satisfy local laws. Lugging an empty 50-gallon holding tank all over the world—with space aboard being at such a premium—isn't practical.

Non-U.S. vessels calling at U.S. ports without holding tanks haven't been universally hassled so far. Although it's unethical to advocate the flaunting of any law, the old saying, "It's easier to get forgiveness than permission," has a place in the scheme of things. A foreign vessel entering U.S. waters for the purpose of sale, however, needs the proper equipment aboard to meet local rulings for a change of ownership to be legal.

Certainly sewage discharge in confined and congested waters is abhorrent, and no responsible sailor should contribute to it. On the other hand, blue-water cruising boats, at sea for weeks at a time, cannot always employ holding tanks. And resources expended for token holding tanks are better spent elsewhere on the boat.

But enough. Direct discharge flows through one-and-a-half-inch plumbing, terminating at a seacock below the waterline. If you have ever witnessed an above-the-waterline head outlet in action, you'll know why it must be underwater. No other plumbing, such as a sink drain, can share this skin fitting, or evil side effects like sewage backing up into the sink will raise your hackles. An inverted U is arranged well above the vessel's waterline. At the peak of the U is a vacuum relief valve, also called an antisiphon or siphon-break valve. This fitting must be at least a foot above the waterline when located near the vessel's centerline and farther above the waterline if placed outboard. The siphon break must not sink below sea level when the boat rolls or heels.

The siphon break stops seawater from siphoning back into the toilet bowl and flooding the boat. The toy ones you see in the marine chandlery shops are not acceptable. They leak and dribble and stink. Obtain a commercial vacuum relief valve like the one Onan uses in its diesel generator-cooling systems.

The U and much of the head outlet plumbing may be constructed of PVC rigid piping and elbows that are more attractive than the traditional black neoprene hose and hose clamps. The traditional bronze U corrodes into ugliness very quickly as well. One-and-a-half-inch PVC tees are available with a female half-inch-pipe thread boss for use at the top of the U. The Onan vacuum relief valve screws right in.

Inlet plumbing for flushing should be a minimum of three-quarters of an inch

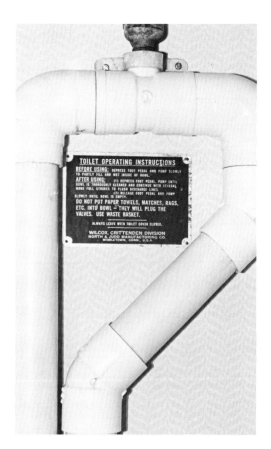

A PVC vented loop running above the water-line. Note commercial-grade antisiphon valve. Head outlets without this feature will flood toilet bowls (Lavac excepted).

inside diameter. If you can't locate the inlet seacock on the opposite side of the keel from the outlet, place it forward and deeper than the outlet. This reduces the likelihood of waste recycling back through the toilet. Inlets are not normally fitted with siphon-break inverted U fittings, because flushing depends on seawater pressure. Inlets for Lavac heads are an exception.

Often a cruising boat anchors or berths in waters infested with debris, and head intakes clog. It's quite a job stripping apart the intake plumbing—or worse yet, the head itself—to clean out blocked passages. This will be a thing of the past if you install a big engine-type intake strainer in the intake line next to the seacock. You won't see a head inlet strainer on one boat in a million, but you'll be glad it's on yours.

A larger head inlet seacock, say one to one-and-a-quarter inches, lessens the chances of blockage, too. Shy away from little half- and three-quarter-inch through-hull fittings for any purpose. They choke up too easily.

PRESSURE SALT WATER IN THE GALLEY

Frequently, yachts have a pressure freshwater system, yet retain an antiquated saltwater handpump in the galley. Why make it easy to use precious fresh water and difficult to use an endless supply of salt water?

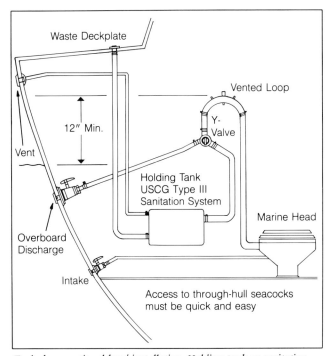

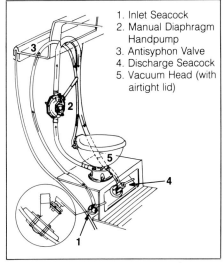

1. Inlet Seacock
2. Manual Diaphragm Handpump
3. Antisyphon Valve
4. Discharge Seacock
5. Vacuum Head (with airtight lid)

Typical conventional head installation. Holding tank or sanitation system optional.

Blake's Lavac head installation differs from conventional setups. An antisiphon valve is necessary in the inlet line because there is no inlet valve on the head. The outlet plumbing needs no antisiphon valve because the manual diaphragm discharge pump has built-in check valves. Blake & Sons, P.O. Box 15, Sunbeam Works, Gosport, Hants, PO12 2HG, England.

To facilitate daily dishwashing, install a pressure saltwater system with a pivoting spout. The galley slaves can clean those dishes 'til the cows come home, letting salt water run and run. And you'll have more fresh water left for important things like showering.

It won't be necessary to fit a complete pressure system in the normal sense, just a delivery system. A small 12-volt pump like a Jabsco, an inlet seacock with a strainer (or teed off another seawater intake), a switch, and a swing spout are all that's needed. Delivery is either on or off. Considering you'll want both hands free for the job, a knee- or foot-activated switch is the most convenient. Anchor windlass deck switches with rubber boots are just the ticket.

Even tiny 12-volt pumps may deliver too much salt water. You may be better off using a 24-volt pump running on 12 volts to cut down output. Add a variable rheostat to the pump circuit so you can adjust pump speed precisely for just the right water flow.

ADVANTAGES OF A WATERMAKER

When it comes to living the good life afloat for extended periods in remote locales, independence and cruising comfort are firmly linked. For example, crews that wish to spend months in the Tuamotu atolls of French Polynesia are often forced out of the area prematurely because their freshwater supply runs low. Either that, or they go on strict rationing to hang on a bit longer, which takes the fun out of life. With a watermaker aboard, your lifestyle gains welcomed flexibility.

A watermaker contributes to healthier cruising by eliminating disorders stemming from infected water supplies. The Aztec two-step isn't worth experiencing, and hepatitis could ruin your whole trip. Desalination equipment also saves you the trouble of ferrying jerry-jugs of fresh water by dinghy to the mother ship in remote anchorages. It's seldom possible in outlying regions to bring a yacht alongside a wharf for watering. Either there is no wharf, or the water alongside is too shallow for anything but small native fishing canoes.

Self-contained watermakers in ready-to-install cabinets occupy as little as two cubic feet and deliver ten, 20, even 40 gallons of fresh water per hour, converting ordinary seawater. Belt-driven component kits take up less room and are more suitable for yachts. The hardware looks a lot like mechanical refrigeration componentry.

The principle of operation is simple. Seawater is forced against a man-made, semipermeable membrane; the water molecules pass through the membrane, but the sea salts do not. The process requires a pump to force the fresh water past the barrier at a pressure between 700 to 950 psi. Most of the energy for desalination is consumed by this pump. Prefilters remove solids larger than five to ten microns from seawater so the membrane doesn't clog up and lose efficiency. Sensors monitor salinity and automatically divert the product over the side if the salt content is too high for safe human consumption. Gauges

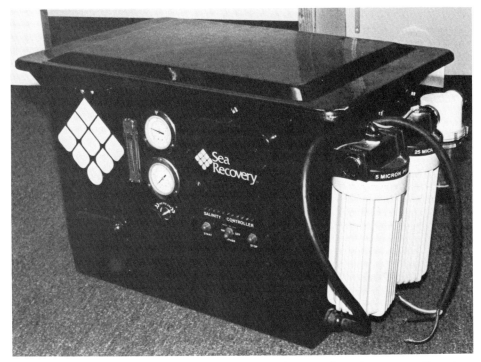

Sea Recovery's self-contained, AC-powered desalinator housed in a weather-resistant GRP cabinet. Output, 100 to 600 gallons per day; other models, up to 1,200 gallons per day. Note external inlet filters and strainer to protect the equipment's membrane. Sea Recovery also manufactures component systems for custom installations.

indicate flow rates into the ship's tanks. And an alarm warns you if the seawater intake or membrane becomes plugged.

Most watermakers in ready-to-install cabinets are powered by AC electrical energy, consuming 3,000 watts and up. Component kits with engine-driven pressure pumps nibble a meager six amps or so of 12-volt current during operation for the monitoring circuitry. Regardless of the energy source— mechanical or electrical—the ability to produce gallons of fresh water while motoring, charging batteries, or pulling down a refrigeration system is a boon. Custom systems that harness a freewheeling propeller shaft to spin the pump are available, too, although of modest output. Imagine making fresh water under sail and ending ocean passages with full tanks!

But the cruising sailor can't rely on a watermaker entirely. Sufficient tankage is still necessary as a backup in case the watermaker takes some time off. And remember that sufficient tankage must be available to absorb the watermaker's output; it'd be a pity to make tons of fresh water and have nowhere to store it. So a watermaker will not answer all your problems; it simply provides an alternate source of drinking water, thereby increasing your independence.

Desalinators are a good value for the money as it is, but a percentage of the cost is offset because tankage on a long-range boat can be safely halved to about 50

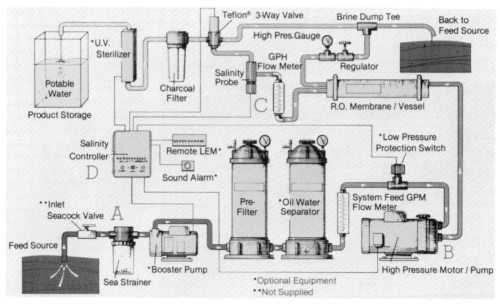

Sea Recovery Reverse Osmosis Desalinating System (Sea Recovery, Box 349, San Pedro, CA). Courtesy of Sea Recovery.

gallons per person. Water tanks are costly, and there's a real savings when total capacity is reduced.

Space occupied by a watermaker is nothing compared to space gained by less tankage. The net result is extra storage—lots of it. Vessels with watermakers are bound to be lighter, too, perhaps by as much as 1,000 pounds. This is a bonus, since overall weight of a fully laden cruising boat is one thing that's difficult to keep down.

BILGE PUMPS

Bilge pumps may not be as exciting as the prospect of unlimited freshwater showers with a watermaker. Unless you need a bilge pump desperately, that is— then they will will be very dear to your heart!

Several bilge-pumping systems are necessary to protect your investment and your crew. The first line of defense against flooding is an electric pump, such as the PAR unit discussed earlier for the sump tank. A positive-displacement bilge pump with a diaphragm pushing water past check valves has advantages for cruising over the more popularly accepted centrifugal-type bilge pumps seen in recreational use.

Centrifugal bilge pumps have two potential liabilities. First, they are vulnerable to choking: small debris can jam the impeller or cause it to cavitate, and pumping ceases. Second, although they look good on paper, the volume of water expelled by centrifugal pumps falls drastically with increased head pressure. Since centrifugal pumps live down in the lowest part of the bilge where the water is (they are submersible-type units and not self-priming), they frequently must overcome a great discharge gradient, and output suffers accordingly. Cruising boats tend to be substantial vessels in terms of displacement, with bilge sumps far below the waterline. The vertical distance is increased by the need of a siphon-break loop rising some feet above the waterline.

Positive-displacement bilge pumps might not, at first glance, seem to throw out volumes of water like centrifugal pumps, yet in actual service they can actually throw out more. Diaphragm pumps have some virtues worth considering. First, they are hard to choke. Second, they are self-priming and don't need to be right down with the bilge water. This means they can be positioned with maintenance in mind.

The price paid for choosing a diaphragm pump is increased maintenance. They have more working parts (diaphragm, check valves, connecting rod, belt) than centrifugal pumps have. A good centrifugal pump such as a Rule will give trouble-free service for years. Chances are the PAR will need to be rebuilt once every year or so for top performance, although this is no great chore.

So how do you decide between a centrifugal and a diaphragm pump? If your boat has immaculate bilges, as it should, and the bilge sump isn't too far below the waterline, then a centrifugal pump will fill the bill. However, if your boat has very deep bilges, and you already have a diaphragm pump for sump or shower discharge, then it's a good idea to install an identical model as a bilge pump and consolidate your spares inventory.

If you opt for a centrifugal unit, give attention to the problem of surge in the discharge line. The pump will dry out the bilge and shut off, then the water in the outlet line that didn't make it over the hill will rush back down through the pump into the bilge. This may cause the float switch to cycle on and off. To cure this, locate the float switch an inch or two higher or install a check valve (a large one that won't restrict the pump's output) near the pump's outlet port in the discharge line. Your pump manufacturer should be able to advise you on this. (Diaphragm pumps don't have this problem; their internal check valves, if in good order, inhibit backfeeding.)

The companion feature of an electric bilge pump is the float switch. This automatic feature is important, acting as a sentinel against a flooded bilge. A float switch is particularly important on unattended vessels. For this reason, an automatic bilge-pump system should be wired independently of the master switch, directly to a battery bank. When you shut down the main electrical circuits, the pump must remain on duty.

Motor-driven accessories like bilge pumps require a big surge of current to get them rolling. A fuse near the value of the pump's advertised electrical consumption will wear out from momentary starting loads and eventually fail even though no problem exists. Remember: it's best to use slow-blow fuses for momentary overloads and replace them periodically for extra protection. A bilge pump that goes on strike secretly is no friend. Use the same reasoning with a circuit breaker in a bilge-pump circuit—fit a slow-trip one of a higher value (say, 50 percent over rated pump consumption).

Most electric bilge pumps are supplied with a switch panel holding a single-pole, triple-throw toggle switch. This provides three positions: manual, off, and automatic (float switch). The switch should be left on automatic, but it's a good practice to toggle the switch each day to the manual setting. Listen to the pump until it sucks air. This tells you how much water, if any, the vessel made since yesterday, and also lets you listen for unhealthy sounds in the pump. If you do this as a matter of routine, whether you are in harbor or at sea, you'll avoid nasty surprises.

No single system for a vital task can be trusted absolutely. That's why a manual bilge-pumping setup is fitted as a backup. Manual diaphragm pumps pass an exceptional amount of water and are resistant to clogging. Provide a completely separate plumbing network for each bilge-pump system so a common problem won't put several systems on the blink all at once. For example, bilge pumps should not be teed into other drainage plumbing. Electric and manual bilge pumps teed into a cockpit drain for economy could both be out of order if weeds or barnacles blocked the through-hull. For the same reason, bilge pickups should never be shared. Discharge outlets should be placed above the waterline to minimize pump-out resistance. Besides, above-the-waterline drains are less subject to marine growth.

All bilge-pump discharge plumbing should be arranged with short runs to keep internal friction down for maximum volumetric efficiency. No sharp bends, elbows, or restrictions from components that reduce a plumbing's inside diameter can be tolerated. Electric bilge-pump discharge lines should be at least one-and-one-quarter inches inside diameter, and manual outlet lines should be one-and-one-half inches inside diameter or larger to suit equipment outlet nipples.

Another manual diaphragm bilge pump mounted on a board with ten feet of inlet and ten feet of outlet hose makes a handy portable unit. This adds another backup to the ship's inventory and is convenient for pumping out dinghies or transferring water or fuel. Make sure your portable pump has a chemically resistant diaphragm, check valves, and hose.

Yet another manual diaphragm bilge pump and plumbing network serves the chain locker sump, which should be isolated from the vessel's bilges by a watertight bulkhead.

COCKPIT DRAINS

Cruising cockpits should be designed so they don't hold enough water if flooded by the sea to affect the vessel's trim. Nor should a flooded cockpit pour into the accommodation via the companionway (a high bridge deck and stout dropboards prevent this). High cockpit coamings attached to the deckhouse must be cut away somewhere to let water escape instantly down to deck level.

Seats sunk below deck level should be avoided on an oceangoing yacht. It's best if only the cockpit well is a receptacle for seawater; it won't hold much compared to the rest of the cockpit. Lockers accessible through hinged cockpit seats don't belong on oceangoing boats either. It's better to reach under cockpit stowage from below decks and preserve watertight integrity.

Traditional cockpit drainage emphasizes large scuppers. But even gargantuan drains won't empty an oversized cockpit quickly. Safety depends more on cockpit design. Drains should only be asked to cope with spray and rainwater.

Nevertheless, try for the best cockpit drainage you can arrange. The cockpit sole is built to slope aft slightly to avoid a wet spot at the companionway, and drains are positioned in each aft corner. Designers have advocated some fancy footwork by crisscrossing drain lines, but nothing beats the direct vertical shot. Through-hulls should exit the hull above the waterline. This speeds drainage and eliminates two unnecessary underwater fittings.

Check valves (floating rubber balls) in cockpit drains restrict flow. Instead, cockpit soles should be far enough above the waterline so backfeeding from the sea into the cockpit in rough weather is not a problem. Grids on cockpit-drain hardware serve one purpose: to keep your valuables from going down the spout. A crossbar over the hole is more efficient for drainage than a perforated cover plate.

Test your drains by plugging them and filling the cockpit. While you are at it, check the trim. And see if water flows below decks, either through the companionway or those dreaded cockpit lockers. Release the plugs and see how long it takes for the cockpit to empty; it'll probably take longer than you think.

Don't overlook cockpit seat drains, or a pocket of water will pool in seat corners when the boat heels under sail. Low spots on deck that collect rainwater or spray should also be dealt with by scuppers or limber holes.

Some cockpits have massive tubes leading straight aft through the transom for drains, or more daring, open transoms adjoining the cockpit. In a heavy following sea, this kind of thinking is all wet.

CONVENIENCE IS THE KEY

Shipboard plumbing systems should *seem* to act much like shoreside systems. This means automatic, hands-off operation whenever feasible. Manual features have a habit of interfering with one's life. Reliable self-tending systems do take more initial effort to plan and implement, but they are worth it in the long run. The best-loved features and systems aboard ship are the ones you hardly notice. They don't attract any attention because they work.

4▶ The Engine Room and Its Machinery

The rig towering above decks is an evident part of a sailboat's character, liable to comment and attention. Engine rooms hide below, out of the limelight; thus, no admiration for them—just abuse or mishandling when something goes haywire.

For serious cruising, be it local, coastal, or far afield to overseas ports, the boat must function as a sailboat *and* a motor yacht. Although the rig propels the boat through the water most of the time, it doesn't dominate the cruising life as it does recreational sailing. The engine room, on the other hand, although playing a minor role in recreation, gets top billing on a cruise. Someday, reliable machinery may be all that stands between your ship and harm, especially in emergencies when the rig is useless windage.

And the engine room has roles other than locomotion. Through long intervals in harbor it slaves away, giving freedom and pleasure. At sea, it's critical to security.

Armed with the basic rules of system design—simplicity, accessibility, and ease of maintenance—get down on your hands and knees and give the engine room the tender loving care it deserves. If you run across any cancer, cut it out, or it'll kill your voyage.

HOW MUCH POWER?

Sometimes the owners of cruising boats don't have much say about engine selection. What comes in a production boat is pretty much potluck. Economics play a part, since production builders are influenced by cost, thus limiting customers' options. Custom vessels offer freedom of choice, and of course, people who build their own boats have total control. But even with freedom of choice, the decision won't be easy. Certainly, diesel power for dependability and economy. But how much?

To nail down horsepower, first figure out your power plant's responsibilities. Is the prime objective extreme range under power? Or more speed with less emphasis on economy? How about responsive maneuvering? These things call for a different approach to power.

Economical, long-range cruising under power, at, say, 0.7 to 0.8 of the boat's theoretical hull speed (roughly five to six knots for a 40-footer) takes about one-and-one-quarter horsepower per ton (continuous). A 40-foot yacht, displacing 15 tons, traveling conservatively for optimum endurance, uses a steady 20 horsepower. Fuel consumption is about three-quarters of a gallon per hour. This only applies in calm conditions when there's no extra resistance to forward motion such as headwinds, wave action, or a badly fouled bottom.

More power is necessary to travel faster, near hull speed (approximately 7.5 knots for a 40-footer): about two horsepower per ton of displacement, or 30 or more continuous horses for the 15-tonner. The extra couple of knots practically doubles fuel consumption, greatly decreasing the boat's range under power. Lesson: speed costs.

For jackrabbit maneuvering, a further increase in horsepower, sometimes a colossal increase, is required. A 15-ton yacht could benefit from 100-horsepower bursts while jockeying in a tight spot. There's nothing so satisfying as surplus muscle in close quarters, either. Fuel consumption doesn't matter a damn for momentary spurts of raw energy—the object is overcoming inertia instantly. The heavier the boat, the more power you need.

Power, then, must take into account various conflicts of interest. For extended cruising, range under power is important (see section on tankage). However, it's shortsighted to choose an engine sized for minimal fuel consumption alone. It will generally prove too weak. A slightly larger engine won't be quite as stingy, because it won't operate in the most efficient rpm range or at optimum loading for ideal volumetric efficiency. Yet some surplus power is vital.

Since the cruising yacht must be, in many respects, a powerboat, too, good performance while motoring is essential. The rig and hull present quite a resistance to a headwind. And head seas reduce speed. To move against both requires a considerable increase in thrust over calm conditions. Also, fully laden boats in cruising trim are weighty, despite intentions. And weight is a factor to be reckoned with in close-quarters maneuvering. Reserve power is an important safety factor when fighting a pass against a strong current, too, particularly with some growth on the bottom.

A workable compromise is an engine sized to move the vessel at hull speed with a few ponies to spare, continuously, with a fouled bottom over a fairly calm sea. Figure on three to four horsepower per ton of displacement, or, in the case of our 15-ton 40-footer, 45 to 60 horses (continuous, not intermittent).

If you plan to drive a cluster of auxiliary equipment off the propulsion engine, you'll need more horses so the vessel's performance remains the same. Engines under 50 horsepower are sensitive to loads from extra generators and compressors, because a larger percentage of the engine's total output is diverted from the propeller to run them than is the case with bigger engines.

WHAT TYPE OF DIESEL?

An engine's continuous power capabilities are often a far cry from maximum advertised horsepower. Once you've an idea of the continuous power you need, decide on the type of engine in order to nail down the maximum rating required. A heavy-duty power plant is normally rated for continuous duty at maximum output; higher speed diesels have intermittent maximum ratings and lower ratings for continuous, day-in, day-out operation.

True slow to medium-speed marine power plants weigh at least twice what high-speed engines with the same advertised power rating weigh. And slower speed engines may be twice the size, physically. The obvious difference is height: heavy-duty engines have longer strokes and more sump capacity for larger oil reserves. They stand tall. Real marine engines have bigger bores, too; the engine block is longer, cylinder for cylinder. They make up for slower rpm's with increased cubic capacity. This, and heavy construction, makes them wider. Huge flywheels for smooth running add width and weight as well. Most heavy-duty marine power plants in the ten-to-100-horsepower range have maximum engine speeds between 750 and 1,200 rpm. They're found in workboats but rarely in yachts anymore because of weight, bulk, and astronomical initial cost.

Medium-speed engines, however, are found on quality custom vessels. They top out at or under 2,000 rpm and cruise at about 1,200 to 1,400 rpm for peak efficiency. If asked, engines of this type operate for long periods at or near their maximum ratings.

On the other side of the coin are engines that started life in industrial or agricultural applications and were converted for marine use. Many power plants installed in production boats are of this type. They are compact, lightweight, and much less expensive—sensible attributes for casual recreation, where anything more would be a waste of money. High-speed diesels top out between 2,500 and

3,000 rpm, some higher, and cruise between 1,500 and 2,800 rpm in auxiliary sailboat applications. Rpm ratings go higher in runabout and planing-cruiser applications.

Traditional marine power plants have advantages. They are built for reliability and longevity in severe service. Weight is not shaved at the expense of strength. Structurally superior engines turning more slowly require much less maintenance than do lightweight, high-revving power plants. Cooling is greatly improved by larger radiating surfaces and capacious lube oil sumps. Large oil reservoirs mean less frequent oil changes, too. Valve clearance adjustments, after the engine is run in, are infrequent. Husky, slow-turning components—camshafts, injector pumps, and crankshafts—and reciprocating components like valves and pistons—go on forever. Bearing surfaces are massive and durable. Seals last longer. Volumetric efficiency is higher, producing more horses per gallon of fuel. Brute strength allows high-compression ratios, furthering efficiency. Higher compression ratios contribute to easy starting without glow plugs or intake air heaters in cold weather. Hand-starting is a common feature, too, even on engines of 100 horsepower, whereas it's not seen on high-speed diesels.

Real marine medium-speed propulsion engines are designed for maintenance. They have individual cylinder heads that are convenient to remove and lug around. Inspection ports in the crankcase facilitate the removal of connecting rod caps for bearing inspection and, if necessary, replacement. Often the cylinders are individually removable, too; engines can be completely rebuilt right on their mounts.

Other design features increase dependability. Pumps are normally gear driven, eliminating a symphony of vee-belts and a forest of mounting brackets. Tall engines require fewer cylinders for a given capacity. This means fewer pistons, valves, bearings, injectors, etc., to inspect, adjust, rebuild, and replace.

A well-built cruising vessel lasts decades. How sensible to fit an engine that's a permanent part of the boat, rather than a temporary fixture. A slow to medium-speed engine can last ten times as long as a lightweight, high-speed one. And there's nothing like them for sure starts, year after year.

Your vessel's ability to carry weight and the vertical space that can be designed into her engine room influence engine selection. Medium-to-heavy-displacement boats allow more latitude. They have more internal volume and tolerate more engine weight per foot.

In the long run, a genuine marine engine is less expensive, if you can stand the initial jolt. If you plan to own your boat for years and sail to far places, it's an investment that can pay.

THE DRIVE TRAIN

Efficiency can be improved with an engineered drive train. In the quest for the last 0.1 knot under sail, the motoring qualities of a sailboat are downgraded. If you sail all the time, okay. But you won't on a cruise.

For propulsion efficiency, propeller shaft speed should not exceed 700 rpm (at cruising speeds, not flat out). Then a larger diameter propeller can be fitted for more efficiency against headwinds and head seas. Shaft speed depends on engine rpm and the reduction-gear ratio. For cruising, medium-speed diesels are usually fitted with two-to-one reductions; high-speed engines, three to one.

Efficiency under power in displacement boats is at an all-time low with direct-drive (no reduction gear), two-bladed propeller drive trains. Cruising depends too much on motoring performance to consider anything but the smoothness and efficiency of a three-bladed propeller coupled to a reduction gear.

Variable-pitch propellers, mentioned earlier for freewheeling charging systems, seem the answer— full feathering for low drag under sail and optimum thrust under power. A fixed propeller is only right for one loading condition and a little bit wrong the rest of the time, while a variable-pitch prop can be set to match all conditions (motorsailing, powering in a calm, powering against a headwind, etc.). But it's difficult to engineer reliability into small variable-pitch systems, and only first-class gear should be considered. Also, although variable-pitch systems are claimed to eliminate the need for a reverse gear, maneuvering in tight quarters (backing and filling) is less nerve-racking with the instant response of a shift lever rather than the clumsier pitch control wheel.

All things considered, including cost, the best setup is a fixed, three-bladed prop of generous diameter, but with thinner blades than a powerboat prop to reduce drag under sail. At least this alternative is 100-percent dependable.

ENGINE LOCATION

A separate engine room with full standing headroom, although a blessing, isn't practical on most boats under 50 feet. The exception, the center-cockpit configuration, offers the potential for spacious machinery spaces, which no other layout can match.

Aft-cockpit yachts often have unacceptable machinery spaces. The first thing a knowledgeable designer does is avoid the use of vee-drives: they shoehorn an engine out of reach and shift too much weight toward the stern, increasing polar inertia. They also place the engine higher, raising the vessel's center of gravity. There's not always a way around stuffing engines under aft cockpits. However, it helps when the boat is designed *around* the engine instead of the engine being squeezed in as an afterthought. Remember: the farther forward the engine, the more room around it.

Every component in the machinery space must be easily reached for inspection and maintenance. Production yachts vary in emphasis given to machinery spaces, but all too often the more obvious features that further the cause of marketing receive priority— and what's out of sight is seldom examined. Sales commentary such as, "The engine's back there, out of the way," probably means the engine is crammed in an improbable hole that only a chimp can reach. Maintenance of that engine will expand your vocabulary.

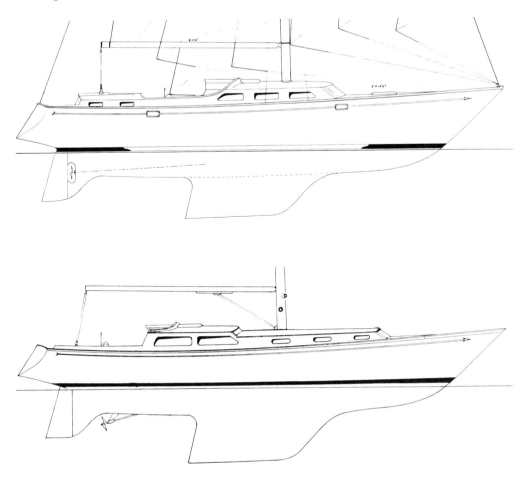

These views of a Salthouse 46 show a nice medium-displacement cruising profile with ample keel and a solid skeg. Note the prop-shaft location for each. By raising the propeller and moving it slightly aft, the center-cockpit version achieves a nearly horizontal shaft. Thrust is directed right at the rudder for more responsive static maneuvering, too. The aperture is placed correctly in the skeg; apertures in rudders make them difficult to construct, and when the helm is hard over, the prop wash blows right through the hole, and static maneuvering (with no way on) is more sluggish. Courtesy of Salthouse Design Services, Ltd.

Some machinery spaces underneath aft cockpits should be illegal. If access to the gearbox, shaft coupling, stuffing box, exhaust system, and rudder gland is through a removable cockpit floor or through cockpit locker hatches, you need to be a human pretzel. Removable cockpit sole panels almost always leak, bathing the equipment beneath in salt water. They can take forever and a day to remove, too. In an emergency, in case of a strange noise or burst pipe, cockpit hatches are criminal. When it's pouring rain, and you're slogging along in rough weather, they should be a hanging offense.

Engines are also installed in the galley inside a box. This certainly offers better access than a cramped cave under an aft cockpit. But engine boxes lack space for equipment and extra engine-driven accessories, and there's the difficulty of ventilation, sound deadening, and routing the exhaust system. The galley itself is compromised by less stowage and floor space. How would you like a diesel engine in your kitchen ashore?

Engines live under cabin soles, too, notably in vessels with high doghouses allowing raised cabin soles to clear the machinery. Generous hatches must be built in the floor as the only access is from above. In a rolling seaway, big horizontal hatches are awkward, and once opened, they create a gaping hole filled with roaring machinery—a devil's playground. Still, this layout lets you reach things, and it offers precious standing headroom.

In aft-cockpit boats under 50 feet, it's often possible to design a sizable engine room under an athwartship double berth in a stateroom just forward of the cockpit. This has advantages. The engine moves forward out from under the cockpit, where the hull is wider. More room is available around the power plant for access and additional equipment.

ENGINE-ROOM ATTRIBUTES

Wherever your engine sits, the machinery space must be sealed from the rest of the below-decks accommodation (see chapter on ventilation), and noise must be dampened by sound-deadening materials. Maintenance should be geared for offshore conditions, when a breakdown is hardest to deal with and when the engine and its machinery are vital to security.

An engine room should be painted white and have bright, multiple lighting. It should be clean as a whistle—no fuel or oil leaks anywhere. A twice-a-year wipedown with a rag lightly dampened with kerosene should keep the engine spotless.

When looking at designs to build from or boats to buy, you should ask hard questions of the engine room. Can the cylinder head be easily removed? (Unbelievably, some designers force you to pull the engine first!) Can you conveniently remove an engine's inspection covers to inspect bearings? Can the transmission and reduction gear be removed without pulling the engine? Can you get at all the pumps, the starter motor, alternators, heat exchanger, injector pump, and so on for maintenance, replacement, or quick inspection? What about adjusting valve clearances? Can you change fuel and oil filters without getting oil and fuel all over the place? Will a job like this ruin your whole day? What about checking the dipstick?

If every potential customer looking for a cruising boat would insist on witnessing an oil change, stuffing-box adjustment, seawater pump impeller replacement, and a valve-clearance job *before* discussing personal finances and

Engine room in Dolphin Queen. *Seat in foreground (partially shown) allows comfortable sitting with major components close at hand. Note hot water heater, engine-room exhaust blower, and Formica-covered bulkhead for equipment mounting. This engine room, located under an athwartship double berth, has three access doors and a removable bunk panel. Engine: Lister HRW3, 45 horsepower continuous.*

The aft bulkhead of a 45 footer's engine room under a center cockpit. Note sink for washing up, aluminum catwalk over prop shaft, variable-pitch propeller handwheel, cockpit drain hoses on each side, safety grab bar, and fire extinguisher (which, incidentally, needs a backup or two outside the engine room).

means of payment—then there'd be progress. As a final test, how easy is the engine to align?

ENGINE HEIGHT AND ANGLE

Engines are heavy. The lower they sit, the more they aid stability. In this sense, they can be looked at as very expensive ballast. Yet some of the boat's bilge volume should remain below the engine so partial flooding won't submerge it.

One offshoot of engine position is propeller-shaft location. Ideally, the prop shaft will be almost half the vessel's draft below the waterline. Then, in rough conditions, the prop bites solid water instead of air. Lightweight boats make this impossible.

For propulsion efficiency, the propeller shaft should be horizontal, not angled. That way, thrust is directed in line with the boat's travel, and power isn't wasted trying to lift the stern. Maneuvering performance, particularly in reverse, is improved; the boat backs straighter. Again, lightweights lose out because level shafts are not practical.

In medium-to-heavy-displacement yachts, a level prop shaft can be arranged, but it sometimes positions the engine too low. This makes the power plant more difficult to reach for maintenance and more susceptible to flooding. To counteract this, the standard reduction gear should be replaced with an offset unit, raising the engine three or four inches. It can make all the difference. It's simple to organize during construction and a terrible project later on.

THE ENGINE BEDS

It may seem a foregone conclusion that your engine is permanently affixed to the boat—but don't bet on it!

Engines *have* rejected their yachts far from civilization, and the consequences are a show stopper. If it happened to you, a great part of the time and money you allocated for the cruise would be squandered to cover the blunder.

Marine power plants are heavy, and inertial loads in severe circumstances fierce. An engine won't stick around of its own accord; it must be held there. Imagine your boat laying over on her side and being dropped—hard—as happens sometimes on beam reaches in big seaways. The boat heels to her railcap, snaps upright as a wave passes underneath, and then falls over on her side again. The motion strains engine mounts and beds, trying literally to toss the engine off the beds or tear the engine *and* the beds loose from the hull.

Engine beds are best built as lengthy fore-and-aft stringers. They should be an integral part of the vessel's hull, not tacked on as afterthoughts. Long beds reduce localized loading on the hull skin, spreading weight and stress over a large area.

This serves two purposes: the engine enjoys a firm foundation, and the hull is stiffened.

Strong engine bearers in steel and aluminum yachts are not hard to arrange. Fore-and-aft members are welded permanently in place to the vessel's ribs. Engine beds in ferrocement craft are welded to the steel framework as well before plastering. Traditional wooden boats have substantial wooden beds bolted and bedded to the frames. Cold-molded boats often use box-section bearers fabricated of plywood or laminated sheets and solid timber, which are bolted and glued in place. They are stiff and durable.

The beginnings of a trade and a tradition were evident early in GRP's history. Then came the choppergun, wet-out systems, mass-production shortcuts, and the end of product continuity. Nowadays, most recreational yachts are laminated like shower stalls and spa pools by people who know nothing whatsoever about marine construction—just cheap labor. And too many construction decisions are made by accountants. Unless a boat has a Lloyds of London certificate, it's hard to tell whether it's sound unless you are an expert.

As a rule of thumb, beware of boats with bonded GRP hull liners. This shouts production-line expediency. Liners prevent access to all the nooks and crannies below decks, hiding system components and covering craftsmanship, or the lack of it. They make hull repairs difficult, too.

When liners form engine beds—watch out! A shiny engine pan with molded mounts looks smart, but how is it laminated, reinforced, and attached to the hull?

Some liner-type engine beds are tacked to the hull at the edges only, and they flex, allowing the engine to dance around. This strains engine brackets and mounts, transmission bearings, and propeller-shaft couplers and prematurely wears prop-shaft bearings. I have friends, owners of a popular heavy-displacement production boat, who have had to replace a flexible engine-bed liner with proper engine beds 10,000 miles from home. Their boat's manufacturer, who flaunted the vessel as a world cruiser in high-profile campaigns, didn't want to hear about the problem.

THE ENGINE MOUNTS

Flexible engine mounts are here to stay so long as shaky one- and two-cylinder diesels are installed in lightweight racer/cruisers. This kind of marriage needs a buffer between engine and hull, or the cream will jump out of the coffee.

More substantial cruising boats with quality marine engines have no need for flexible engine mounts. Their hull/deck structures are composed of fairly rigid skins backed up with a complete framework of stringers, ribs, partial and full bulkheads, deck beams, bonded furniture, and, if necessary, keel floors. The engines are designed to exacting standards, balanced with big flywheels and counter-rotating balancing weights, if required, to run smooth as glass despite cylinder configuration. Some examples of smooth-running engines are Lister, Kelvin, Gardner, Sabb, and Marna. When a well-built vessel is fitted with a real marine power plant, it's smoother under power with solid mounts than a recreational craft with a flex-mounted, throwaway thumper.

Solid-mounted power plants have three main advantages over flex-mounted engines. First, plumbing, wiring, and cables don't whip in endless frenzy while the engine runs. This reduces chafe and general wear and tear, contributing no end to trouble-free, long-term operation. Second, the propeller shaft is kept in strict alignment. Bearing wear and vibration from momentary misalignment from flex mounts is eliminated. Finally, only solid-mounted engines can be linked to power take-offs, the best way to drive auxiliary equipment.

Solid-mounted power plants also eliminate the need for flexible couplings between the reduction gear and prop shaft, a weak link in power transmission that can let you down in the boondocks.

Ideally, a length of angle iron a bit longer than the engine is bedded and either lag screwed or bolted (preferably) through both faces to a good hardwood engine bed. The engine mounts are bolted to the angle iron by drilling and tapping bolt holes or, if the angle iron is too thin for adequate thread depth, by through-bolting. This spreads the load. It also places some bolts in tension and some in shear, because both surfaces of the angle iron are fastened to the bearer. The result is stronger than simply lag bolting engine-mount feet directly to the beds. Angle-iron engine-bed facings are a truer surface to move the engine around on for alignment purposes. And iron bed facings offer a hard bearing surface for shims. Perfect alignment is easier to achieve and maintain—indefinitely.

There are many ways to mount an engine, so don't panic if your boat is set up differently or you're building with another system in mind. Just make sure the loads are distributed over a large area and the holding power of mount-to-bed fasteners is beyond reproach.

And finally, beware of GRP-encapsulated stringers unless you know what's inside them and how they're laminated to the hull.

ENGINE ALIGNMENT

In an existing engine installation, the engine is aligned to the propeller shaft; the prop shaft is never manipulated to comply with engine position.

Before attempting alignment, the cutlass bearing, stern tube, and stuffing box must be scrutinized to make certain the shaft passes through them all squarely. This can be checked by trying to move the shaft at each bearing point back and forth, laterally. The shaft should rattle slightly in the bearing, indicating a smidgen of clearance.

If the shaft is locked solid at a bearing point, it passes through at an angle, and alignment cannot proceed until the bearing itself is straightened. Installations with only one bearing—a cutlass bearing at the stern and a hose-mounted, self-aligning stuffing box—need a temporary support to firmly locate the shaft dead center before alignment proceeds.

After the shaft is located (longer shafts require some upward pressure at the coupling end to take the weight of the shaft so it floats in the bearings without distortion), then the engine is moved around until the coupling surfaces mate exactly. Clearance is measured with a feeler gauge. Four-thousandths (0.004) of an inch is tolerable, but try for two-thousandths (0.002) or better.

Aligning an engine is a finicky chore. But it's worth every effort to get it right. Bearings last longer, and vibration is kept to a minimum. The engine delivers more power to the water, too.

Don't take it for granted that your engine is anywhere near aligned unless you check it personally. Once it's dead on, check it again periodically. A new boat needs a checkup a few weeks after launch and another in six months. If alignment's still okay, a once-yearly inspection is sufficient as long as the boat remains in the water. Check again after each haulout.

THE COOLING SYSTEM—CHECK FOR FREE FLOW

Even if you have owned your boat for a long time and the power plant runs great, a voyage to the tropics could overtax the cooling system. Engine rooms can be 30 degrees warmer in Papeete than in Seattle due to higher ambient air and seawater temperatures. This makes cooling systems work harder.

To inspect the system, follow flow in and out of every component. First, look at the skin fitting and the inlet valve. All engines, regardless of horsepower, need cooling inlet through-hulls and valves no smaller than one-and-one-quarter inches inside diameter. One-half-inch to one-inch hardware is too easily choked by marine growth. To make certain your engine intake doesn't latch onto something it can't swallow, install a grilled cover or choose a through-hull with grillwork. To repeat: the inlet must freely ingest small things and keep out what it can't swallow.

Next in line is an intake strainer. Make sure it's at least a liter in capacity, regardless of engine size. Junk and refuse in the water does not come graded to suit different size engines. Choose a strainer with a see-through cylinder and mount it close to the inlet where it's visible, easy to clean, and over an area not bothered by a deluge. The strainer must have large ports matching inlet hardware.

Do not use 90-degree elbows or plumbing reducers or incorporate sharp bends in water hosing between the seacock and the strainer. *Do not* attach the seacock to the skin fitting with a 90-degree elbow or reducer fitting, either. Otherwise, refuse can jam in a bend and choke the intake.

A free-flowing intake fitting lets in garbage without choking on it, and a big strainer acts as a holding pen. Both work in harmony for reliable power-plant operation.

The foregoing will prevent 90 percent of your potential cooling-system headaches on a cruise. The hardware involved is cheap insurance against big trouble. The rest is straightforward until the seawater leaves the engine. Follow good plumbing practice with short, efficient runs, no sharp bends, and no restrictive components. Make sure the hoses are well supported and in no danger of chafe from vibration or moving machinery such as vee-belts. If your engine has flex mounts, observe the show while it's galloping around to be certain nothing important is being squeezed to death or slowly cut in half.

CHECKING COMPONENTS IN EXISTING INSTALLATIONS

If your power plant is not brand-new, pull the cover off the saltwater pump. Check for wear on the back face and inner face of the cover plate and inspect the impeller for cracks or missing bits of vane. Check for oil or water leaks, too. This pump is the vulnerable part of the cooling system, and a complete standby unit should be aboard for quick exchange in circumstances when a rebuild isn't practical (as at sea). Stow several saltwater pump rebuild kits, which will include the neoprene impeller, end plates, gaskets, water seals, and oil seals.

Then examine all heat exchangers to make sure the tubes are clear. Remove hoses or, when present, end caps from both ends and shine a light through the tubes. Blocked tubes should be hand-reamed with bronze welding rod until they're spick-and-span. Even partially obstructed tubes reduce cooling efficiency markedly.

If your engine has a saltwater-cooled exhaust manifold, check the water jacket for salt deposits that constrict flow. Salt deposits insulate the manifold so heat is not transferred to the cooling water as efficiently. If the manifold must be removed to ream out the deposits, do it!

Hopefully, your engine is freshwater cooled via a saltwater-cooled heat exchanger. If not, check all the engine block passages to ensure that they are free of salt deposits. Cleaning these can be a major undertaking; you might have to pull the engine to pieces to do it right. After this chore, consider installing a heat exchanger and circulating pump so you never have to do it again. Raw-seawater-cooled engines are not suitable for tropical service, because coolant temperature must be held at or below 140 degrees F. to prevent rapid salt buildup. Low operating temperatures are more difficult to maintain in high ambient temperatures (the greater the temperature differential between coolant and seawater, the greater the heat transfer).

Freshwater-cooled engines operate at higher temperatures, around 180 degrees F., improving engine efficiency and cooling reliability.

COOLING-SYSTEM PROTECTION WITH ZINC ANODES

While you have the heat exchanger pulled to bits, make sure the materials are compatible where they contact salt water and that there are zinc anodes present. The saltwater side of the heat exchanger contacts the sea just as skin fittings do, so galvanic and electrolytic protection is necessary. Scrape the paint and/or internal deposits off the end caps to see what they're made of. They *must* be bronze. Some engine manufacturers make end caps of cast iron—a definite no-no! They'll crumble to dust on your cruise. If you are stuck with cast-iron ones, use them as a pattern to make identical replacements cast of bronze and machined to fit. Make sure the new end caps have a cast boss that can be drilled and tapped for pencil zinc anodes.

THE FRESHWATER CIRCULATING SYSTEM

Marine freshwater circulating systems resemble automotive cooling systems except that a seawater-cooled heat exchanger is used in place of an air-cooled radiator. A circulating pump moves cooled fresh water from the heat exchanger through the engine passages where heat is absorbed and back to the heat exchanger again, continually. A thermostat controls the rate of flow to keep engine temperature stable at a preset value. Hoses and pipes connect the components.

Ask your engine manufacturer to recommend a suitable rust inhibitor/ antifreeze solution. This reduces internal corrosion in cooling passages and lubricates the circulating pump for longer life.

Spares for the freshwater cooling system include all gaskets, O rings, and seals for every component; a circulating-pump rebuild kit and perhaps a spare pump; zincs; an extra thermostat; and a tube of gasket sealer.

THE EXHAUST SYSTEM

Traditionally, exhaust systems were lagged (insulated) runs of black iron pipe routed from the engine up above the waterline near the deck, where seawater coolant was injected. From there the system was fabricated of hose for the downward journey to an outlet in the transom. To avoid metal fatigue, the pipe was coupled to the engine's exhaust manifold with stainless bellows-like tubing, which absorbed vibration.

It was functional. The dry part of the exhaust lasted years and years. But corrosion occurred where seawater entered the hot piping. If this part of the system was made of stainless steel, it still corroded. Other variations used a stainless standpipe muffler at the high point where water entered the system; they rotted, too.

Water-jacketed piping made from stainless steel, nickel bronze, or copper pipe has been substituted for dry, lagged piping. Although more expensive by far, it also lacks long-term reliability.

Today, sailboats are built with water-pot or waterlift exhaust systems that give lasting service and are easier and less costly to install. Coolant is injected with the exhaust gases immediately after the manifold via a water-cooled exhaust elbow.

This cools the entire exhaust system, and even the vessel's interior stays cooler. Exhaust hose is used from start to finish, which absorbs vibration and some sound.

The guts of a waterlift system is the pot, serving as a collector, muffler, and ejection device all rolled into one. It mounts below the exhaust manifold; waste cooling water flows downhill to it. The pot's outlet is spaced an inch or two off its bottom. Coolant and exhaust gas flow into the pot, and when the water level inside reaches the outlet port, it's forced out with the exhaust gases through the rest of the exhaust system and overboard. A waterlift system is engineered so velocities and back pressures are controlled. Outlet plumbing that's too small chokes an engine with excessive back pressure; too large an outlet causes water to pile up and exit in gouts, rather than mix evenly with the gases in a continual spray.

The outlet hose rises high under the deck, a few feet above the waterline, then slopes down again to the transom outlet fitting. This prevents a following sea from entering the exhaust and filling the pot and the exhaust manifold.

If waste salt water from the heat exchanger or exhaust-manifold water jacket is led directly to the exhaust manifold's water-cooled elbow, there's potential trouble when the engine is shut down. Exhaust gases no longer force water out of the pot, and since the pot is below the waterline, it's vulnerable to flooding from the intake seacock. The only thing in the way is the seawater pump. A new pump might stop the flow; a worn pump won't. To prevent a flooded pot, waste

GRP waterlift pots are the heart of a modern exhaust system. Note molded exhaust-hose connections that do away with metallic pipe components for longer life. This design also eliminates the traditional internal standpipe, increasing flow-through efficiency.

seawater is routed well above the waterline, near the vessel's centerline, and then back down to the exhaust fitting where water is injected. At the top of the loop lives an antisiphon valve.

Siphon-break valves are not necessary in exhaust systems that inject water up near deck level. This arrangement presents a natural break. And the coolant joins the exhaust gases on the far side of the hill, anyway, and will only flow out the transom.

Waterlift systems do reduce exhaust noise considerably, but if your boat still sounds like an earthmover, install an additional muffler. The rubber ones are very effective and last indefinitely.

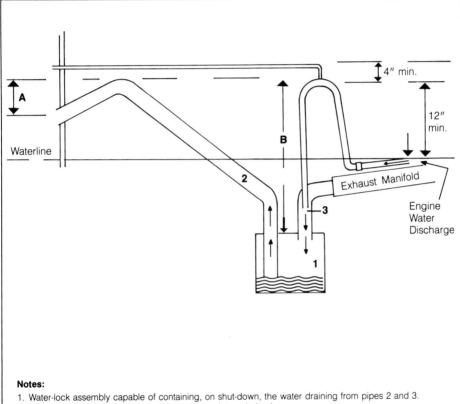

Notes:
1. Water-lock assembly capable of containing, on shut-down, the water draining from pipes 2 and 3. (Correct outlet from the water-lock is the longer internal pipe.)
2. The pipe feeding water into the exhaust system should be looped at least 12 inches above the waterline between the engine discharge and water injection points. At the highest point in this pipe, a means of preventing a syphon must be incorporated. This can be a vacuum relief valve or a permanent bleed. A permanent bleed using 3/16-inch-bore pipe out the side of the boat would provide an easy visual check of water circulation.
3. The dimension "A" must allow complete drainage of the pipe outboard of the peak of the loop in pipe 2 and discharge above the waterline.
4. The maximum dimension "B" should be stated by the exhaust system manufacturer with reference to volume of (1) above.

Typical waterlift exhaust system.

Nonferrous standpipe exhaust systems are still made for larger yachts. Note the stainless bellows to eliminate vibration between the engine exhaust and the muffler. Waste saltwater coolant injects at the top. Inside, a deflector plate prevents coolant from reaching the engine. The rubber hose at the bottom leads to overboard discharge.

If your boat has a transom, the exhaust must exit on that surface. Outlets in the topsides dip in and out of the water when a vessel rolls or heels, creating disturbing sounds. Topsides quickly blacken with soot and oil film, too. And exhaust noise is more noticeable exiting alongside, nearer the cockpit.

Be careful not to place an exhaust outlet too low on the transom, though. In your mind's eye, you may see the waterline as absolute. However, as a boat moves through the water, her wake rises up at the bow and stern. Exhausts that look right on paper often end up gargling salt water. If you're faced with this annoyance, it's better to admit defeat, plug and refinish the old hole, and relocate the fitting higher.

Serenity aside, it's an old wives' tale that just because an exhaust exits underwater it hurts engine efficiency or performance. Some charter boats purposely have their exhaust outlets six or eight inches below the waterline for quieter operation. These systems have been scientifically tested for back pressure, and received a clean bill of health.

WHAT FUEL CAPACITY?

An interesting topic of conversation out in the cruising grounds is fuel capacity—what's a good range under power? Opinions differ considerably between first-time sailors and veteran voyagers. Often what seemed adequate beforehand—isn't.

Fuel tankage follows a logic similar to water tankage: a cruising yacht must be self-sufficient for long periods. Like water, fuel is often inconvenient to obtain in overseas ports, particularly in island nations. Sailors with small tanks resort to the jerry-jug juggle, ten gallons at a crack, standing beside roadways hitchhiking back and forth between the anchorage and the filling station. Filling stations never seem to be near anchorages. They are located to service cars and trucks, not yachts. Commercial harbors don't always cater to yachts, either: Frequently, one must make an appointment, move the boat to a wharf designed for ships, not small craft, and laboriously drag huge hoses aboard. Tricky manipulations with a giant handwheel meant for bunkering commercial vessels might get diesel fuel into the tanks without polluting the harbor, and it might not. Then you go across town to an obscure office somewhere to pay the bill. Roadsteads are another exciting place to fuel up. You become proficient at running a surf in a dinghy full of fuel jugs. Once in a while, desperation overcoming good sense, you buy from a questionable source. For no extra charge you get a few quarts of water, all kinds of refuse, and a fistful of dead insects. The filters make heavy weather of it, and the engine eventually dies just when it's needed most.

Aside from letting you pick and choose where and when you refill, generous tankage keeps the show on the road. Imagine yourself on a flat sea without a breath of wind. Let's say it's your third day of stationary life. What fuel you have you're hording for the landfall, when you will need the engine to get you into harbor or through a pass in a coral reef.

Most cruising people weigh days out of their lives against the cost of burning fuel and gladly burn it if they have it. On long passages, ample fuel reserves can save days when you strike windless weather—days that are better spent at anchor.

Shoot for tankage that gives you at least 1,000 nautical miles at cruising speed. Blue-water sailors heading for remote areas may wish to bunker for 1,500 miles. Most cruising boats around 40 feet can do this with 200 U.S. gallons.

Generous fuel tankage also extends cruising endurance. You may wish to take a long ocean passage to a place that doesn't have fuel, spend a month or two there charging batteries and pulling down refrigerators every day, and then make another long passage to the next destination where fuel is available again. Fuel is freedom.

THE FUEL TANKS

GRP water tanks are one thing, but avoid GRP fuel tanks. Fuel is harder to contain than water; its low viscosity lets it ferret out microscopic tunnels in GRP gelcoats and laminates. Boats with integral GRP fuel tanks have been plagued by fuel seepage right through the hull. Yuck!

Integral fuel tanks should not be built into GRP or timber vessels, anyway. Use metal bolt-in tanks. Aluminum is the number-one choice. The panels are thicker than stainless and hence allow wider, thicker welds with less chance of pinholes. Stainless steel is fine for fuel tanks, too, despite criticism about crevice corrosion. Tanks built of either material should be baffled to reduce sloshing and increase strength.

Although they've been used, black iron tanks are not suitable for yacht building. Interior corrosion is inevitable—it's just a matter of time. Fuel tanks are normally permanent, confined by built-in furniture. Pulling a tank is something you never want to face. The money saved building with black iron is not significant, anyway.

Integral tanks make sense in steel or aluminum yachts having hull materials that encourage this technique. Integral tanks in metal boats save space and reduce cost; part of the tank, the hull surface, is already built. Metal tanks in metal boats also strengthen hulls.

Inspection ports on fuel tanks are potential leaks. A tank built of first-class materials won't contribute to contamination. This, combined with care during filling to screen out big lumps, keeps the tank clean.

Sediment traps have drawbacks for cruising. Sediment can slowly build up over months of harbor life, and it gets stirred up the next time the boat goes offshore. Suddenly, a huge quantity of contaminants flows into the filters all at once, raising havoc. It makes more sense to draw fuel right from a tank's bottom and let the filters chew on smaller quantities of water and debris on an ongoing basis. This keeps tanks clean and prevents unpleasant surprises.

However, a fuel tank should have a drain at its low point so it can be flushed out if necessary.

FUEL-TANK PLUMBING

The first objective is: getting fuel into the tank fast, while letting the air it displaces out—just as fast. Recreational fuel inlets are commonly one-and-one-half inches inside diameter; for cruising, this isn't adequate. Foreign fuel trucks and fueling wharfs don't always cater to small deck fills. Large inlets allow bigger funnels and decent-sized Mexican fuel filters to fit, too, and fuel from any source flows readily into the tanks, not over the decks and through the scuppers. Flows at commercial fueling depots can be gushers, making for excitement when there's a person at the valve who doesn't speak your language. Whatever happens, you've got to be able to take it! Consequently, don't install deck hardware and inlet plumbing less than two-and-one-half inches inside diameter.

Vents must match fuel-inlet performance. Three-quarter-inch-inside-diameter vent lines and fittings prevent choking and backfeeding while filling. Fuel vents, as opposed to water-tank vents, must be external. Fuel vapors and accidental overfills will make a shambles below decks. An inverted U at the top of the vent plumbing, with the vent positioned lower, keeps salt spray out of the tank. Locate vents adjacent to their respective fills so it's obvious when a tank is full (gurgling noises through the vent warn you).

Fill and vent plumbing should have no horizontal runs, elbows, or restrictions. Vents must be plumbed vertically, or nearly so, with a continuous gradient up to the U to prevent fuel pockets from forming in the line and then spurting over the decks during filling.

A good cruising fuel setup can take all a home-heating fuel truck can deliver without misbehaving. Try it!

Deck fills should be electrically bonded to the fuel tank to ground static discharges. The tank, in turn, is electrically connected to the ship's bonding network to ground the entire installation.

FUEL-SYSTEM PLUMBING

Copper tubing was once used to route fuel to the engine, with a short length of hose at the fuel pump to absorb vibration. Although copper tubing works, fireproof, reinforced neoprene hose is easier to work with and plenty safe. It's also nonconductive, offering no ground to a potential short circuit.

Connections should be made with brass barbed fittings, the kind that holds hose on permanently without clamps. Then clamp them for good measure.

Route fuel lines by following good plumbing practice: even support, no sharp bends or elbows. Use continuous runs from component to component—no joints. Joints and elbows collect debris and contribute to clogging. Fuel lines are vulnerable to clogging between tanks and filters. The initial part of the system should be plumbed oversize (three-quarters-inch inside diameter) to reduce the chance of blockage. The same strategy is used for fuel-tank outlets to filters as is used for saltwater cooling inlets to strainers: impurities and refuse must have free passage for safe entrapment. This keeps tanks clean by allowing what goes in to come back out freely. After the filters, short runs of fuel hose can be as small as three-eighths-inch inside diameter for diesels up to 100 horsepower.

Many diesel engines have a fuel-return line from the injector pump. Let's say your boat has two saddle tanks, each outboard of the engine, a common configuration. Place a Y valve in the injector bleed-off return line to divert overflow to either tank. Then the tank feeding the engine can receive what's returned, too. This makes it easier to keep track of consumption and prevents the embarrassment of an overflow (when an engine draws from one tank and the surplus secretly overfills the other).

Fuel tanks should have a 90-degree cock at the outlet so any problem component in the system can be isolated from the supply. Some governments insist on standpipes so fuel is drawn from the top of the tank, not gravity-fed from the bottom, to safeguard against a flood of fuel should something break or fire breach the plumbing.

FUEL FILTERS AND BLEEDING

There is no substitute for massive fuel filters. Engine size does not determine filter capacity, and quantities of dirt and moisture in fuel tanks have nothing to do with engine horsepower. A good system has two outsized filters, at least one liter each, and another smaller one downstream toward the engine. The first big filter can be used without the filter element, acting solely as a water trap and coarse catchment basin. The second big filter traps middle-of-the-road junk. Downstream of the two giant filters and the smaller hedging-your-bets filter is the standard filter on the power plant.

Racor filters work great. They have see-through bowls (a must), drain petcocks, O-ring-sealed tops, and quick-change cartridges. Don't use filter units with metal cannisters. They hide dirt and water, and checking them is a messy, counterproductive chore.

Locate the top of a fuel filter below the bottom of a fuel tank whenever possible. Otherwise, bleeding with low tank levels is difficult. You have to pressurize the tank through the vent to do it right.

Normally, to bleed a filter, the top is cracked until the unit overflows with fuel. Start at the filter assembly nearest the tank and work your way along to the engine. To make bleeding easier, drill and tap each filter lid at its high point and screw in spring-loaded aircraft-type wing tank drains. Henceforth, air is purged conveniently without spilling fuel or taking apart filters.

Filters must be located for visual checks and easy access for draining and maintenance. Install drip trays under them to keep spilled fuel out of the bilges so the boat won't smell and the harbor isn't polluted when you pump the bilges. A valve on the bottom of the drip tray allows excess fuel to be drained into a jar or bottle for stowage and eventual disposal. If the spilled fuel is reasonably clean, pour it back in the tank!

FUEL GAUGES

Sight gauges are the most accurate and straightforward way to determine fuel level. New tanks should be calibrated by filling them five or ten gallons at a time

Dual Racors featuring see-through bowls, O-ring-sealed quick-release tops, and drain petcocks. Note stainless drip tray beneath.

and marking an adjacent surface next to the sight tube. Sight gauges must be fuelproof and structurally bulletproof. Locate them in protected areas and, if necessary, install guards. Valves are required at the bottom and top of each sight gauge where it connects to the tank so the fuel can be isolated for maintenance.

Dipsticks are lousy fuel gauges. At sea, when the vessel rolls and pitches, dipstick readings—always hard to determine in the best of times—are meaningless.

Instrument-type fuel gauges, regardless of their method of operation or high-tech hocus-pocus, give readouts too crude for ocean sailing.

A gauge must indicate the exact quantity of fuel in gallon units. There may come a day when you're caught short and need to account for fuel precisely so you can decide whether to burn some to motor through a calm or charge depleted batteries, or hold off to use the remaining supply for powering through a pass in a reef at a landfall. Only sight gauges have this accuracy.

ENGINE-ROOM ALARM SYSTEMS AND GAUGES

A full engine-room alarm system can be inexpensive to rig, and it could save thousands of dollars in repair bills. Alarms warn of abnormalities before lasting damage occurs. No sailor keeps an eagle eye on engine instruments every second to safeguard equipment against a sudden malfunction; it's not humanly possible.

The most important function to monitor is saltwater coolant flow. Should this cease, the saltwater pump self-destructs (unless it was the perpetrator and has already bitten the dust). Once saltwater flow is interrupted or restricted, the engine and exhaust system overheat. An in-line sensor warns of the malfunction instantly, before the engine heats up one degree, regardless of whether the problem is pump failure, a blocked intake, or choked plumbing. A simple spring-loaded gate in the sensor closes and activates a switch when flow falls below a safe rate. Although supposedly the spring is preset, you may have to tweak it so it won't activate the alarm when the flow is sluggish at engine idling speeds. Aqua Alarm and others make good, inexpensive flow sensors. Install one in a cold part of the system somewhere after the inlet strainer and before the first heat exchanger. Consider a flow sensor standard cruising equipment. Charging batteries in commercial harbors results in a blockage sooner or later—those bloody plastic bags are everywhere.

Fit a coolant sensor to monitor engine temperature, too. This warns of fresh-water cooling problems. Two types are available: a contact sensor attaching flush to the upper engine block near the cylinder head, or a screw-in sensor contacting the freshwater coolant directly. Either is fine. Then you'll be forewarned of things like thermostat failure, inadequate coolant level, a burst hose, or circulating pump malfunction, all separate phenomena arising from saltwater flow problems.

Next—but not least—tee in a low-oil-pressure-alarm sensor. This sings out if the oil level in the crankcase falls below the oil-pump pickup. An engine losing oil through leaks or worn rings can drink itself dry without you knowing it (you might have other things on your mind and forget to check the level someday). A sudden and massive oil leak, for an unforeseen reason, could totally destroy the power plant, too. Without an alarm, you would never know about it until the engine was scrap. In rare instances, the oil pump itself might even go on strike. The lubrication system is the engine's lifeblood. There's a fine line between year-after-year dependability and a smoking ruin.

Another sensor, similar to a contact engine-block-temperature sensor, warns of an engine-room fire. It mounts high in the machinery space, where heat would be most intense, and has a preset value of around 180 degrees F.

Boats with hydraulic transmissions benefit from low-oil-pressure and high-oil-temperature sensors that warn of gearbox cooling or lubrication troubles.

All the above sensors are energized automatically when you start the engine by an on/off oil-pressure switch. Make sure the oil-pressure-alarm sensor has a higher trip rating than the alarm-system pressure switch so low oil pressure trips

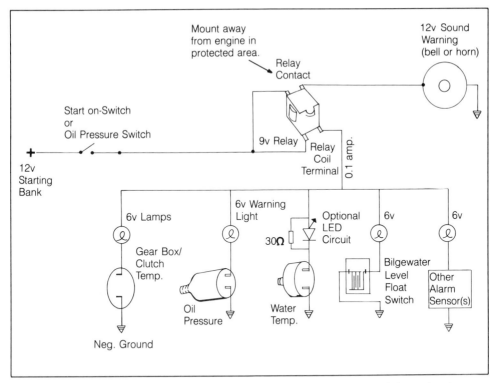

Simple and effective 12-volt engine-room alarm system. Six-volt indicator lamps labeled as to function are wired in series between the sensors and the relay coil terminal providing approximately 0.1 amp to trip the relay in event of a malfunction. The water-temperature circuit shows an LED (light-emitting diode) in lieu of a standard six-volt incandescent light bulb; either type of indicator is fine. The 30-ohm resistor diverts sufficient current around the LED to trip the relay. Without the resistor shunt, an LED will overload and self-destruct when the sensor activates. (Ocean Energy Systems)

the alarm instead of shutting it off. Wire each circuit to its own siren or whoop-whoop horn (or share with the burglar-alarm horn).

One final sensor activates the alarm horn from a power source that's energized all the time, whether the engine is running or not. This is a bilge-pump float switch positioned a few inches above the one for the bilge pump. Thus, for the cost of another float switch, you have a high-bilge-water alarm, too.

You can install all of the above for the price of a big night out on the town. The protection is worth a hell of a lot more.

ENGINE GAUGES

Alarm systems do not take the place of engine-monitoring instruments, nor do idiot lights. When an idiot light flashes, the only thing that's for certain is a functioning light bulb. In bright sunlight, you may not even see it unless you accidentally look. Gauges, on the other hand, are visible night and day and tell exactly what an engine is doing. They also show trends, warning of possible trouble in the future. Alarms and idiot lights don't.

A tachometer indicates engine speed (rpm). Two types exist: mechanical ones that couple to a rotating engine component via a flexible cable, and electronic instruments that are excited by the alternator's AC frequency before it's rectified to DC. Motorola makes a range of alternator-excited tachometers. If your boat has no tach at present, they are inexpensive and easy to install. Borrow a hand tach to calibrate it, and you're set.

Tachometers are not optional. Guessing revolutions by engine sound alone is like trying to determine engine temperature by laying a hand on the block— impossible. Occasionally, an engine needs winding up to full revs to check that all is well with it and the drive train. Accurate rpm's help zero in belt-driven AC alternators, too. And a tach is another check on boat speed, once a speed-to-rpm conversion table has been worked out. Powering at precise rpm's allows you to predict fuel consumption accurately as well. A tach is also handy for resetting the engine when somebody inadvertently knocks the throttle lever.

Temperature gauges reveal critical intelligence about the engine's behavior by showing subtle temperature fluctuations. Abnormally low operating temperatures indicate a sticking thermostat. Temperature spikes—erratic readings— warn of a dying thermostat, low water level in the heat exchanger reservoir, or an intermittent blockage.

Capillary-type gauges with bulb sensors and a little tube leading to the instrument head are more accurate and more reliable in offshore conditions than electric gauges. Capillary gauges also continue to indicate temperature after the engine is shut down, whereas 12-volt instruments read nothing once the circuit is broken.

Oil-pressure gauges also indicate trends and fluctuations. A slight drop in oil pressure as a vessel rolls at sea can mean the oil level is too low. A steady reading slightly below normal often means oil dilution from contaminants (too many hours between oil changes), a dirty oil filter, or oil that's running too hot (plugged oil cooler or cooling-system malfunction?).

Hydraulic transmissions are safeguarded by an oil-temperature gauge to warn of overheating from a plugged oil cooler or low fluid level. A transmission oil-pressure gauge warns of low oil level caused by a leaky seal or an internally corroded heat exchanger and can also tell of worn internal components or excessive operating temperatures.

A pyrometer is an optional instrument for special applications. It's basically a high-temperature thermometer monitoring the diesel's exhaust-gas temperature. Boats fitted with variable-pitch propellers need them to indicate optimum pitch settings. Propeller loads, and hence engine loads, are directly related to exhaust temperature (your engine manufacturer will supply a recommended operating range).

Mount gauges that monitor vital engine functions so they are visible from the helm. The front of the cockpit well offers a good location. Protect gauges with a sheet of bedded Lexan. They must be totally sealed from moisture and spray. Never mount them out in the weather as RV folks do. Try to position the gauges so they are visible from below decks somehow. While charging at anchor, it's inconvenient to climb out in nasty weather to see what's what. If you can crane your neck from the companionway to see gauges in the cockpit well, fine; otherwise, double up on key instruments.

Try to avoid mounting gauges on pedestal steerers. They are hard to protect from the weather there, and their umbilical cords are unnecessarily long and cumbersome to rig.

A final gauge, the engine hour meter, lives on the main electrical distribution panel below decks. It lets you schedule and record engine-room maintenance: valve adjustments, oil changes, injector calibrations, combustion chamber de-coking, valve grinds, bearing inspections, transmission-fluid changes, fresh-water coolant changes, battery filling, etc. An hour meter logs engine hours offshore and at anchor, giving you a breakdown of the power plant's contribution to your lifestyle. The hours will mount up quicker than you think!

POWER TAKE-OFFS

Most engine rooms have an array of engine-driven accessories for cranking out comfort: additional 12-volt alternators, perhaps an AC alternator, maybe a refrigeration compressor, a deck-washdown pump, and possibly a hydraulic pump for powering high-capacity gear. Each piece of equipment needs a home.

Twelve-volt alternators and refrigerator compressors are sometimes tacked on power plants, but this is best avoided. Heat and vibration are transferred directly to the equipment. Complicated mounting brackets and nested equipment make servicing and inspection difficult. Cantilevered brackets are very susceptible to fatigue and fracture. And a stack of vee-belt pulleys on the crankshaft strains its snout and prematurely wears the front main bearing. It's a shaky way to transfer power, an invitation to mechanical catastrophe far from home.

Engines manufactured for serious marine applications have crankshaft snouts machined for a keyway and engineered to power accessories (often up to the maximum rated output of the engine). This is an important feature to keep in mind when choosing an engine.

A well-designed power take-off consists of a keyed shaft rotating on solid-mounted, self-aligning bearings. The shaft is positioned in line with the crankshaft snout and coupled to it; dangerous side loads from stacked vee-belt pulleys are removed, and crankshaft loading is harmless torque. Whenever the engine runs, the power take-off spins. Accessories requiring on/off intermittent or cycling operation have their own clutches, either manual or electromagnetic, depending on system design and/or convenience required. Alternators spin continually without clutches.

This power take-off on a 45 footer has a nylon coupler to reduce shock transfer. It rotates on self-aligning bearings, driving a washdown pump (right), a hydraulic pump (left), and a DC generator (belts leading out of photograph to left). For further information, contact Berg Evans Chain, 217 S. Findlay, Seattle, WA 98108.

A power take-off shaft must be the same diameter as the crankshaft stub. This simplifies coupling and allows accurate alignment. Coupling types vary as to alignment tolerances. Usually, they must be within three degrees of true. This is simple to achieve with shims and slotted bearing feet.

Equipment is mounted to each side of the power take-off shaft (and above, if necessary). Structural hull components like stringers and bulkheads provide good strong points for mounting brackets, and additional bases or pads are made to suit. Once the equipment is bolted down, vee-belt length can be determined. Vee-belt alignment is fine-tuned by sliding pulleys back and forth a mite on the power take-off shaft.

Mounting brackets must have generous travel for belt tensioning. Otherwise, there's too little leeway in vee-belt length (it might be hard to find the right belt and a gut-buster to fit it). Brackets need some means to provide leverage for tensioning. Large, heavy accessories with double belt drives cannot be tightened by hand. An elementary but effective method has a fulcrum tab welded or bolted on so a lever can be used to pry an accessory over. Better yet, equipment slides away from the power take-off with the aid of adjustment bolts (and lock nuts for securement).

Long belts are vulnerable to harmonics. In most cases, pulley center-to-center distances should not exceed 18 inches. Flapping vee-belts strain equipment mounts and bearings. If there's no option, install an idler pulley to eliminate belt jump.

Power take-offs are the only satisfactory solution for spinning multiple accessories dependably, year after year. That's why commercial vessels use them exclusively. Unfortunately, the advantages are not available to sailors with flex-mounted engines, as mentioned. A rigid power take-off shaft coupled to a bucking engine will break the coupler overnight.

THE LAY SHAFT

Power take-offs require space in front of the engine. The boat must be designed with this feature in mind, and many designers don't think about it. If your engine is smack against an engine cover or bulkhead, there's another alternative. If the engine has no stub shaft, all is not lost either. As long as you can fit a hefty, two-groove vee-belt pulley to the crankshaft or flywheel (some manufacturers have a bolt-on pulley option), you can still spin the goodies that make life worthwhile.

The lay shaft (also called a jack shaft) is similar to a power take-off, but it's positioned alongside the engine. Instead of a direct-drive coupling, the lay shaft is driven by vee-belts. Two C-section belts will deliver enough energy to operate a variety of accessories. A lay shaft imparts some side load on the crank, but two pulley grooves closer to the front crank bearing don't have nearly the lever arm of stacked pulleys.

DON'T GET CAUGHT SHORT

Engines turning a variety of ancillary equipment won't have quite the power to twist the propeller, as previously mentioned. A few alternators charging at high output, a refrigerator compressor making ice, and a big washdown pump can easily absorb ten horsepower. The boat's propeller must be sized for conditions when all the gear is running. This prevents overloads, and it's preferable to run the engine a bit light now and then rather than risk abuse.

Even when a prop has been sized for running accessories while powering, as a matter of seamanship, always maneuver with them switched or clutched *off* so all your horses can be brought to bear at the drop of a hat. Once you are safely away from an anchorage, or clear of a marina, the gear may be activated.

HYDRAULICS

A hydraulic system is simple and hence reliable. Power is created by a pump belted off the engine or power take-off. In low-power applications (under five horsepower, intermittent), pumps have an integral oil reservoir and resemble an automobile power-steering unit. Systems working harder in continuous duty need separate, larger oil reserve tanks and heat exchangers to cool the circulating oil. Pumps are rated in gallons per minute. Their motors are selected to function at a given rpm and torque rating for a particular job. Hydraulic motors are marvelous for marine use—compact and absolutely weatherproof.

Oil is pumped through a closed circuit, applying pressure to vanes or gears in the motor and producing rotation. High-pressure hose or piping connects all the hydraulic components. Any number of accessories may be activated from a single pump, so long as the system is designed for it. All hydraulic systems require a pressure bypass valve, which pops off if an accessory is overloaded, thus safeguarding equipment from damage (1,200 psi on small systems).

Examples of hydraulic benefit to cruising are anchor windlasses (nothing beats hydraulic windlasses), high-capacity pumps, power capstans, AC alternators (some have built-in oil-flow regulators for constant speed), and bow thrusters.

A simple hydraulic system powering one accessory such as a windlass has an electromagnetic clutch to spin the pump on demand. A foot switch operates the clutch, and the windlass acts just like an electric one, except it will be a stump puller. Systems with multiple motors have valves to control each piece of equipment separately or in unison; either the pump spins continually or it's activated by a manual clutch.

Hydraulics are used extensively in commercial marine applications to cope with severe service and harsh environmental conditions. Widespread applications are found in industry, too. Consequently, equipment is reasonably priced, because it's universal. If you plan to drive something requiring brute power or absolute dependability, hydraulics is the last word.

THINK NOW—RELAX LATER

Before leaving the engine room, sit down for a minute and think again about your machinery. If anything bothers you—a suspect installation, sagging wiring or plumbing endangered by heat or chafe, borderline equipment—remount, replace, or reroute the culprit now. If you haven't made friends with something, ask around or read up on it. Mechanics are fundamental to the cruising life. There's no escaping them.

To further the cause, see if you can devise a better way to reach important gear. Equipment that's buried is often ignored and seldom serviced. Hidden things often suffer from sloppy installations, too; craftsmanship thrives best out in the cold light of day. Perhaps an extra removable panel, another section of lift-out flooring, another inspection port or hatch, or other access scheme can be worked out for a difficult area. If not, you have no choice—remount equipment where you can lay a hand on it.

Engine rooms can be improved with simple things: another light, a handhold, a little step for your foot so you can lean comfortably over something, a fold-out

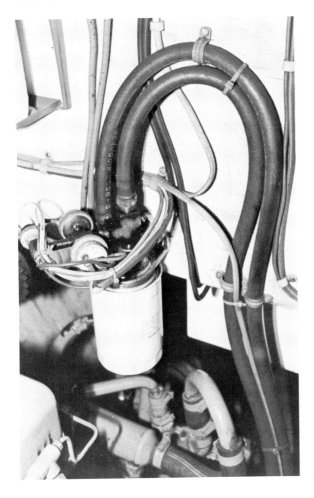

A remote oil filter setup with Aeroquip high-pressure hose makes filter changes a snap. Note teed oil-pressure switches and low-oil-pressure alarm sensor.

or permanent seat, a component shifted to a better location, a painted plywood panel for mounting system components (fuel systems, refrigeration, desalination, etc.). Just a good cleanup and a coat of paint works wonders.

What can you do to make chores easier? How about a bulk lube-oil tank holding four or five oil changes, plumbed and valved for simple operation? A sump tank to drain old oil into for holding until it's convenient and responsible to dispose of it? Why not mount a remote oil filter if the one on the engine is awkward to service and install a drip tray underneath it? This is easy with Aeroquip hose and an off-the-shelf, spin-off filter unit. How about a bracket for a handy squeeze bottle of distilled water for the batteries? Special holders for an inspection mirror, an oil-filter wrench, a flashlight, and a roll of paper towels? A little shelf for tools while you're working in there?

Don't take it for granted everything is okay in your engine room just because someone else did the work. Someone else doesn't have to live with it. Or struggle along in spite of it.

5▶ Refrigeration Alternatives That Work

Since the days of the iceman, refrigeration has been an unsung hero in millions of homes. Your domestic refrigerator sits in the kitchen quietly humming away, a faithful servant year after year. Other than a little attention on cleaning day, it asks for nothing.

Not so with most cruising setups. They are the hungriest consumers of energy aboard, gobbling more energy than all other shipboard appliances combined. Ill-conceived systems give cruising refrigerators a bad name, causing some cruising people to shy away from refrigeration altogether.

A pity. Cruising without efficient refrigeration is a second-rate existence, particularly in tropical climates. Butter is runny and goes rancid; vegetables turn limp overnight; leftovers and surplus fish are wastefully thrown overboard rather than stored for future meals.

Moreover, cruising without refrigeration can kill creativity in the galley and result in lackluster menus. Say goodbye to chilled gelatin desserts, fresh cheeses, whipped cream, fresh meat, cheesecake; say hello to warm beer, warm soft drinks, warm fruit juices, warm salads, warm cocktails, and sour milk. Kiss off your old friend the ice cube, too; ice machines are hard to come by in paradise.

If in doubt about the role refrigeration will play in your cruising life, unplug that trusty refrigerator at home for a month and see how you fare. Chances are, your family will mutiny!

But there's no cause for gloom. Reliable, efficient cruising refrigeration is not difficult to organize when you follow the ground rules and engineer a good system from scratch that suits your lifestyle.

METHOD OF OPERATION

Very likely, you'll have a system that uses the refrigerant Freon 12. First, let's see how Freon works, then discuss how to make it work best.

A refrigeration network is composed of two plumbed segments, the high-pressure side and the low-pressure side. A pump (compressor) charges the high-pressure side of the circuit with pressurized Freon. As the Freon leaves the compressor, it's a heated gas (when a gas is compressed, it warms up). The Freon gas flows through a heat exchanger called a condenser, which cools it to ambient temperatures. As it cools, the pressurized gas changes to a liquid. (Carbon dioxide gas, CO_2, reacts the same way, changing from gas to liquid when it's compressed and stored under pressure in a fire-extinguisher cylinder.) From the condenser, the cooled liquid Freon flows through a filter/drier to be cleansed of impurities.

Next, the Freon enters the low-pressure side at the evaporator located in the refrigerator box. To reach the evaporator plumbing, the liquid Freon squeezes through a tiny orifice, either a capillary tube or an expansion valve. As the Freon jets into the low-pressure plumbing of the evaporator, an instant loss of pressure reverts the liquid Freon back to its free state as a gas. This change of states is accompanied by a massive drop in temperature. (Discharged CO_2 from a fire extinguisher reacts the same way, freezing moisture in the air, which you see as frost.) Heat energy from the evaporator unit and hence heat from the refrigeration cabinet is absorbed by the cold Freon gas as it flows through the evaporator plumbing. From there, the Freon gas travels through the low-pressure piping to the compressor to start the journey again.

The filter/drier protects the orifice in the capillary tube or expansion valve from clogging. The biggest enemy of Freon refrigeration is internal moisture, which, if introduced by a leak, chokes the orifice at the evaporator with ice crystals. If this happens, refrigeration becomes sluggish or ceases altogether until the system is purged of water and recharged with fresh Freon. The orifice is a kind of gauge between the high- and low-pressure sides, metering a precise quantity of Freon and thus maintaining a regimented pressure differential between the sides. This is achieved with a capillary tube or expansion valve that matches the performance of the compressor with the heat-absorbing capabilities of the evaporator.

Simply put, a refrigeration system is a heat pump: the circulating refrigerant absorbs heat when it flows through an evaporator in the chiller box and releases heat via the condenser outside the box.

TROPICAL SERVICE

High ambient temperatures test cruising refrigeration to the limit. Many refrigeration setups that seem okay in cooler regions come apart in paradise. Even systems that perform well in warmer climates like southern California do not always cut (or cool) the mustard in the Caribbean or the South Pacific.

Let's say you live in an area where the average summer temperature is 70 degrees F. (75 degrees in daytime, 65 degrees at night). Although warm, this is nothing compared to the tropics. Average daily temperatures near the equator are at least ten degrees F. higher. While this doesn't sound like much, higher air temperatures are only part of the problem. When it's hot, you as a human being sit in the breeze up on deck. Your refrigerator can't; it remains strapped to its hot seat down in the cabin. Sea temperatures in the tropics may be 20 degrees (or more) warmer than your home waters, too, pushing cabin temperatures up more. And an overhead tropical sun burning the decks hikes cabin temperatures further yet.

High cabin temperatures create huge differentials between the inside and outside of a refrigerator or freezer. For example, a refrigerator holding an ideal 38 degrees F. in a 70-degree cabin has a differential of 32 degrees to maintain. Kick the cabin temperature up to 90 degrees F., and the differential rises to 52 degrees. To you, the rise is only 20 degrees. To your refrigerator, the increase means the differential nearly doubled! The system has to work twice as hard to hold the same box temperature.

Another temperature differential plays an important part in refrigeration efficiency: the variation between ambient cabin temperatures and the temperature of the hot Freon flowing through an air-cooled condenser (or the variation between ambient water temperatures and hot Freon in a water-cooled condenser). In cooler regions, the difference in Freon temperature versus ambient temperature is wide, and standard condensers dissipate heat adequately. However, an increase in radiating surface area is necessary to dissipate heat to cool Freon in hotter climates. A refrigerator's condenser acts like a car radiator. But when the condenser is overtaxed, the refrigeration cabinet won't boil over like a car; the box simply warms up 10 or 15 degrees—spoiling the food.

Remember: When ambient temperatures climb, you lose both ways. The refrigerator box absorbs more heat, and the refrigeration system has a tougher time shedding heat. As a rule, figure on at least tripling refrigeration running times (or else efficiency) when you sail to the tropics.

KEEPING THE COOL

No matter how state-of-the-art your refrigeration componentry is, the system won't be a success unless the chiller box keeps its cool. Production yachts with built-in refrigeration boxes can have mediocre refrigeration performance in tropical waters. Sailors fit refrigeration systems to existing iceboxes in good faith, innocently believing the cabinets will cope. Sometimes their hopes are drowned out by the roar of struggling refrigerator components battling thawing steaks.

Sloppily fitting, poorly insulated doors, thin cabinet insulation, inferior insulation materials, water leaks in cabinets, and conductive material connecting the inner compartment with the vessel's structure are inefficiencies to watch for.

If you are buying a boat with an insulated box in place, it won't hurt to oversee its construction. Otherwise, order the boat without a box and do the job right yourself—from scratch! If you're already stuck with a box that insulates like a sieve, rip the whole works out and start over. It's almost impossible to patch up an existing failure.

A tropical refrigerator should have four inches of poured urethane foam between the liner and the outside walls. A freezer, because of the greater differential between box and ambient temperatures, requires six to eight inches of poured foam. This may be more insulation than advised by experts not familiar with tropical conditions. But foam insulation is dirt cheap compared to the overall price of the system. And it's a one-time expense, saving you energy and headaches in the years to come.

Poured foam is superior to sheet foam because no joints exist that can collect moisture and conduct heat into the box in case of condensation or a leaky liner. And poured foam fills odd-shaped nooks and crannies so common on boats.

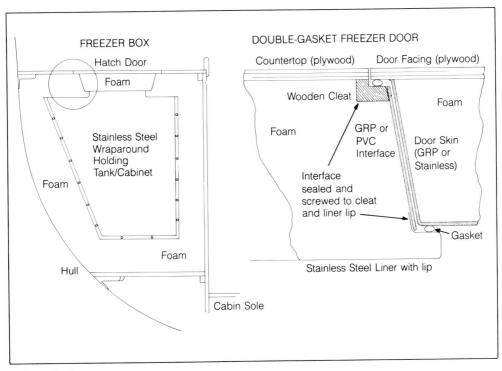

Refrigeration box.

Avoid supports between the inner compartment and the outer structure of the chiller box. The entire liner should float on foam except at the door opening where it interfaces with the outside structure. All paths that conduct heat into the box must be eliminated. Most of the time we think of insulation as keeping cold *in* a refrigerator, but technically speaking it keeps heat *out*.

The interface between the liner and the exterior of the cabinet forming the access opening is often a source of heat leakage. Keep it thin by avoiding the use of plywood. Instead, mold a thin laminate of GRP or PVC to resist heat transfer. If the inner box is to be constructed of plywood, make sure it's waterproofed so no moisture infiltrates the insulation or seeps behind the door-opening interface to conduct heat. Formica looks nice on a liner, but the joints, even when bedded with marine sealant, eventually leak moisture. A smooth GRP laminate painted with polyurethane paint makes an attractive, easy-to-clean, watertight surface. If a stainless steel liner is used, do not be tempted to use the metal for the entire interface at the opening. This looks nifty and is often done, but it forms a path for heat transfer. There must be a break in the stainless surround covered by GRP or PVC.

The door sides must not conduct heat, either. Construct a door skin of thin GRP laminate in a one-off waxed plywood mold. Pour the foam in before releasing the door skin from the mold so it keeps its shape (door insulation must be the same thickness as box insulation). Screw the insulated door skin to a stout outer panel of teak or mahogany or Formica-covered plywood for decoration and strength. Do not use stainless steel for the door skin unless it stops short of the outer gasket. Otherwise, heat will be conducted into the box at the edges.

A novel approach when space is limited. Chart table slides back to reveal freezer compartment beneath (insulated freezer lid not shown). Since freezer access is sporadic, there is no great inconvenience.

Door hinges and latches must be stout to exert firm pressure on a double set of gaskets. Top-loading doors held down by a wing and a prayer invariably leak heat into the box. Hatch-type doors need flush-fitting hinges and latches. An inner gasket (use soft vinyl extrusions designed specifically for refrigeration) seals the door's inner face, and an outer gasket seals the timber door facing to the outer surface of the refrigerator box. This way, an insulating dead air space is trapped between the two gaskets. Adjust the door by shimming the hinges and latch so the gaskets are compressed evenly to form an absolutely airtight seal. This is critical.

Traditionally, freezers are built for top loading so less heat invades the box when the door is opened. This design suits an under-the-counter space in a galley perfectly. However, an upright refrigerator with a well-sealed door may be preferable for the sake of convenience.

It's a finicky chore to build a good refrigeration cabinet, particularly the door and all the mating surfaces in the box opening. But out in the cruising grounds, there is no substitute for quality. First-class craftsmanship and generous insulation will save hours of compressor time each week. Remember, heat rises, so the coldest part of your refrigerator will be near the bottom. An inch or two of extra insulation down there won't hurt.

THINK SMALL

Cruising refrigeration has a better chance for success if you don't expect it to perform like your kitchen refrigerator at home. For one thing, your cruising refrigerator is smaller, so you must cool perishables on a strict priority basis. Bear in mind that much of what lingers inside domestic refrigerators is not highly perishable and doesn't really need to be in there.

For example, foodstuffs such as eggs last several months at ambient temperatures. They don't need refrigeration. Instead of chilling a selection of partially consumed preservatives like jam, refrigerate one at a time. Cool your wine for particular social occasions rather than use the refrigerator for bulk storage. Chill beer on a daily basis; don't keep a week's supply cold. Five kinds of cold fruit juice on tap overcrowds the refrigerator, so drink one variety at a time. Pack food in the cruising refrigerator to conserve space; your refrigerator at home contains more air than anything else. Slightly altered habits allow great reduction in cabinet size without sacrificing convenience.

And you'll be rewarded for your efforts to adjust to a smaller refrigerator. A smaller box has less surface area to transfer heat, which translates into less energy consumption. You'll find you can cram an amazing amount of goodies into a two-and-one-half-cubic-foot refrigerator. Freezers as tiny as one-and-one-half cubic feet are very useful, often holding enough frozen meat, fish, and cheese for a month. Efficient insulation cuts down net capacity for a given space, anyway. Don't worry about it. A little gem is a lot better than a big energy hog.

Two-cubic-foot refrigerator cabinet with double gaskets, holdover plate, and a minimum of four inches of poured foam insulation. The door is made of Formica-covered plywood filled with foam, a small source of heat leakage. A GRP door skin would have been better. Compressor is a Danfoss 12-volt unit.

HOLDOVER PLATES

Traditional, mechanically driven cruising refrigeration systems, freezers in particular, rely on heat absorption to hold down temperatures over long periods. The evaporator, which is often referred to as a holdover or eutectic plate (or a series of plates), is really a stainless steel tank containing a solution of water and minerals or water and alcohol, which, when cooled, converts to semisolid form. This happens at a lower temperature than that required to turn plain water to ice. In fact, it takes a massive dose of energy to convert the liquid solution to slush; therefore, it follows that an equal amount of heat energy will be absorbed from the foodstuffs to convert the eutectic solution back to the liquid state (less what energy is wasted through box leakage). Think of the eutectic solution as an encapsulated block of super-cold ice that melts slowly, keeping the box below freezing temperatures, then is refrozen with a burst of compressor time to melt and cool again.

An engine-driven compressor works to cool a plate or series of plates directly, and food is kept cold indirectly. Having insufficient plate capacity is like trying to cool an icebox with an ice cube instead of an ice block. The eutectic solution warms too quickly, and once plate temperature rises to equal box temperature,

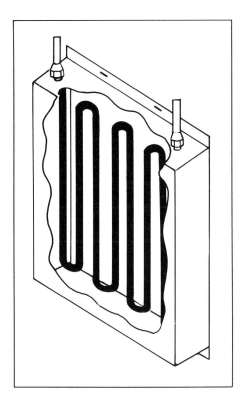

Single tube holdover plate.

holdover ceases. From then on, box temperature rises, too. Inadequate plate volume also means the compressor has less heat to remove each time the system operates, which wastes a powerful condensing unit's heat-pumping potential. Once a plate is brought down to minimum temperature, the compressor must be shut down, regardless of plate capacity. The plate capacity and box efficiency then determine whether the box stays cold for two hours or two days.

For tropical service, eutectic plate size—and the length and diameter of Freon tubing immersed in the plate solution to match the plate volume—must be far greater than what copes in cooler climates. Long holdover in hot climes depends upon continued, large-scale heat absorption. Within limits, it's impossible to err with excess holding-plate capacity for a freezer, so long as the rest of the system is engineered to suit. Naturally, you need some room left in the box for food!

Plates are usually fastened directly to the box liner. Indeed, some boxes are built entirely of double-walled stainless steel to form a wraparound holding tank. This is a terrific way to gain generous plate volume, and the stowage area is clear of bulky, bolt-on plates. Plates mounted flush to the insulation expose only part of their surface area to the foodstuffs. Consequently, they provide longer holdover, provided their total capacity is sufficient to keep the box cold despite this reduction (about 40 percent) in the rate of heat absorption. Plates spaced from the box surfaces or plates used as shelving or dividers absorb heat nearly

Construction of a double-walled freezer liner with integral, wrap-around holding plate and Freon tubing. This keeps bulky plates out of the box and provides a massive heat sink for long-term holdover.

twice as fast, because the entire plate surface area is exposed. Only about half the plate capacity is necessary to maintain box temperature, but the system will need pulling down twice as often.

In summation, holding-plate absorption (measured in Btu's) must exceed box leakage (also measured in Btu's) over the period desired between pulldowns. Additionally, plate capacity should reasonably match compressor capacity (measured in Btu's per hour). It's important to realize, for example, that a 15,000-Btu compressor will take about the same time to pull down a 2,000-Btu plate as it will to pull down a series of three, four, or five 2,000-Btu plates.

ENGINE-DRIVEN MECHANICAL REFRIGERATION

When a big deep freeze is required—six cubic feet or larger—you are stuck with the traditional engine-driven mechanical setups with the brute power to suck heat quickly from large plates.

The rate of heat transfer in good mechanical systems is such that air-cooled condensers big enough to work are too bulky to fit aboard. Instead, water-cooled condensers are installed in line with the diesel engine's seawater intake plumbing (taking advantage of the existing saltwater flow when the engine runs), or a separate water pump (belt driven or electric) and seawater plumbing system are arranged.

If an adjacent parasitic refrigerator feeds off the freezer—a popular expediency on cruising boats—there must be provision for adjustable temperature balancing. Even so, there can be problems maintaining temperature stability, and food frequently takes a shellacking. Refrigeration, as opposed to freezing, does not

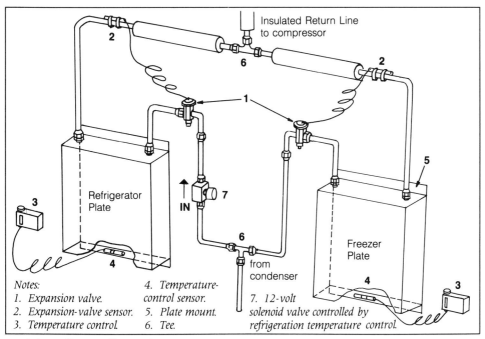

Dual plate refrigerator/freezer schematic.

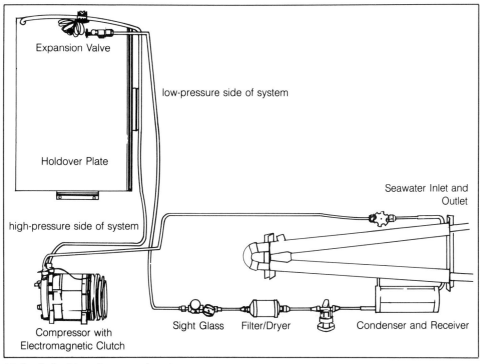

Mechanical refrigeration network and components.

lend itself particularly well to one burst of energy per day. Box temperatures fluctuate during the holdover cycle; food warms just prior to pulldown and may be cooled too vigorously during and just after pulldown. Parasitic refrigerators do work when balanced for a particular climate, but on a long-distance voyage from temperate to tropical areas, the setup can be a crude way to keep the coleslaw.

Separate refrigerator and freezer cabinets, each fitted with its own evaporator, can solve the temperature-fluctuation problem. A smaller capacity holdover plate with a higher melting point solution is installed in the refrigerator compartment. Autonomous refrigerators and freezers sharing a single compressor each have their own expansion valve(s) and monitoring systems. They are engineered so that the Freon supply to the refrigerator evaporator is cut off via a solenoid valve first, diverting the entire flow to the freezer until compressor shutdown.

A direct-drive compressor inadvertently run too long can self-destruct by creating too much vacuum and overcooling the low-pressure system, thus causing the pump to eat liquid Freon instead of gas. To prevent this, a pressure switch is plumbed into the high-pressure side, which disables the compressor's electromagnetic clutch if abnormal pressures (set around 180 to 250 psi, depending on the system) occur. Normal regulation is accomplished by a temperature cut-off switch.

Direct-drive systems do not like to be shut down for extended periods, as lack of exercise contributes to leaky compressor seals. And the sheer complication of elaborate direct-drive setups means a lot of parts flying in loose formation. It's best to keep them simple. According to Murphy's Law, the more that can go wrong, the more that will, and when something goes wrong, it will only get worse. When cruising remote areas, you must be capable of servicing the system, or someday you may have to feed a freezer full of thawing food to the sharks (two-legged or finned). In addition, it's prudent to carry comprehensive spares and Freon for recharging when you cruise away from civilization for long periods.

Mechanical refrigeration regiments your daily life out in the cruising grounds. Each day, an engine must be fired up to pull down the system (an excellent setup will hold over for two days, but most don't). While there is some latitude in the timing of this chore, it does have to be done at regular intervals. Poorly engineered systems need to be pulled down in the morning and again in the evening! Only you can judge if the benefits of a large-capacity engine-driven system outweigh this inconvenience.

PARALLEL SYSTEMS

Mechanical engine-driven systems have another drawback: they can't take advantage of shore power when it's available, and the diesel engine still needs to be run dockside. To circumvent this, holding plates are built with dual Freon

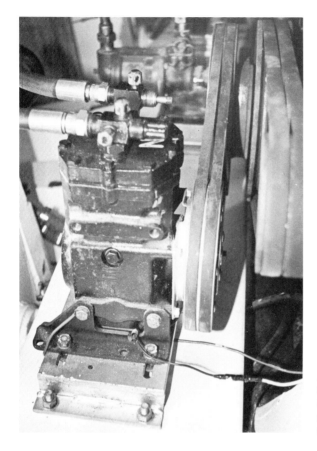

Belt-driven compressor with electro-magnetic clutch. Note dual belts, slotted mount for adjusting belt tension, and maintenance valves atop compressor.

circuits (plate size being increased to compensate for the displacement of extra piping), so that a parallel refrigeration system may operate from either 12- or 110-volt electrical power at the dock. Although a parallel system sharing the same holdover plates provides backup capability when the vessel is equipped with adequate electrical generation to run it, the whole thing becomes intricate, bulky, and expensive.

Although single and parallel holding-plate refrigeration has been honed to a fine art by firms specializing in it, and although the systems have the potential for reliability when expertly done, there are alternatives that may better suit living aboard on the move.

12-VOLT CUSTOM REFRIGERATION

Traditionally, 12-volt refrigeration has been dismissed as a joke by cruising sailors, yet with advances in 12-volt charging and refrigeration technology, the tables have turned. A vessel with a sound 12-volt base can use it to power refrigeration, even in the tropics!

Auxiliary charging devices—windmill alternators, solar panels, and water-powered alternators—can supply ample 12-volt current for refrigeration, rarely calling upon the diesel engine for supplementary charging. This enhances cabin comfort; there's less engine heat and noise to contend with. And less regimentation, to boot.

Operating refrigeration (as opposed to freezing) off the 12-volt system has further advantages. The equipment suckles power on demand just like the refrigerator in your kitchen ashore. Box temperature remains perfectly stable round-the-clock with an adjustable thermostat that cuts in and out automatically. And happily, 12-volt refrigeration is at home at the dock while the converter (battery charger) is plugged in. It greatly simplifies the cruising life when everything aboard runs off a common energy source. That way, the engine won't have to be fired up specifically for an oddball chore.

If you expect 12-volt refrigeration to perform, you must be hard-nosed about equipment, insulation, and box size. Just as importantly, the more diversified the 12-volt charging network, particularly equipment that charges compliments of Mother Nature, the more direct-current refrigeration will be a self-tending convenience. When all else fails, substantial engine-driven 12-volt alternators offer quick recharge, and daily running time will be no more than what's required for engine-driven mechanical compressors—if you've done your homework, perhaps less. Moreover, schedules for battery charging are more flexible than schedules for mechanical refrigeration pulldown.

One efficient alternative is a custom cabinet combined with a system designed around the 12-volt Danfoss compressor, either the commercially available precharged component kits or, even better, an energy-saving one-off system with an outsized air-cooled condenser for hot weather efficiency. The pure simplicity of the 12-volt Danfoss system is a bonus. The compressor is hermetically sealed like your shoreside refrigerator; there are no external Freon seals to leak.

Expensive, bulky holding plates are dispensed with. Although you can mate a holdover plate to a Danfoss system, there is no advantage in doing so and good reason not to. With a plate, the system will cycle less frequently, contributing to temperature fluctuations in the box. This is avoided by choosing an evaporator that has minimal heat-absorbing properties, increasing the incidence of system startups per day and reducing running times for each session. More frequent cycling maintains steady box temperatures—no warm beer or frozen lettuce. Evaporators of this kind look like freezer compartments in old-fashioned shoreside refrigerators. There's room for a few icecube trays and a small amount of frozen food.

To further simplify the system, a capillary tube is used instead of an expansion valve. This reduces cost and complication and increases reliability. No monitoring sensors are necessary other than a temperature-controlled on/off switch. A Danfoss system is much less powerful than the engine-driven types, and an air-cooled condenser (either natural convection or the more efficient 12-volt, fan-assisted radiator type) is all that's necessary. This eliminates complication and maintenance associated with water-cooled condensers.

A custom 12-volt condensing unit with a Danfoss compressor, 24-volt cooling fan (12-volt ones are too energetic), and a large air-cooled condenser for tropical service. Black box at left is the Danfoss electronic monitor, which prevents low-voltage damage and flat batteries. Power consumption while running: five amps. Unit is hung under the afterdeck with generous natural circulation.

Energy consumption in tropical weather is around 45 amperes per 24-hour day with a well-insulated, two- to two-and-one-half-cubic-foot box (the Danfoss compressor consumes about five amps per hour when running). Exact power drain depends upon users' habits, actual ambient temperature, and the quality of components such as the condenser and box. Expect power consumption to drop by half or two-thirds in cooler climates. Compared to the raw power required for belt-driven mechanical systems, the outright efficiency of quality 12-volt refrigeration is commendable. In fact, it works so well that a little insulation (neoprene foam) glued to the outside surface of the evaporator might be required to keep the food *outside* the freezer/evaporator from freezing, too.

Danfoss compressors are supplied with an electronic brain to monitor battery voltage. If the voltage drops below 11.5, the compressor is not allowed to start. The unit continues to test voltage periodically and automatically resumes normal operation when sufficient power is again available. This keeps a bank from ruin and protects the compressor from low-voltage damage. Good engineering!

Make sure to provide sufficient battery banks for three days of operation so lulls in natural charging won't instigate immediate engine startups. Since only half a battery's rated capacity can be safely tapped for cruising purposes, and since other 12-volt appliances will also be consuming power, a 50-amp-per-day refrigerator needs about 500 amps of storage.

You can set yourself up in style by installing a second Danfoss system to service a small freezer box. Then you have two independent setups, which together, by the way, cost less than a single engine-driven mechanical system. When the freezer is not needed, it can be shut down to save energy. These systems don't mind inactivity the way their engine-driven cousins do. At times when minimal refrigeration suits you, the larger refrigerator can be inactivated and the small freezer's thermostat reset for refrigeration temperatures. The result—super energy conservation.

Apart from obvious flexibility, two completely separate systems offer total backup capability should unlikely problems develop with one of them. Remember to complement the two systems with matched battery and charging capacities. It won't be necessary to double electric production and storage, though; another 200 amp/hours in battery capacity and another 60 or 70 amps of charging capacity will do for the second system.

Maintenance with 12-volt Danfoss systems is nil. And there is no user intervention required once the thermostat is set. Just be certain to install the compressor/condenser unit in a well-ventilated location so heat is not trapped around the components, artificially raising ambient temperatures. No matter who tells you differently, *don't* install the compressor and air-cooled condenser in the engine room!

Custom 12-volt refrigeration and a good windmill alternator will silently convert a breeze into ice cubes for cocktail hour. It sure beats sitting in your own smoke.

HEAVY-DUTY 12-VOLT REFRIGERATION

Those of you requiring larger refrigerator and/or freezer spaces that can't be efficiently cooled by small Danfoss systems—but still desiring the flexibility of 12 volts—have the option of installing larger capacity 12-volt condensing units. These resemble smaller versions of direct-drive setups except the cast-iron piston-type compressor is belt driven from a 12-volt electric motor. Condensers are water cooled to cope with greater heat transfer, and due to higher Btu ratings, a holding plate is normally used in lieu of a little aluminum freezer compartment. Naturally, electrical consumption is higher—you don't get something for nothing—but an engineered 12-volt base won't mind.

OFF-THE-SHELF 12-VOLT UNITS

Some chest-type, off-the-shelf refrigerators don't do too badly if your needs are modest, although they cannot be expected to be as efficient or powerful as custom 12-volt setups. I've been shipmates with Norcold's smallest chest-type

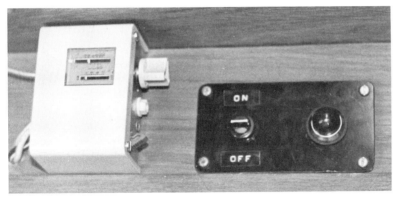

Danfoss automatic temperature switch for the condensing unit pictured on page 153. Note manual switch (to override automatic operation) for pulldown while motoring to a new anchorage, etc., saving a few amps later on. Manual switch cools plate below normal refrigeration temperatures for icemaking, too.

refrigerator/freezers on two transpacific voyages, finding them reliable and appreciated. If you are riding the fence on custom refrigeration because of cost or space, consider taking along one of these compact, ready-made refrigerators.

They are tempting stuff for the home boatbuilder due to easy installation and low cost. In cool climates, they work after a fashion, sometimes managing with great fanfare to make an ice cube. But high ambient temperatures cause them to huff and puff continuously, seldom cycling, sucking the life from a battery bank

The larger, upright, 12-volt marine refrigerators won't be successful in tropical conditions. They have too much surface area and fairly thin insulation—killers to efficiency in high ambient temperatures.

THERMOELECTRIC 12-VOLT REFRIGERATION

The thermoelectric bolt-in modules rely on the principle of an impressed current through two dissimilar sandwiched conductors—one side that becomes warm and the other cool. Heat dissipates off the warm side of the plate outside the box and is absorbed by the cold side of the plate inside the box. Aluminum fins and little fans speed heat transfer.

Be warned: these modules are *worthless*. And they are shaped wrong to use as a dinghy anchor.

They are tempting stuff for the home boatbuilder due to easy installation and low cost. In cool climates, they work after a fashion, sometimes managing with great fanfare to make an ice cube.But high ambient temperatures cause them to huff and puff continuously, seldom cycling, sucking the life from a battery bank like a vampire. Small thermoelectric modules are rated around 3.8 amps per hour. At the end of a hot 24 hours, total consumption is on the order of 80 to 90 amps, and the beer's still warm! Think of what a custom 12-volt system can do with 90 amps.

The similar-looking Freon-type modules are far superior to these greedy thermoelectric tragedies, although even they fall short of the mark.

HEAT TO MAKE ICE

Ammonia gas is used as a refrigerant in a type of refrigeration that functions on the heat-absorption principle. Instead of using mechanical or electromechanical energy to power a compressor, ammonia refrigerates directly from heat energy. It may sound strange to use a flame to cool a bottle of wine, but that's exactly what happens. Absorption refrigeration has a few things in common with a Freon system—there is an icecube-tray evaporator inside the refrigerator cabinet and a condenser outside—but there's no compressor. Not even any moving parts.

These are off-the-shelf appliances meant for domestic use in shoreside areas where electricity is not available. Absorption refrigerators work on boats, too— sort of.

Fuel is either kerosene or LPG (liquid petroleum gas). As such, absorption refrigeration has the advantage of silent running, never imposing on the vessel's power plant as an energy source. Kerosene is the preferable fuel; it's easily stowed in a bulk tank and is not explosive. Although LPG refrigerators are identical to the kerosene models, with the exception of the flame fixture, enough bottled gas for a remote cruise is ponderous to stow (figure on going through a 20-pound cylinder every two to three weeks in warm weather). And living with a deck cargo of LPG would turn most sailors into nervous wrecks, even if the refrigerator had safety features to cut off gas flow to the burner in the event of a flameout (most do).

In calm anchorages, absorption refrigeration is quite successful, particularly in cooler climates. Unfortunately, the motion offshore reduces performance, because the plumbing network must remain on level footing for the ammonia to circulate efficiently. This can be overcome by swinging the refrigerator athwartships on pivots like a galley stove.

Motion creates an erratic flame in the kerosene units from surge in the fuel tank, too. This can be minimized by stuffing the fuel reservoir with brass wool. Kerosene burners need their wicks trimmed regularly to keep the flame burning cleanly and evenly. The fuel tank needs topping up every few days.

Heat from the flame of kerosene or LPG refrigerators raises cabin temperatures. For tropical service, it's smart to fit an insulated through-deck flue.

Insulation, as in most off-the-shelf vertical-door refrigerators, is marginal for tropical use. Although an absorption unit may crank out a few trays of ice each day in hot weather (nothing to sneeze at!), the rest of the refrigerator space may be lukewarm. This can be partially remedied by cementing additional foam sheeting on the cabinet and door surfaces. But there still will be some heat infiltration via the original sheet-metal surfaces.

Despite its drawbacks, absorption refrigeration cannot be faulted for reliability. It keeps trying, even if efficiency in hot weather isn't always 100 percent. Since the components are not designed for marine use, some external corrosion is to be expected unless you apply additional, after-market coats of paint.

REFRIGERATION DRAINAGE

If you are serious about energy conservation, you might decide against refrigeration-box drains. They are a small source of heat leakage, even when designed properly with a water trap. A drain in a freezer is no great asset, anyway. It's not much trouble to defrost it on cleaning day and bail it out like a dinghy (as you do with a chest freezer ashore).

Water pools in refrigerators from evaporator condensation, particularly in hot, humid weather. If you don't install a drain, the water must be periodically sponged out. A drip channel or tray positioned to collect dripping condensation from the evaporator compartment or plate helps keep foodstuffs dry. Don't store items directly on the bottom surface of the refrigerator liner; use a cake rack to space items up out of the damp.

THINK BEFORE OPENING

While energy-efficient refrigeration is the ticket for tropical cool storage, further savings are yours with a little discipline. Ashore we browse glassy-eyed into an open refrigerator out of habit; aboard ship, this wastes energy. Remember what foodstuffs the refrigerator or freezer contains and open it with a definite purpose in mind.

Don't leave chilled foodstuffs out to warm up needlessly if they are going back in the refrigerator. Why waste all the work the system has done by making it do the job all over again? The goal, particularly in hot weather, is to minimize how often and how long chilled provisions are exposed to warm ambient temperatures. This saves energy—and importantly, it saves the need to produce more energy.

THE DILEMMA OF CHOICE

For comfortable cruising, some form of refrigeration is essential. The system you eventually choose depends on your philosophy of energy production, your deep-freeze needs, your budget, the space available for the chiller box and its components, and how you rate a particular system's inherent complications or hassles or inadequacies versus its benefits.

A large percentage of refrigeration energy is consumed by the freezer (it maintains a greater differential between box and ambient temperatures than does a refrigerator). In practice, it's the refrigerator, not the freezer, that sustains a good lifestyle by supplying cold drinks and chilled desserts and providing day-to-day preservation of dairy products, vegetables, meats, and leftovers. A reliable refrigerator containing a small freezer compartment for a few food items and a couple of icecube trays could satisfy most of your cravings. A big freezer, although enviable, should be considered as secondary.

⑥▶ Ventilation in All Climates

Whether you plan to sail to tropical ports of call or cruise the higher, temperate latitudes, only a first-rate ventilation network has a prayer of sustaining a reasonable level of creature comfort in daily, liveaboard life. A diverse ventilation system works by flushing all the nooks and crannies below decks with an ongoing supply of fresh, outside air—rain or shine, through gales and calms, at sea and at anchor.

Ventilation is fundamental to overall climate control. It's the only way to maintain a sweet smelling, dry, and habitable accommodation 24 hours a day, seven days a week. Without it, the quality of life aboard a cruising yacht is doomed, and refinements such as heating systems won't have half a chance to do their stuff.

Dead air spaces cost you a big slice of comfort by contributing to a stale, muggy environment in the cabin. Inadequate air circulation costs money, too. Offshoots of poor ventilation—mildew, condensation, and rot—will plague you to the end of your liveaboard days. Boatbuilders don't universally understand the ventilation facts of life unless they've lived aboard. Fewer yet appreciate tropical conditions and know what to do about them.

Flush vents are okay for refreshing moored vessels or for chainlockers or lazarettes on liveaboard boats, but they don't move enough air through living spaces to be of much value. If you use them, you must find a way to cap them in heavy weather.

There are four basic ventilation strategies: cowl vents on dorade boxes, opening ports, hatches, and forced-air extraction. No single ventilation method stands alone. The individual elements or components for ventilation are arranged so they work separately and in harmony to cover a wide variety of climatic and weather conditions.

To function with distinction, any system must be designed with ultimate adversity in mind. Ventilation is no exception. In this case, ultimate adversity is the sticky combination of high humidity, high ambient temperatures, and heavy rain. A ventilation network that copes with this will handle anything.

COWL VENTILATORS

On racer/cruisers, cowl vents are losing popularity and flush, dish-shaped vents (the ones that look like a Frisbee on deck) are becoming commonplace. Don't let this trend lead you astray when outfitting for a blue-water cruise. The flying-saucer-shaped, deck-hugging vents are an economic compromise that bolt down quickly. They are fine on unattended, moored vessels where minimal circulation is all that matters. But they do virtually nothing for liveaboard comfort.

The advantages of a cowl vent over a Frisbee vent are critical. A large cowl vent sits up high on its dorade box to catch the breeze; Frisbee vents crouch low where the breeze is likely to be obstructed. A cowl vent can be rotated into the wind to divert the maximum volume of air below in any mooring or sailing situation, or it can be aimed away from the wind to act as an extractor. Frisbee vents don't have this flexibility or performance, being fixed, omnidirectional units with tiny inlets. Mushroom vents are similarly inflexible and weak lunged. The role a cowl vent plays to rid a vessel from accumulated moisture-laden air in all kinds of weather cannot be overstated. Flush-fitting vents are also susceptible to flooding when green water comes aboard uninvited. Dorade vents thrive in rough weather. It's true that Frisbee and mushroom vents have one advantage—they don't foul sheets. However, this is academic when cowl vents are placed thoughtfully out of the line of fire and sheets kept under control with fairleads and blocks.

For tropical duty, a cowl ventilator should have at least a four-inch throat. The diameter of the cowl itself should be nearly twice that, say six to eight inches. Height off the dorade box should be 12 inches or more, to place the intake up in clear air. A vent of these dimensions diverts large volumes of soothing air down into the accommodation, creating a drier, cooler atmosphere in steamy conditions. If you can't find large off-the-shelf cowl vents, create your own, starting with a mold and laminating the vents with GRP. Don't be tempted to compromise with smallish cowl vents. They are your last line of defense, staying on the job in conditions that put other ventilation features out of action.

DORADE BOXES

Cowl vents have a partner called the dorade box, an on-deck water trap. Every cowl vent should have one. Rain or spray that sneaks down the cowl vent's throat runs back out on deck again through a drain hole and not below to soak the accommodation. Basically, a dorade is divided into two sections inside by a dam. Air flows over the dam and into the boat through the deck aperture, but water, because of its greater weight, falls by the wayside on the ventilator side of the dam. A variation on this theme, serving the same purpose, has a fiberglass or PVC pipe rising up in the box.

To be effective, a dorade box must match its cowl ventilator. No restriction can exist within the box with less cross-sectional area than the vent's throat. The usual impass in a poorly designed dorade box is the space over the water-stop dam (or above the deck-aperture tube, as the case may be) and the deck opening itself.

SECURING DORADE VENTS

Each compartment below decks should be served by at least one dorade vent, more often several. In hot, humid weather the vents join forces to draw volumes of fresh air in and expel stale air, but in cooler weather the air flow must be restricted to keep the crew warm and toasty. Sometimes it's a simple matter of aiming a vent away from the wind to reduce the invasion of cold air. However,

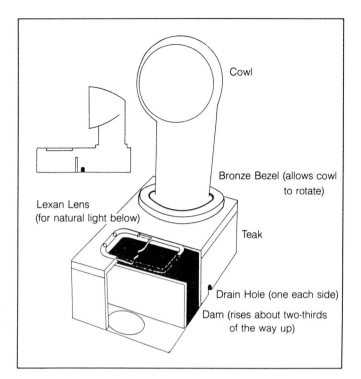

Cowl

Bronze Bezel (allows cowl
to rotate)

Lexan Lens
(for natural light below)

Teak

Drain Hole (one each side)

Dam (rises about two-thirds
of the way up)

Large cowl vents with free-
flow dorade boxes are all-
weather ventilators. There's
no substitute for live-aboard
comfort at sea or at anchor.

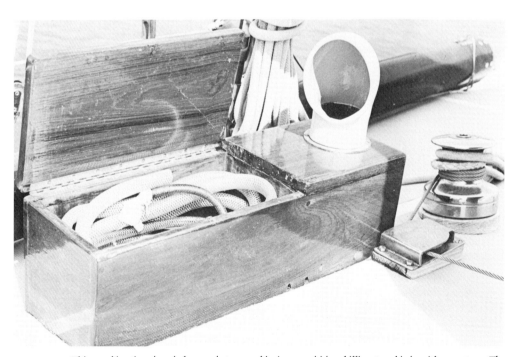

This combination dorade box and stowage bin is a good idea, killing two birds with one stone. The
winch, turning block, and cable leading across the deck, however, are bad news.

in extremely cold weather, some of the vents must be blocked off. And also, in rare instances at sea, vents must be closed off because of heavy weather to deny seawater entry into the boat.

Traditionally (and nonsensically), dorades are capped by removing the cowl ventilator and replacing the cowl with a screw-in cover. But imagine scampering about on deck in the middle of a gale on a dark night with an armful of vents and caps. What a stupid chore! Or just as ridiculous, imagine yourself quitting a cozy bunk in an anchorage to go up in a pouring rain to fit a cap or rotate a vent.

To short-circuit the inconvenience (and possible danger) of capping dorades on deck, each through-deck aperture should be fitted with a plastic inspection port with a screw-in cover (the kind with an O-ring seal). The outer ring is mechanically fastened and bedded to the deck opening underneath (when the vessel is built, it's simple to cut the hole to size). Then the vent aperture may be secured absolutely watertight from below decks without exposing a soul to the elements. Each screw-in cover is stowed in a handy spot near its respective deck opening. Dorades with a deadlight lens over the deck aperture use translucent screw-in caps.

In the event of heavy weather, you'll be reassured by the knowledge that the yacht's vents are sealed to keep the sea outside the hull, where it belongs. The inspection ports are stronger than they look and positioned where they are not easily damaged. Even if an unfriendly wave boards you and rips a few dorade boxes out by the roots, the yacht remains tight as a drum. Not so with the old-fashioned caps on the boxes; if the box goes, the cap goes along with it, and suddenly there's a gaping hole in the deck.

OPENING PORTLIGHTS

Like the dorade vent, the opening portlight is an endangered species. Racer/cruisers are resorting to one-piece Plexiglas or Lexan sheeting for cabin windows. And that's what they are—windows, not ports. Again, it boils down to boatbuilding economics: screw-on sheeting is cheaper in material cost and labor content than individually fitted opening portlights. Yet a cruising boat seldom benefits from production-line expediencies; she must have ports, not windows, if there is to be a prayer of comfort in steamy, tropical climates.

Opening portlights are the prime fixtures that encourage generous, soothing cross-ventilation. They allow the breeze to blow literally right through the boat, just as open windows do in a house. Imagine a house built in a hot climate with fixed windows and no air conditioning, and the role opening ports play becomes clear. During occasional broiling days in paradise, you'll forget all about the cost of your opening portlights and pity neighboring sailors who are sweating it out without them.

Ideally, every port should open. Think of each one that does not as a permanent wall to a cooling breeze. Forecabins require two on each side; the

Ventilation aids for the aft stateroom of Dolphin Queen *include a skylight hatch, a large dorade vent, and five 7 x 16 opening portlights (one on rear of cabin). In all, the vessel has 19 opening ports, and in the tropics each one is a blessing. Dorade at upper right is over the companionway. Dorade in the foreground serves the engine-room exhaust blower. All cowl vents are custom made of GRP with teak boxes and bronze bezels for rotation.*

head compartment *must* have at least one; the saloon, at least two per side; and the galley, several. Quarterberths tucked alongside the cockpit—marginal places for habitation, anyway—are improved with opening ports in the side of the cockpit well.

Opening ports not only refresh in sweltering weather, but they brighten the vessel's interior with natural light, making the boat feel bigger and cooler. Because of this, they are particularly at home in the hulls of flush-decked vessels, so long as they are strong fixtures of bronze with thick, tempered glass. In addition, hull ports should be fitted with removable, clear Lexan shutters that bolt on for ocean passages to protect against the possibility of damage in a heavy seaway. Heaving-to could be more than a hull port will bear unless it's stout and well protected.

There's nothing wrong with polycarbonate opening portlights in a vessel's superstructure, however. They are fairly strong, light in weight, and less expensive than their bronze counterparts. Yet, glass resists abrasion, scratches, and fogging over the years, while polycarbonates and acrylics don't. Even mar-resistant Lexan deteriorates quickly in cruising service.

HATCHES AS VENTS

Centrally hinged, winged, skylight hatches are rarely seen on new vessels anymore. These masterpieces of joinerwork bathed majestic saloons of yesteryear with natural light and fresh air. They've faded into history, replaced by aluminum-framed, off-the-shelf, bolt-on hardware. Neither really suits the cruising yacht. The old beauties tended to leak like sieves and the new breed of aluminum/acrylic or aluminum/polycarbonate hatches make poor ventilators.

In any case, once again, the racer/cruiser merchants have taken the path of least resistance, and bolt-on hatches have become standard throughout the industry. In all fairness, the bolt-on hatches are okay for casual recreation, and they do have one redeeming feature: they don't leak when dogged. But their prevalence on recreational craft should not lead you to think they belong on a cruising boat. Because they don't!

Hatches serve several purposes. They offer passage spaces for people, sails, and supplies. With acrylic or polycarbonate inserts, they act as skylights. And when cracked, they ventilate, helping to eliminate a multitude of sins such as galley smoke, moisture, and heat. You needn't do much to make a hatch ventilate—just open it—until rain or spray enters the picture, that is. Then, if the hatch has not been designed with a water-trap feature (and this is where the bolt-on hatches fall down), you have to part company with some of your comfort.

To work as a ventilator, a hatch should sit off the deck on coamings so seawater jumping aboard in heavy offshore conditions is less able to climb over the edge and invade the boat's interior. Wind-driven spray or rain, either at anchor or at sea, must be excluded from the accommodation, too. This requires a special hatch with double coamings. The hatch cover is hinged to an outer coaming, which, in the closed position, provides structural integrity. Inner coamings that are spaced an inch or two inside the outer coamings rise up to meet the underside of the hatch cover. A watertight rubber gasket is located at this interface. Drain holes in the outer coamings let any water blocked by the inner coamings escape. Hatches built like this may be left ajar a few inches in wet weather, allowing air to flow in and out. Perversely, ready-made bolt-on hatches sitting flush on deck offer an open invitation to rain, spray, and the odd gout of green water.

Triangular hinged side flaps block the sides when a hatch is cracked, leaving just the back open to the elements. The spray and rain then find it much harder to sneak below decks. The side flaps fold underneath the hatch cover when it's dry.

Hinged hatches are more effective at anchor (and in reasonably gentle weather offshore) if they have two sets of hinges, dogs, and adjusters. They can be propped up to scoop air below decks when the wind is on the bow during clear weather, or cracked, normally using the front hinges, in wet weather. The ability to scoop is welcomed over sleeping quarters in hot, muggy weather, contributing no end to a decent night's rest.

Hatches that leak are a terrible bother. Often it's the companionway sliding

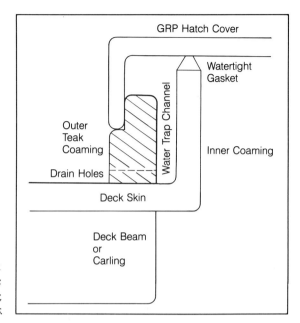

Water trap hatch coaming schematic.
Without this feature, exposed hatches
must be dogged in rainy weather,
and cabin comfort declines.

hatch that dribbles down your neck when rain or spray is lashing the decks. To stop that forever, this hatch should slide into a watertight envelope bedded to the deck or cabintop. The envelope is critical to the success of a water-resistant dodger, too, as we'll see later on.

Typically, recreational sailboats have a single sliding companionway hatch and a single forehatch. For tropical cruising, this is by no means adequate, regardless of boat length. Additional hatches over the saloon and galley are mandatory. A saloon hatch smothered by a chocked dinghy won't contribute much light or ventilation, either. If you are faced with this situation, install smaller hatches outboard of the dinghy.

Aft sleeping cabins need a hinged hatch, too, even if they already have a sliding companionway-type hatch for entry. Sleeping cabins deserve the best ventilation you can possibly arrange, or the accumulated moisture from breathing and sweating will grow a bumper crop of mildew that will play havoc with clothing and shoes.

A final but vital word about hatches: build them as if your life depended on them, because it does. Use only beefy metallic bronze or stainless hardware for hinges and latches (dogs). Make dead sure the outer coamings and the hatch covers themselves are structurally bulletproof. Hatches protrude off the deck, thereby offering a purchase to a boarding sea. If you ever are unfortunate enough to get nailed, weak hatches could leave you vulnerable. Super-strong hatches pay for themselves by giving security and priceless peace of mind offshore where it counts. It won't hurt to bolt a cleat on each side of a hinged hatch as an extra precaution, either. That gives you the option of lashing the hatch cover down if worse comes to worst. If you prepare for nasty weather, you'll proably never experience it. If you don't, you will.

Skylight hatches over saloons let in natural light, dispelling gloom. Also, when covered by an awning or fitted with water traps, they ventilate an important gathering place.

A companionway hatch sliding into a GRP envelope bedded to the cabintop. This, and the wooden dams to each side for fitting a cockpit dodger, are the basis of a dry accommodation.

THE SUPERVENT

Sometimes, because of restrictions in deck layout, it's impossible to fit a hatch over the saloon table, yet there is dire need for generous air flow there for dining and cocktail-hour comfort in hot weather when the cockpit is uninhabitable because of rain. A similar problem exists over a berth in a sleeping cabin, particularly in the case of a double berth, where two people sleeping in close quarters in hot weather demand copious ventilation. This dilemma can be solved with a huge cowl vent that force-feeds a cabin a flow of fresh air.

The vent should be two to three feet in height, six inches across the throat, with a cowl diameter of one foot. If you could stow a gadget of this size somewhere when it wasn't in service, even if it had to be lashed under the deck in the chainlocker or hidden away in a chocked dinghy or an engine room, a supervent could be your salvation. But vents like this have to be custom made of copper or fiberglass. Don't let that put you off, though; it could be cheap at twice the price, compared to living in a sauna.

A large custom vent is designed around whatever readily available hardware is chosen to mate it to the deck. Locate a six-inch brass or bronze threaded deckplate (you have to secure the hole in the deck when the vent is not used, anyway). Buy two caps for the threaded deck flange. One cap will be sacrificed for its threads, which are bonded or soldered to the vent's lower throat for mounting.

The vent's cowl should overhang the throat, with the top of the cowl projecting a few inches farther yet, so rainwater won't run down the throat when the vent is positioned with its back to the wind. Even positioned for wet weather, the vent does you a service by exhausting stale cabin air. A dorade box for a vent of this stature is hardly feasible—it's basically a fair-weather feature. Install a crossbar handle in the vent's lower throat for rotation from below decks.

Although primarily a feature for harbor use in special circumstances, a supervent would also be an asset during hot times offshore in docile conditions.

IMPROVING CIRCULATION BELOW

Hatches, opening ports, and dorade vents take care of the cabin-to-cabin and cabin-to-outside air circulation. But a boat is chockablock with smaller compartments: lockers, drawers, bins, and bilges. Every one of these subcompartments must be ventilated.

Louvered doors, traditional features seen on better yachts for generations, still present the only means to ventilate vertical lockers and particularly hanging lockers fully. No matter how thoroughly the bulkheads and sub-bulkheads adjacent to the locker spaces are perforated with a hole saw, mildew will gain the upper hand without a free-breathing, louvered door. There is simply no substitute!

Louvered doors on all lockers help fight mildew.

Drawers can be a problem, too. Even though they are open on the top, it does not follow that the compartment they slide into is anything but dead air space. So the confines of this space must be perforated, too. Instead of installing brass drawer pulls, which cost money and tend to snag passers-by, cut an elongated opening in the drawer face for a pull. The cutout performs double duty as a vent.

Stowage bins must be attacked with a hole saw to promote maximum circulation. Whatever the bins will eventually contain, the same rules of ventilation apply—no dead air spaces. The disappointment from rusty tins of food or a mildewed photo album will be remembered long after the sweat to cut the holes has dried. Visible inboard faces of bins must be ventilated, too. Decide on the method early in construction so the hardware used to beautify ventilation holes is consistent throughout the vessel. If the pressed stainless steel louvers sold by marine outlets are too garish for you, hunt around for plastic soffit vents at your local building-supply center. These inexpensive, press-in vent plugs are used to ventilate eaves in housing and are less of an eyesore than the stainless marine variety. Some sailors bore neat holes, paint them, and leave it at that.

Bilges must not be left as dead air spaces, either. They have to breathe to stay healthy (in wooden vessels, this is crucial to continued preservation). Perforate bulkheads under the floorboards, arrange venting spaces outboard of flooring into lockers, and provide an avenue for air flow into the engine room (more on this in a minute).

AREAS OF INDEPENDENT VENTILATION

Three areas aboard ship must be absolutely self-contained, sealed from the rest of the accommodation. Ventilation to these areas must not depend on compartment-to-compartment flow. If this philosophy is applied religiously, you're guaranteed a better standard of living on your cruise.

The Chainlocker

A chainlocker must have its own bilge, isolated from the rest of the vessel's bilges by a watertight bulkhead (which can serve double duty as a crash bulkhead). The reason for this crops up after several months of cruising: accumulated harbor goo and sand create a mess, occasionally a smelly mess. Despite a good job of rinsing the anchor chain on its way into the locker, some mud and sand always lurk in the links. In the event of a hurried departure, there may not be an opportunity to rinse the chain at all. If muck is allowed to infiltrate the entire bilge system, you'll have a cesspool that's the devil to clean.

A separate bilge solves the problem. And as an added bonus, the chain may be washed conveniently right in the locker. A diaphragm bilge pump in the chainlocker ejects muddy leavings from weighing anchor or cleaning the chain. It's a system you'll enjoy year after year.

It follows that a chainlocker's ventilation system should never breach a watertight bulkhead, either. Mud odors must be barred from the accommodation. If there's access to the chainlocker from the forecabin, install a tight-fitting solid door, not a louvered one. Vent the chainlocker to the deck only. The crew living in the forecabin will be forever grateful.

The Head

Similarly, separate ventilation is called for in the head compartment. Except here we are not talking about mud! Head compartments aboard yachts can be a source of embarrassment, needlessly. Why should crude amenities be acceptable aboard a boat when they are not ashore?

Yachts are compact dwellings, and it's not unusual for the throne to be bolted down within spitting distance of the saloon. How many houses have a toilet at arm's length from the dining table? It just isn't done. However, this situation aboard can be salvaged by making the head compartment *feel* dissociated from the adjacent accommodation, despite its proximity.

A tight-fitting solid door isolates the head, forming a barrier against embarrassment. This also furthers the function of an independent ventilation system, which pulls outside air in and expels less fragrant air continuously. The head door should remain tightly closed at all times, whether the facility is in use or not. Obnoxious odors will be contained and dispersed without permeating the rest of the boat. It's the only civilized alternative.

The Engine Room

Here's another compartment that generates unpleasant odors, requiring separate ventilation and no circulatory interchange with other areas below decks. Otherwise, the interior of the boat will smell of diesel oil, lube oil, and hot machinery. In lumpy weather at sea or at anchor, engine-room odors can be cruel to sailors with weak stomachs. Engine-room fumes take the edge off a fine dinner, too. So, like the chainlocker and head, the machinery space must be a tightly sealed area with solid doors and inspection panels—no louvers! Solid doors reduce noise, too.

FORCED AIR EXTRACTION

Natural circulation meets ventilation needs most of the time if it's methodically arranged. But there are three problem areas that need more vigorous air flow to remain pollution free. They must be fitted with 12-volt exhaust blowers to drive out the poison. The blowers are cheap comforts that should be seen as standard equipment, not luxuries.

The Head

A 12-volt blower is a definite requirement in the head compartment to supplement natural ventilation. When the blower is switched on (all blowers aboard can be controlled by a rheostat so speed is adjustable), outside air is pulled through the head's cowl vent(s) and expelled through the blower's vent; air exchange is practically instantaneous. The advantages of forced extraction are appreciated by the ship's company during times of intermittent noxious odors. On paper this may seem amusing; aboard ship it's not.

Forced extraction is an absolute must for showering. If allowed to dissipate naturally, water vapor from regular showers dampens the boat from stem to stern, resulting in mildew. The head compartment remains perpetually damp, speeding the growth of bacteria (and hence, odors). Without forced extraction, towels never quite dry between showers, either, and there's going to be something rotten in Denmark, or whatever state you're in. The extractor whisks away shower steam like magic.

*A squirrel-cage blower in a head
compartment sucks out the poison.
Life's grim without one!*

The Galley

Consider the worst conditions for cooking—wet, calm, roasting weather. Out of
necessity, some of the hatches and ports are partially secured to keep out rain.
Your dinner guests arrive and are quickly invited below out of the weather. The
cook of the day gets cracking in the galley, pressure-cooking a pot roast, boiling
potatoes and vegetables, and, with spur-of-the-moment inspiration, frying a
dozen oysters for hors d'oeuvres. In no time, the atmosphere becomes thick from
warm bodies and cooking. Portlights steam up; grease smoke hangs heavy.

Offshore with the boat buttoned against flying spray, the story is much the
same. Particularly in hot, steaming weather, when the stove adds additional
doses of heat and moisture.

An extractor over the galley stove changes the picture completely. At the flick
of a switch, the steam, the grease smoke, and cooking heat vanish. There's no
substitute for a galley extractor.

The Engine Room

The case for forced air extraction in engine rooms used to be based on safety
when gasoline engines were installed in sailboats. Although diesel power has
replaced gas engines, there are compelling reasons to keep installing blowers. In
the tropics, the heat generated by the power plant for battery charging or
spinning refrigeration compressors will raise cabin temperatures significantly
unless the heat is expelled swiftly from the boat. Long spells of powering in hot

An anodized Breidert-type aluminum vent directly coupled to a blower under the deckhead. Note custom stainless steel guard. After a Pacific voyage, no corrosion.

weather will heat up the vessel's interior beyond comfort, too. Natural ventilation cannot be expected to cope. Only high-volume air exchange gets the job done.

There are more reasons than comfort to have engine-room extraction. In high ambient temperatures, an engine room will be a furnace without it. This is harmful to componentry dependent upon air cooling: voltage regulators, alternators, rotary converters, inverters, etc. When these things overheat, efficiency and/or service life is reduced.

Even water-cooled machinery like the propulsion engine and reduction gear depend greatly on surface radiation to keep cool. In tropical conditions, a power plant that functioned perfectly in temperate climates can mysteriously develop cooling-system problems when engine-room temperatures soar. Lube oil thins out, losing some of its lubricating properties; engines don't live as long.

The engine-room blower has worthwhile side benefits. While forcing air out of the machinery space, it creates a slight negative pressure (partial vacuum) in the compartment, and all fumes and smells shoot up the spout rather than waft past cracks and gaps in access doors and panels into the accommodation.

Twin-squirrel-cage blower efficiently cools a large engine room with an auxiliary diesel generator.

Providing the bilges vent into the engine room and have air inlets at their extremities, the slight vacuum produces an air flow through them. Stale, damp bilges are refreshed; things stowed there have a better chance for survival.

The engine-room blower is a godsend, especially when you have to work on or near hot machinery, which sometimes happens to the best of us. Without the blower, it's hotter than the hinges of hell; with it, you bask in a cooling breeze.

EXTRACTOR VENTS

A squirrel-cage blower works best when coupled directly underneath a dorade vent. The blower itself can sit right out in front of God and everyone, or it can be disguised by cabinetwork, as you prefer. Other kinds of vent hardware work with exhaust blowers, too (mushroom, cowl without dorade, and Breidert-style omnidirectional), but they don't incorporate the vital water-trap feature. The ship's blowers should be free to operate in all weather. The worse the weather, in fact, the greater a blower's value.

The small, three-inch, plastic-cased bilge blowers are fine for the head and galley. But the engine room needs a husky four-inch unit, because the job there is the toughest. Make certain the cross-sectional area of the inlet vent(s) in the head is *more* than equal to that of the exhaust blower and vent. If air cannot get into a compartment efficiently, a blower cannot expel it efficiently. The engine compartment should have inlet vents totalling *twice* the cross-sectional area of the exhaust blower and vent so the partial vacuum induced there is kept to a minimum. The engine, like the blower, sucks air from the engine room, too, and

Custom ship-style stainless ventilator with internal water baffle coupled to the twin-cage blower pictured on the opposite page.

restrictive inlet venting could prevent the power plant, which is designed for ambient atmospheric conditions, from operating at peak power and economy.

Wide separation of inlet vents and extractors induces a flow of air completely through a compartment and helps eliminate dead areas. For example, an engine room could draw air from vents on the afterdeck, sweeping the lazarette, exhaust system, and the entire length of the machinery space with a cool, dry breeze. This does away with mildew, heat, and moisture in a large portion of the vessel's interior that otherwise is prone to stagnation. When the blower is shut down, the squirrel cage won't block the natural flow completely, either; even an idle blower contributes to ventilation.

Extractor dorade vents, like the other deck vents, must be set up for capping in severe weather. This can be done on deck in the traditional manner, or the blower can be installed on a hinged or sliding bracket so it can be swung aside, the vent being capped with a screw-in inspection cover. The latter makes more sense; the more holes you can plug from the security of the cabin, the better.

WHEN ALL ELSE FAILS

Voyages to the tropics expose the crew to weather conditions that sailors in temperate climes can't fully appreciate. Although a tropical lagoon is heaven for

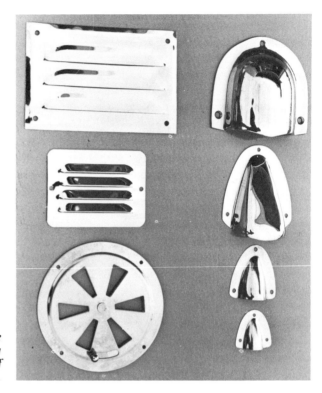

This kind of hardware has no place on the exterior of an oceangoing boat unless it can be closed off watertight.

outright cruising pleasure, no place is perfect, and there will be random intervals of discomfort caused by temporary lulls in tradewinds. During calms, when temperature and humidity both soar into the 90s, even the best ventilation system may be hard pressed to cope.

To anticipate these inevitable extremes of heat and humidity, grace each berth with a small 12-volt fan. Locate the fan at the foot, near the deckhead. There will be times when it makes the difference between contented sleep and sweaty insomnia. And that's saying something!

Small automotive fans are inexpensive comfort. They won't break the battery bank, either. Most eat less than 0.5 amp, no more than a tiny dome light.

While you are at it, find homes in the saloon and galley for a few fans. They'll convert a hot box into a decent place to live.

A THUMB FOR EVERY DIKE

A blue-water boat must be set up to be made fully waterproof at the drop of a hat. Cast a critical eye over your boat. If you see any vent holes or other apertures that cannot be instantly plugged with on-board hardware, rectify the situation before going offshore. Sometimes, production yards install daysail-type recreational hardware such as clamshell vents, which let seawater hose freely into the cabin if the boat becomes momentarily immersed. Hardware like this must be replaced.

7▶ Shipboard Heating for All Seasons

The objectives of a marine heating system are twofold: lowering humidity below decks while at the same time raising cabin temperatures to a comfortable level. An all-weather ventilation system is fundamental to a heating system's success. The heater will only deliver the goods—a toasty, bone-dry accommodation—if it's complemented by efficient, natural circulation.

THE ENEMY: CONDENSATION

Boats are moisture traps. In a house, there is likely to be ten times the air to absorb water vapor generated by people and their activities. Aboard ship, the production of moisture from cooking (both as a byproduct of combustion from burners plus steam from the cooking food), showering, evaporation from wet clothing and gear, and water vapor from breathing humans is just as great, but it's concentrated. This raises relative humidity to unacceptable levels unless something's done to get rid of it.

In warm weather, moisture isn't much of a problem if a good ventilation system is operating at full tilt. In cold weather, wide-open ventilation chills a crew to the bone, so the boat's buttoned up. Then, without heat, the below-decks atmosphere hovers at the saturation point, day and night. Cold inside surfaces— portlights, hatches, and uninsulated deck and hull areas—lower the temperature of contacting saturated air to the dew point; condensation dampens or soaks curtains, upholstery, bedding, clothing, personal possessions—the works! In the morning, when condensation's at its worst (hull/deck surfaces are the coolest around daybreak), entire deckheads weep, dripping portlights form pools, and skylights sweat like pigs.

Shipboard life in these conditions is grim. And it doesn't have to be all that cold to dash hopes of comfort, either. Mild temperatures in the 60s (F.), although reasonably comfortable in a house, are likely to be miserable aboard.

CONTROLLING MOISTURE AND HEAT LOSS WITH INSULATION

Insulation materials slow down the transfer of heat from the accommodation to the outside world. The best insulation is composed of tiny air bubbles (foam). The less insulation weighs per cubic foot, the more air it contains, and hence, all things being equal, the better it performs. Before modern technology got into the act, cork was accepted as insulating material. But cork is heavier than modern foam insulation, containing less air, so nowadays it's second rate.

To reduce condensation to a minimum—it's probably wishful thinking that it could ever be totally eliminated on a yacht—all inside surfaces of the hull and deck require attention. Heat transfer must be retarded so interior surfaces stay warmer than out-of-doors, closer to the cabin's ambient temperature. Then saturated air won't drop its cargo of water through condensation. And importantly, moisture remaining in the air as water vapor can be deported.

An effective insulation program depends on the hull/deck material of your boat and the climatic conditions of your cruising grounds. Steel or aluminum boats have to be more heavily insulated, because metal conducts heat rapidly. Urethane foam is popular because of its spray-on qualities and superior insulation properties, plus it tends to seal a boat's surfaces against moisture (a metal hull or deck must still be corrosion-proofed before application, though).

If you are building a vessel for hire, check with appropriate authorities. Urethane foam gives off poisonous gases in combustion and is not approved for commercial marine use in some countries.

A fiberglass vessel needs less insulation than one built of metal. But GRP is still a poor insulator, definitely needing attention unless cored with PVC foam. Wood core materials do not guarantee the boat will be insulated effectively. For example, a composite, strip-planked, cedar/GRP vessel may fight off condensation without further help, whereas an end-grain-balsa/GRP composite may not. How well wood insulates depends on its thickness and the amount of resin it absorbs (resin reduces insulation qualities by filling air cells).

Sheets of quarter- to three-eighths-inch closed-cell neoprene wetsuit material cemented directly to a fiberglass surface stop condensation in its tracks. Wetsuit sheeting is available finished on one side with a smooth, tough skin that is easy to clean. Instead of using contact cement or Neoprene cement, which bond permanently at the slightest touch, try a rubber-based linoleum paste. It cures slowly, allowing the material to slide to and fro for accurate positioning. Use less expensive, unfinished sheeting in areas where it's covered with ceiling, vinyl sheeting, or where you're not concerned with appearance.

Solid timber boats sometimes squeak by without insulation because, unlike GRP or metal, wood has natural insulation properties. Covering traditional, planked hull surfaces with insulation can be a risky business, anyway, encouraging rot if moisture is trapped between the insulation and hull. A cold-molded wood/epoxy boat sheathed with GRP doesn't absorb water into the hull like a traditional planked boat and can be more safely insulated with spray-on foam (on top of water-barrier coats of epoxy).

Insulating against condensation and insulating for minimum heat loss are two different things. Just because condensation is under control does not imply heat retention. Nevertheless, a vessel may be heated comfortably in mild climates (above freezing) if the hull is simply insulated against condensation and the deckhead, where most heat loss occurs, is insulated thoroughly with one-inch Styrofoam or urethane sheeting. A well-insulated overhead retards the leaching of heat into the accommodation from hot decks, too. This keeps the boat warmer in winter and cooler in summer or tropical weather. You win both ways.

DRY HEAT WITH A STACK

A heating appliance has to do more than supply warmth. Since boats have such a problem with internal moisture, the heater must never add to below-decks humidity. This narrows down the hunt for a boat heater, since only those with stacks will expel moisture and combustion pollutants. Any heater without a through-deck stack or flue must be crossed off your shopping list.

High on the blacklist are cooking stoves. The shortcut of running an open burner hasn't a hope of offering comfort in cold weather. One of the byproducts of burning petroleum products or alcohol is water! Sure, a cookstove burner warms the cabin a bit, but humidity climbs right along with temperature, and the ship stays damp. The safety of an open cooking burner being monitored by the cook is one thing; an unattended burner left to its own devices for heating purposes is another story altogether. If the flame goes out and the fuel continues to flow, watch out!

Likewise, infrared or catalytic liquid-petroleum gas heaters produce moisture without ridding the ship of it and are not suitable for liveaboard use. The same is true of portable kerosene heaters. Avoid them. While not having an open flame *per se*, the byproducts of combustion from these heaters are contained within the boat. Using LPG for heating fuel, by whatever means, leaves much to be desired so far as convenience is concerned, anyway. Heating requires a lot more energy than cooking, and LPG cylinders need frequent refilling. Out in the boondocks, this is either a hassle or an impossibility.

A heater fitted with a stack or chimney performs other valuable services. Not only do pollutants and moisture from combustion get the bum's rush, but the updraft exiting through the stack causes fresh outside air to be drawn into the cabin spaces via ventilators—ventilators that, with cabin heat, may be cracked instead of tightly shut. This interchange gives you the same level of comfort as if the ship was opened up in warmer weather. Moisture you've kept up in the air with good condensation-stopping insulation is swept up the stack to vanish forever. And importantly, the cool, fresh outside air drawn into the boat and warmed by the heating system keeps the boat drier (when air is warmed, its relative humidity drops).

STACK DESIGN FOR NATURAL-DRAFT HEATERS

Before looking at the types of heating units that work in cruising service, there are a few points to ponder that apply to most of them equally. A natural-draft heater, whether solid or liquid fueled, will only operate at peak efficiency if the chimney design and installation induce a healthy updraft. A weak draft hurts combustion, causing excess smoking and less heat output and wasting fuel by incomplete combustion. A weak draft also leaves the heater vulnerable to backwinding, when, for an instant, reverse air flow in the stack caused by a wind shift or a gust fills the cabin with smoke—nauseating!

If feasible, a chimney should run vertically from the heater through the overhead and then continue straight off the deck to the smokehead. Every bend causes a slight restriction, partially reducing draft velocity. If a bend is inevitable, it should be gentle, not more than 20 or 30 degrees. Forty-five- to 90-degree bends are likely to dampen your heater's performance.

Stack diameter must be consistent. No constrictions should exist, lessening cross-sectional area. This includes the through-deck fitting and smokehead, too.

Stack length is critical to heater performance. If it's too short, the draft is lethargic, combustion suffers, and backwinding is more likely. Too long, and excess draft velocity may broadside combustion efficiency. Most natural-draft liquid- and solid-fuel heaters for boats like stacks between six and seven feet, as measured from the heater to the smokehead. Check with your heater manufacturer for exact specifications.

OMNIDIRECTIONAL SMOKEHEADS

An important attribute of a heater stack is the ability to exhaust reliably in a wide variety of wind conditions. Wind velocity and direction should never affect

On-deck stack for a natural-draft diesel heater. Breidert-type smokehead as shown is effective against rain and violent squalls. Smokehead must clear the vessel's superstructure, or turbulence will backwind the heater.

Dickinson stainless deck iron for routing a natural-draft-heater stack through the deckhead. Deck aperture is cut with plenty of clearance around the stack for an insulating airspace.

performance. The heater must do its thing in squalls and gales, at anchor or offshore. This is achieved by good stack design and an efficient smokehead.

A good Charlie Noble or smokehead lets combustion byproducts out of the stack while preventing rain or spray from entering it. To do so, it must be designed to perform regardless of wind direction. This means symmetrical design. If a smokehead looks the same to you from all points of the compass, it will look the same to the wind, too. T-shaped smokeheads don't contribute to consistent heater performance. The most efficient and reliable smokeheads are Breidert types, which perform beautifully in gusty conditions.

A smokehead must protrude above a boat's superstructure into clear air. If it's partially sheltered from the wind at certain angles, it will be subject to turbulence, and stack velocity and heater combustion will be inconsistent.

The portion of the stack above decks must be simple to remove and replace with a watertight cap in case of heavy weather offshore.

Dickinson's Arctic diesel heater in Dolphin Queen. *Note stainless bulkhead shield (asbestos backed), safety grab bar, deckhead fan, and plastic swivel hangers for drying clothes. Adjacent panel shows the hot water circulating temperature and the freshwater system pressure, with controls for the start-up blower and hot water circulating pump speed.*

NATURAL-DRAFT HEATER INSTALLATION

Heat rises. A heater installed low in the cabin warms upholstery and carpeting better. The chimney is the hottest part of a natural-draft heater; therefore, a low position exposes maximum stack length within the boat, and more heat is radiated into the cabin spaces, and less heat is wasted on the outside world.

The heater should be located centrally so the boat is heated evenly. Ideally, a heater lives next to a bulkhead, somewhere out of harm's way in the galley/ saloon space. Try not to place it too close to a settee, or you'll have an uninhabitable hot seat when the heater is operating.

Protect the heater's home with fireproofing and insulation so the heater burns only its fuel, not the boat. Polished stainless sheet metal spaced from the bulkhead a half-inch or so forms an insulating air gap, or it can be fitted flush with an asbestos backing (wear a mask when handling asbestos). This spruces up the boat's looks and prevents a scorched bulkhead. Ceramic tile is an elegant alternative. Remember, that stack is going to be hot, so keep it spaced at least three inches from the insulated bulkhead all the way up.

Hot heater stacks can be a safety hazard. When the boat rolls or lurches, it's instinctive to grab anything handy to brace yourself, even if it's a scorching heater stack. Thus, an unprotected stack could mean a serious medical emergency aboard your boat one day. To prevent accidents, install a stout safety bar parallel to the stack and/or fit a spaced shield around the stack.

IMPROVED HEAT DISTRIBUTION

All natural-draft heaters have a hot spot where the stack exits the deckhead. This wastes heat energy. Natural convection induced by heat rising from the heater isn't vigorous enough to distribute heat collecting there to the far reaches of the cabin. An electric fan tucked next to the stack improves heating efficiency tremendously (and doubles comfort!). Aim the fan downward at a 45-degree angle toward the accommodation. Heat will be dispersed low in the boat to warm furniture, flooring, and feet. Without the fan, heat hovers high in the cabin, and lower areas stay cool. In summertime or in the tropics, the same fan cools.

Most 12-volt fans sound like miniature hurricanes when they're fed their full ration of volts. Since the fan runs to improve circulation whenever the heater operates, nerve-racking noise won't be appreciated. It doesn't have to be a holy terror to do the job, anyway; a gentle breeze removes the hot spot. A 24- or 32-volt fan running on 12 volts works discretely at a walking pace. If you can't find a 24- or 32-volt fan, wire a fixed or variable resistor (rheostat) to a 12-volt unit to slow it down.

SOLID-FUEL HEATERS

Marine solid-fuel heaters resembling tiny fireplaces have been around for a long time. They provide dry heat and make fine boat heaters if the fuel is handy to obtain and easily stored aboard. This can be a problem on a long-distance cruise. Solid fuel, whether wood, briquettes, carbonettes, compressed sawdust logs, or coal, is bulky and sometimes messy. Only you can decide if a solid-fuel heater's liabilities concerning fuel availability and storage are worth it. Also, solid-fuel heaters require considerable operator intervention. Some folks enjoy fooling with a fire; others find it a nuisance.

Solid-fuel heaters are less costly than more elaborate setups. Fuel is often inexpensive—sometimes free. If you decide to go with solid fuel, give appliance selection more than passing interest. The cast-iron heaters, really small potbellied stoves, are a good bet. They are robust, their thick construction radiates heat evenly, and they are designed to encourage good combustion and draft. Little potbellies usually have a hot-plate top for boiling water or warming coffee, too.

Fancy bulkhead solid-fuel heaters featured in marine chandlery shops look the part. And some do work beautifully, burning clean and bright. Others look cuter than the dickens until you light them. As a point of caution, never buy a solid-fuel heater, particularly the decorative bulkhead type, without seeing it work in another boat.

Solid-fuel stoves and heaters need adjustable air inlets to control the rate of combustion. Heaters claimed to burn coal should have a double set of air intakes: lower ones for burning the carbon solids on the grate and higher inlets above the grate to oxidize gaseous volatiles that otherwise exhaust unburned.

PRESSURE KEROSENE HEATERS

Heaters based on kerosene Primus or Optimus burners have been around for years, the Taylor being the best known. They are fed by a pressure tank like a kerosene-fueled galley cookstove. Although the least expensive liquid-fuel boat heaters, they are also the most primitive. They do exhaust through a stack to purge moisture and combustion pollutants from the accommodation, but they have their drawbacks.

First, the reliability and dependability of pressure kerosene burners is suspect. The tiny orifice is prone to clogging by carbon deposits, decreasing combustion efficiency. A problem burner is obvious on a cookstove, but heaters tend to be ignored once lit, and faulty combustion may not be noticed for some time.

Controlling flame intensity is bothersome. As fuel burns, the pressure drops in the tank, and the flame shrinks. A fuel-network under pressure is never as trustworthy as gravity-fed fuel systems, either. If the fire blows out for any reason (low pressure, down draft, child playing with control knob), the fuel continues to flow unabated. Not a pleasant thought!

A pressure kerosene heater needs close watching, which restricts personal freedom. Every time you take a nap or go for a row in the dinghy, you'll wonder what the damn thing is doing. Letting it hiss away overnight is chancy; therefore, each morning begins uncomfortably (and damply) in the cold until the heater's lit. The same can be said of solid-fuel stoves, most of which are stone cold in the morning, too, but at least the best of them burn up the fuel supply and die safely after you go to bed.

A classy brass solid-fuel heater. Although impressive, the installation has faults. Located at the end of a set-tee, instead of in its own alcove, the heater compromises seating space during operation. The location also places the heater higher off the cabin sole. The bends in the stack are gentle enough, but vertical stacks are best. Brass heaters require much polishing to stay shipshape.

The kindest thing to say about pressure kerosene boat heaters is: they are better than nothing.

DIESEL POT BURNERS

For convenience and around-the-clock warmth, a diesel-fired heater can't be beat. Ample quantities of the fuel are aboard for propulsion, so no special arrangements need be made for another type of fuel and a separate fuel system.

Despite its disadvantages, this stainless pressure kerosene heater helped a crew survive a liveaboard winter on a 36 footer. Note stack shield and good mounting position near the cabin sole.

Dickinson's diesel-burning Alaska heater is available with floor or bulkhead mounting. Maximum output is 9,750 Btu's. A real beauty for smaller cruising boats up to 36 feet. Photo by Jon Skoog.

Pot burners are fed by gravity from a small day tank, often five gallons or less. The tank is filled from the vessel's existing fuel system by a manual pump or, more conveniently, by an automotive electric fuel pump. A sight gauge on the day tank makes it easy to keep track of fuel consumption. Fuel flows from the tank through a filter and then on to the heater's metering device. A shut-off valve at the day-tank outlet is used as a safety precaution when the heater's off.

Combustion takes place in a burner, the critical component of a diesel heater. The burner's design has much to do with efficiency, and all diesel heaters are not equal. Among the best in the world are Dickinson Marine's range of heaters made in Canada. Both the bulkhead-mounted Chesapeake and the larger, freestanding Antarctic (formerly Arctic) are excellent investments in year-round shipboard comfort, not to mention being attractive additions to a cabin decor. The Antarctic has a hot-plate top for keeping hot beverages at the ready.

Diesel pot burners are regulated precisely by fingertip control. Some have a simple drip-feed metering valve; better models have float-controlled, jetted-fuel metering systems. Float-regulated metering systems have an antiflood feature, too. If the flame goes out, the pot won't overflow with fuel, because the float shuts off the fuel supply automatically when the fuel reaches a certain level—an important safety feature.

When choosing a pot-burner heater for cruising, consider the location of the fuel-metering apparatus in relation to the burner. Both must remain on the same plane when the boat heels. A heater mounted facing fore-and-aft needs its metering system either directly in front or directly behind the burner, parallel to the boat's centerline. A heater mounted facing athwartships must have the fuel-metering device located to one side of the heater. If this is neglected, the burner floods or starves, depending on the tack, and achieving reliable heat underway is impossible.

Four-gallon gravity diesel-fuel tank supplying a Dickinson Arctic heater. Note 12-volt electric fuel pump for filling, shutoff cock, and water separator. Sight glass out of view at right.

An electric combustion fan is a handy feature to have. During start-up, it increases draft so the heater gets up to operating temperature quickly. Once the heater is burning cleanly, the fan is switched off—a quality, properly installed diesel pot burner doesn't require forced combustion for normal operation. It burns cleanly by design.

DIESEL POT-BURNER COOKING STOVES

Cooking stoves operate on the pot-burner principle, too. Once again, Dickinson's are first class. These appliances have large, cast-iron or cast-aluminum cooking surfaces and sizable baking ovens. They are popular with commercial fishermen and cruising yachtsmen in cold climates where heat is desirable nearly year-round. Vessels heading to warmer climates need alternate cooking facilities, because the heat from a diesel cooker is too much of a good thing in hot weather. Also, a diesel stove takes some time to reach cooking temperature and is not practical for casual use; it's either running all the time or shut down. A boat fitted with a regular marine cookstove and a diesel pot-burner cookstove has all the bases covered.

HOT AIR HEATING

Diesel can also warm you with a minifurnace, similar in concept to diesel central heating in homes. Combustion does not depend on natural draft; the little stack pipe can be routed horizontally with less regard for bends and elbows.

Hot-air furnaces are true central-heating setups, with hot-air ducts to the cabin areas of your choice. Cabin temperature is thermostatically controlled, and the heater is conveniently self-starting by electric spark. An integral pump forces fuel through a vaporizing nozzle into the furnace's combustion chamber, just as in shoreside furnaces. Heat energy is transferred by heat exchanger; the combustion chamber and heat-distribution network are isolated from each other.

You need a few amps of 12-volt current to operate combustion and circulating blowers, plus a momentary fraction of an amp to incite starting. If this seems a disadvantage, remember that solid-fuel and diesel pot-burner heaters also require modest 12-volt current to run an overhead fan.

Forced hot air heat offers much to liveaboards. When the boat feels cool, turn the thermostat up a hair, and the heater kicks in. Warm air exits through ducts at cabin-sole level for an even temperature throughout the boat. Thorough circulation ensures a dry accommodation.

Hot-air heaters are lightweight and compact. They live out of sight in the engine room or a locker, an advantage on vessels with no space for a bulkhead or freestanding heater. Hot-air heaters operate efficiently without a worry about motion or heeling angle. They are ready to go anytime, at the flick of a switch.

Dickinson's Pacific diesel-fired range with oven (also available for stove oil or kerosene). Heats boats up to 40 feet in cold weather; drives the chill and damp out of larger vessels. Maximum output: 16,250 Btu's. (Dickinson Marine Products (U.S.) Inc., Seattle, WA) Photo by Bill Montgomery.

Espar makes a range of diesel hot-air heaters. Pictured is model D4LK. Output is about 15,000 Btu's for vessels up to 45 feet, depending on climate. Advantages are compactness, automatic thermostat operation, and dry heat. For further information, contact Espar Inc., P.O. Box 2346, Naperville, IL 60566; or Boat Electric Co., 2834 Market Street, Seattle, WA 98107. Photo by Jon Skoog.

HOT WATER HEAT

Small hot water boilers look similar to hot-air furnaces. But instead of heating air, they heat water through a heat exchanger. The water then circulates through a radiator hose to radiators placed in cabin spaces. Circulation is maintained with a small pump integral to the heating unit. To conserve electricity, radiators should be the natural-convection rather than the electric-blower type.

Hot water boilers come in all sizes, from tiny ones suitable for the smallest cruising boat all the way up to commercial models for pleasure vessels over 50

The °Celsius hot water heating system burns no. 1 or no. 2 diesel, JP4, or kerosene. Output is 21,000 Btu's for boats up to 40 feet. Advantages are: dry, even boat heat with convector radiators, hot domestic water heating for galley and shower, engine preheating in cold weather, and fully automatic operation. An oil-fired water-heating setup covers all the bases. Photo by Dickinson Marine Products (U.S.) Inc.

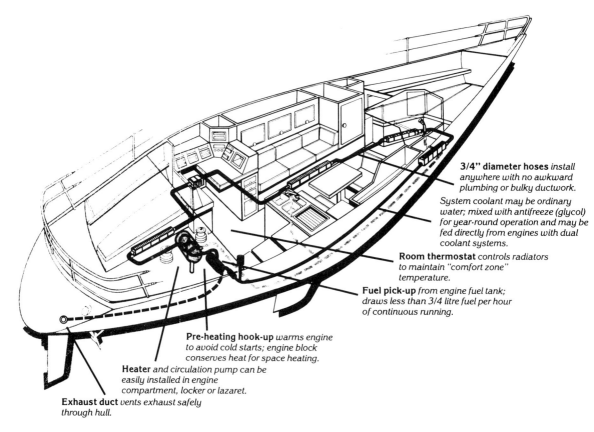

3/4" diameter hoses *install anywhere with no awkward plumbing or bulky ductwork.*

System coolant may be ordinary water; mixed with antifreeze (glycol) for year-round operation and may be fed directly from engines with dual coolant systems.

Room thermostat *controls radiators to maintain "comfort zone" temperature.*

Fuel pick-up *from engine fuel tank; draws less than 3/4 litre fuel per hour of continuous running.*

Pre-heating hook-up *warms engine to avoid cold starts; engine block conserves heat for space heating.*

Heater *and circulation pump can be easily installed in engine compartment, locker or lazaret.*

Exhaust duct *vents exhaust safely through hull.*

Schematic of °Celsius hot water heating system. The exhaust pipe must include a loop above the plane of the heater system to avoid water entering the system. (Heaters Inc., 332 Exeter Road, London, Ontario, Canada N6L 1A3. Also available from Dickinson Marine Products (U.S.) Inc., Seattle, WA.

feet in length. They fire up and regulate cabin temperatures automatically by thermostatic control.

Hot water boilers have one main advantage over hot-air heaters: the ability to heat water for domestic use!

HOT SHOWERS

The next step is interfacing the heating system with the pressure water system so you can enjoy one of cruising's most coveted miracles, the hot shower.

Hot water heating systems give you hot water from a tap on a silver platter. The boiler is plumbed to the hot water tank's heat exchanger (before going on to the radiators). When heat is not required in warmer weather, the radiator part of the system is shut off by a valve, leaving the hot water system intact. Thermostatic control takes care of the rest.

It's not as simple, but far from impossible to heat water with other heating systems. Many solid-fuel heating stoves are sold with a "wetback" option, which heats water from waste energy going up the stack. The hot water is piped to the hot water tank. To function properly, the hot water tank is mounted close to the heater and, importantly, above the heater's hot water coils. Then natural convection circulates the water continually, and a pump is unnecessary (unless long horizontal runs and restrictive bends thwart natural circulation). Water was heated this way for centuries by solid-fuel fireplaces and stoves before the days of central heating.

Diesel pot burners may be fitted to serve as water-heating elements, too. Dickinson offers this useful option, providing stainless steel rather than copper coils in the combustion chamber so the coils are not damaged by heat when dry. Again, mount the water-heater cylinder nearby and higher than the heating coils for convection.

Hot water for showering and dishwashing is worth the effort, so don't give up too easily. If natural convection from a heater to a water tank won't work on your boat, a tiny circulating pump will keep the water moving. It should be 24 or 32 volts for 12-volt service; most 12-volt pumps are too frantic. The aim is constant, easy-going circulation, just fast enough so water does not linger in the heating coils long enough to boil. If the water boils, a vapor lock brings the whole works to a halt (with exciting clouds of steam), and the system has to cool before more water may be added to fill it again—very much like a car radiator that boils over. However, circulation can't be too slow, or the pump will stop when battery voltage drops between charging cycles.

The pump should be located in the coolest part of the circulating system, just before the water enters the coils for heating.

Install an expansion/burp tank (one-quart capacity) at the high point of the circulation system. Air bubbles from overheated water or recently depressurized tap water when topping up can cause air locks. The expansion/burp tank automatically rids the system of air. Make sure the burp-tank cap has a breathing hole to allow for expansion and contraction. Automotive cooling-system expansion tanks are inexpensive and made for the job. Keep the tank half full.

EXCESS HEAT IN A CIRCULATION SYSTEM

One potential snag in making hot water from solid-fuel or diesel-fuel heaters equipped with coils is the tendency for the system to overheat and boil over in very cold weather, when the heater is cranked up all the way. This is aggravated when the hot water tank is already up to temperature, and the water returning to the heating coils is nearly as hot as when it left. If heater-coil length is reduced to eliminate this, hot water production at low-heat settings in warmer weather is curtailed. To cope with a variety of climatic conditions, there has to be a way to keep circulating water below the boiling point.

A few extra goodies will solve this problem. First, a temperature gauge is teed into the system just after the heating coils, where temperature is greatest. This lets you monitor and control your heater accordingly. Even though water doesn't boil until it reaches 212 degrees F., the circulating system should never approach that or excess gas may form that could overtax the burp tank. If the circulating water is too hot, there's no fudge factor left for normal temperature fluctuations, either. As a rule of thumb, the circulating water should not exceed 150 to 160 degrees F. As long as it's hot enough for showering, it's hot enough.

Now for a secret weapon. Next to the temperature-gauge sender, install another sender for an adjustable temperature switch as used in cooling-system alarms. Somewhere after the hot water heat exchanger and radiators but before the heater coils install a radiator with a 24-volt fan (Red Dot makes a good one). Again, a 12-volt system is too busy for comfort. Electrically connect the temperature switch to the radiator fan, and you've done it. Whenever the temperature rises to the preset maximum level of your choice, the fan starts and the radiator dumps heat from the circulating water. The temperature switch cuts in and out, automatically shedding heat as necessary. And the radiator helps to heat the boat in the bargain. A manual override switch allows the radiator to be activated whenever extra heat is required, regardless of circulating temperature.

PREPARE FOR ALL SEASONS

Even sailors heading for extended cruises in tropical climates find marine heating of great value—or at least they do in retrospect. For instance, those who sail to the Pacific Islands from the West Coast of North America or Mexico often visit New Zealand or Australia, too, where comfort depends heavily on cabin heat. After months of acclimation in the tropics, a temperate zone feels like Antarctica, too. And a voyage to tropical waters usually includes plenty of cold-weather sailing to get there and back as well.

Ventilation, insulation, and heating put below-decks climate control in your hands wherever the wind takes you. Houses don't go anywhere, yet most have effective heating and ventilation. Why should a cruising vessel, which has more demanding conditions to contend with, be any different?

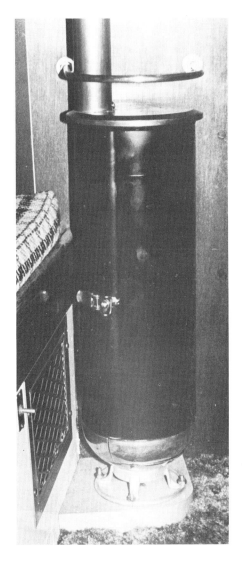

A home-built chill breaker using a modified fire extinguisher to house a large kerosene lamp. Note stack. This vessel has a diesel hot water heating system (adjacent radiator), but the owner wanted something safe and odorless to take the edge off when it wasn't cold enough to run the central heating setup.

8▶ Awnings and Dodgers Against Mother Nature

A sailboat has two levels of accommodation, not just one. The above-deck spaces need special attention, too, to aid comfort in all kinds of weather at sea and at anchor. Once arranged, on-deck protection adds a new dimension to shipboard life. And as it turns out, clever sheltering improves below-decks ventilation and heating performance to round out your climate-control strategy.

Often, deck shelters are glossed over in preparation because a voyage originates in climates where they are not so critical. Not everyone has to live with a burning tropical sun or squally deluges. Nevertheless, you must prepare for conditions outside your experience.

Most temperate sailors realize rain's a killjoy. On-deck projects caught in a downpour are drenched; exposed laundry hangs limp for days. And, for the unprepared, rainy days can mean cabin fever and boredom.

You must recognize the power of the sun, too, for all-around weather protection. Suntanning in higher latitudes is a popular leisure-time activity, particularly after a long, cold winter. But in the tropics, you get more than your share of Old Sol's medicine without seeking it; in fact, you find yourself avoiding it whenever possible.

Comfort aside, there's ever-increasing awareness about skin care, and the sun is being seen for what it is: an enemy to creamy, wrinkle-free complexions. An overdose of sun in remote areas free of filtering atmospheric pollutants is a health hazard, increasing the risk of skin cancer. Although much dreamed about by cool-weather sailors, a hot sun beating down month after month becomes a force to be reckoned with.

Protection from the sun means more than just finding a shady spot to relax in. Accommodations under exposed decks can be ten degrees hotter than those with sheltered decks. What you need is some sort of covering to provide a shady place on deck, where cooling breezes blow.

THE ALL-WEATHER AWNING

Sometimes called a tropical awning, a proper all-weather awning is your number-one defense against the elements in both cold and hot climates while the boat's moored or swinging on the hook. It also remakes an exposed cockpit into a pleasant social center for entertaining. The awning shelters above-deck spaces for leisure activities like reading or people watching, and it allows the companionway to be left wide open in almost any weather for improved below-decks ventilation and the crew's convenience. Further, it shelters other hatches and ventilation aids lying underneath from rain that otherwise inhibits their function.

Nearly 20 years ago, my brothers and I built our first oceangoing yacht and set sail on a circumnavigation. For an awning we used a rectangular canvas tarp edged with grommets. The boom acted as a ridgepole, and the outboard edges of the tarp were lashed to the lifelines, tent-fashion. We soon learned (too late, of course) that that arrangement was a mistake.

Passage forward over the side decks from the cockpit under a tent-type awning is a hands-and-knees exercise, violating the first commandment of awning design: thou shalt have standing headroom underneath. Full headroom lets a person walk to and fro like a human being, upright. There's ample clearance for deck projects, and even room to stretch a clothesline underneath, out of the weather. (Being able to dry clothes in rainy weather is a blessing.) In sticky weather, full headroom cools the crew, allowing unrestricted air flow through the cockpit area. Tent-style awnings block cooling breezes, and while you are sitting in the cockpit, the heated awning material slants down right next to your head.

Having six feet or more of vertical clearance between the deck and the awning requires that the awning be freestanding, independent of the mainboom. To accomplish this, four stiff wooden athwartship battens are fitted to evenly spaced sewn pockets, one at the forward or leading edge, one aft, and two in between. Batten length dictates the width of the awning. Your awning should be a foot or two less than the vessel's beam directly beneath. Then you won't snag it in the rigging of a rafted vessel or against a seawall or lock. The downhauls described below give better lateral support in a crosswind when they lead down to the railcap at an angle, rather than vertically.

A central, fore-and-aft ridgeline reinforces four husky grommets (cringles) located at each batten. These are the strong points to hold the awning aloft; they not only support the awning's weight but also counteract the downward pull of the lines attaching the awning's edge to the vessel's railcap. The forward grommet secures the awning to the back of the mast, and the aft grommet is lashed to the backstay. These two attachment points serve to keep the awning taut along its length. A bridle connects the two central cringles to the main halyard. With this system, the awning may be horizontally positioned at an elevation and inclination to suit.

Each batten end is secured to the railcap by an adjustable downhaul line (after trial and error, each downhaul line may be spliced to its ideal length, making the awning quicker to deploy). Do not lash an awning to the lifelines, or you'll have a renegade on your hands. The awning must be tautly preloaded, forcing the stiff battens (at least one-by-three-inch, vertical-grain fir) into an arc. To repeat: lifelines are too flexible for anchoring the awning downhauls.

To further the cause of rigidity, the aft batten should be made larger than the others for greater stiffness. The outboard forward corners of the awning are secured by lines leading forward to the ship's shrouds, thus tensioning the awning's outboard edges. This forward pull overloads a flimsy aft batten standing alone back there with no means of support.

A slack awning is a menace. Without firm preloading at all anchoring points, it will go berserk in a breeze; in a blow it may commit suicide. An all-weather awning worth its salt must withstand 50- to 60-knot winds (few do, but yours can). If you have to dismantle an awning before every blow or squall, you'll be a full-time rigger, night and day. Once an awning is set, nothing short of a hurricane should interfere with it.

SIDE CURTAINS AND BACK FLAPS

As described, the awning is good protection from a noonday sun and marginal shelter from light, vertical rainfall. Now what about a scorching afternoon sun or a wind-driven cloudburst? The roof alone will not help you with these problems; wide-open sides high off the deck will let in all kinds of misery.

To solve this problem, side flaps (curtains) are stitched to the outboard edges of the awning's roof, reaching down to within a few inches of the lifelines. Pigtails of line at the batten ends are used to secure a bundled side curtain in the raised position, neatly furling it out of the way when it's not required. When the curtain is lowered, a line at each lower corner of the side curtain leads to the railcap (the aft corner may be secured to the stern pulpit) at an outward angle from the curtain's edge, pulling down and away to keep it taut. Sometimes it's a good idea to fit the side curtains with grommets in line with the downhauls and weave the downhaul lines in and out of the grommets. The side curtain slides up and down

Full shelter from mast to stern. Side curtains and back flap (furled) keep rain and sun at bay.

on the lines easily, and in the lowered position the downhauls add extra control to the curtains during a blow.

A back flap is sewn to the aft edge of the awning's roof. When lowered, it ties to the stern rail. Furled, it's lashed to the awning's back edge.

With side curtains and a back flap, you are master of your cockpit's climate. A bothersome late sun can be blotted out by lowering one curtain. The back flap and the other curtain stay furled out of the way so your view and sense of open space remain intact. In wet weather, the side curtains and back flap prevent rain from soaking down the cockpit area. In damp, dewy conditions, the curtains and back flap are lowered overnight, and in the morning the cockpit is dry.

Since the curtains give a blustery wind considerable purchase, they must be furled in a blow. A strong awning with lowered side curtains and back flap lowered will withstand about 20 knots of wind when the boat weathercocks on the hook because the wind blows roughly parallel to the curtains, rather than pushing directly from the side. And the back flap, although square against the wind, is small in area.

When furled, a rigid roof has minimal frontal area for the wind to grip. Provided the awning is taut and well secured as described, you may never be forced to strike it on your cruise. I never did during the liveliest squalls or gales.

This type of awning protects your privacy when moored stern-to at a dock or quay. Lowering the back flap is like drawing the curtains in a house. Strolling rubberneckers can't see into your cockpit, nor can they peer down the companionway hatch into the accommodation. In high-profile situations like Tahiti's waterfront, where curiosity seekers can be inquisitive, this is a bonus.

The above described awning suits a cutter or sloop with an aft or center cockpit. Some ketches and yawls with mizzenmasts smack in the way require a two-section awning, depending on where their cockpits are. Or they make do with less than full mainmast-to-stern shelter.

COCKPIT DODGERS

A well-made cockpit dodger works miracles at sea and at anchor. Without a dodger, a cruising boat's cockpit can be a wretched place, especially when you're motoring beneath a blazing sun or driving hard to windward against a choppy sea; with it, you can thumb your nose at Mother Nature. On the hook, windy, rainy weather can sneak under the awning's lead edge, and the dodger becomes your second line of defense.

As a bare minimum, fit a small dodger over the companionway to shield one person on watch during a passage and to keep the opening dry at anchor when the awning can't cope. Assuming the yacht is equipped with windvane self-steering or autopilot, it's seldom necessary to be physically at the helm if good visibility is available from the companionway, anyway.

Better yet, install a dodger that spans the full width of the cockpit, protecting not only the companionway but the adjacent cabintop as well. Then sailing paraphernalia such as folded charts and binoculars stay dry; wind driven spray and rain are barred from the cockpit area, greatly improving the crew's morale. A good dodger overhangs the cockpit enough so several people remain under cover from a vertical rain or hot sun. Standing headroom off the cockpit sole is appreciated. Stooping for long periods at anchor or at sea is a burden you should never experience.

In rotten weather, dodgers need side curtains that snap or zip into place to enclose the cockpit further. The curtains should have windows of clear vinyl to let light into the cockpit and improve visibility. More elaborate dodgers have back flaps, too, so a cockpit can be entirely enclosed. These are more common in colder regions, where the crew needs an all-'round windbreak to stay warm.

DODGER INADEQUACIES

Some sort of dodger is an absolute necessity on a cruising vessel. However, there are pitfalls to surmount for it to be your best friend, instead of a pain in the neck.

A cockpit dodger with a zip-out windshield panel. Note the stainless grab bar at each side (and at the dodger's back edge)—a smart safety feature.

The first potential headache is a dodger's tendency to restrict visibility. At sea, salt encrusted or blemished vinyl windows are a hazard. Windows must be clean and well polished, or the lookout will be forced to peer over or around them to see, negating the dodger's purpose. At night, visibility through a badly scratched and/or dirty window can reduce watchkeeping to a game of blindman's bluff.

A second potential liability presents itself after a crew reaches its first tropical port of call. Since a cooling breeze arrives from the bow on anchored boats (cross-currents and stern hooks excepted), a thoughtlessly designed dodger can block the air flow to the cockpit, transforming it into a hothouse. Such discomfort is impossible to live with, yet many disgruntled cruising people from cooler climates have no option.

BUILDING A BETTER DODGER

A dodger's job is to enhance cruising comfort, not detract from it, so the front "windshield" must unzip. This allows a foggy or blemished window to be jettisoned in favor of a spare (carry several). Or, in borderline conditions (fog, drizzle, darkness), visibility can be improved by getting the front window out of the road. This can make or break ship safety. Meanwhile, the overhead part of the dodger stays on the job. In dry conditions offshore, the windshield is best removed, anyway.

Unzipping the dodger's front window lets the breeze flow through the cockpit at anchor, too. During a heatwave, nothing must block the breeze. Nothing!

A cruising dodger should have further refinements such as an overhead panel that folds out of the line of fire when you wish to do some stargazing on a clear, calm night at sea. While the dodger needs a generous overhang for full protection during less pleasant times, a permanent roof over the cockpit is too inflexible. It can interfere with sextant work and may be a nuisance when trimming the mainsail.

You won't be impressed by a dodger that leaks like a sieve where it joins the deck or cabintop. A teak dam about four inches high bedded to the deckhead for the dodger to snap onto makes a good water stop. The companionway hatch envelope mentioned earlier allows the dam to span full width without leaving cracks for rain and spray. A hatch sliding directly against the underside of a dodger leaks.

FIXED COCKPIT SHELTER

On larger yachts, it's common to find permanent dodger-type structures made of timber with glass windows. This can be the perfect solution to cockpit shelter, both at anchor and under sail. Nevertheless, a semi-enclosed doghouse must be flexible to fulfill blue-water cruising needs.

Front windows of rigid cockpit shelters must be hinged or somehow

A good dodger with standing headroom underneath and removable overhead panel for sailing. Aft edge is fixed to boom gallows.

removable. Otherwise, the air flow to the cockpit is blocked in hot weather, and the same sad situation exists as with dodgers with permanent windshields—a sauna. Side windows in rigid dodgers must slide or open, too. Any cockpit shelters must deal with a variety of weather.

Similarly, the overhead or roof panels of fixed shelters cannot be decked over solidly. A removable section, a sliding panel, or a fold-over or hinged section is essential to expose the cockpit to the sky when you feel the urge.

Fixed cockpit shelters have advantages. They are stronger and less yielding than aluminum-framed, acrylic-covered dodgers and present useful handholds to crew members as they make their way around the structure from the cockpit to the foredeck and back. Compared with clear vinyl, safety glass or tempered glass offers superior, longer-lasting visibility. Toughened glass is better than Lexan or Plexiglas, too, for long-term clear viewing. Fixed cockpit shelters are ideal structures on which to mount equipment such as foghorns, searchlights, cockpit lights, compasses, echo sounders, drink holders, and stereo speakers, and a shelter provides stowage for charts, binoculars, dividers, flashlights, and so forth.

Design, construction, and aesthetics being equal, a fixed shelter could be your best option. But—and this is the clincher—the design must not hamper efficient shiphandling. Sailhandling and cockpit access must be convenient.

And for safety's sake, a fixed doghouse-type dodger should be expendable. Considering the large surface area of this kind of dodger, it must be built as a sacrificial unit so it doesn't influence the structural or watertight integrity of the ship. In other words, if heavy weather ever damages or carries away a fixed cockpit shelter, the yacht must be left absolutely seaworthy.

Consequently, don't commit equipment to a rigid dodger unless it's duplicated elsewhere. *In extremis*, vital gear could be lost. Consider the vulnerability of gear to theft, too. All valuable items should be simple to remove for stowage below while the boat is in populated harbors.

RAINCATCHING

Awning protection from the mainmast to the stern is essential, but a foredeck awning is worthwhile, too. It doesn't need to be as elaborate as the primary all-weather awning; just a buffer against a midday sun to keep foredeck temperatures down. Rigged as a raincatcher, a foredeck awning provides welcome shade—and fills the ship's freshwater tanks.

A rectangular raincatcher awning can be constructed by fitting a wood batten to pockets in the forward and aft edges. The battens keep the entire awning surface taut when rigged, so it remains impervious to strong winds. Four lines, each attached to a batten end at the corners, lead horizontally to strategic points in the vessel's rigging. These are cinched taut. At the awning's center, underneath, is a D-ring or cringle attached to a hefty reinforcing patch. When a downhaul from the central cringle to a padeye on deck is snugged, the awning takes on a dished shape that catches rain efficiently. A few tether lines from the outside edge to the railcap might be necessary to keep the awning from flapping in windy conditions. But so long as the awning's rigged super-tight, it'll withstand gales without a murmur.

Rainwater is collected by a plastic through-hull fitting at the awning's low point next to the downhaul cringle, and flows through a hose directly to the tank deck fill. The hose fitting must not be bulky, or the awning won't roll up neatly for stowage. With a raincatcher permanently rigged while the boat is in port, the tanks get a free round of drinks every time it rains. Make sure the hose and the awning hose fitting have at least a one-inch inside diameter, or a tropical downpour will overflow the awning's edges and pour through the scuppers. An awning like this can put you into semiretirement from the business of ferrying water jugs.

The main awning can be set up as a raincatcher, too. Each section between the battens on each side of the ridgeline sags a bit when wet. Grommeted drain holes are fitted at the low points in each sector near the awning's outboard edge. A full-length pocket is sewn to the inside corner of the roof and side curtain, serving as a sort of canvas channel. A hose attached to the low end of the channel directs the water to the tanks.

Don't overlook your boat's decks for rain catchment either. Decks have more surface area than awnings, and since area directly relates to catchment volume, the decks can be the most efficient collectors. That is, if deck catchment is planned for during the boat's construction.

Determine the low point in your boat's sheerline—normally about three-fifths of the way back from the bow—and place a set of scuppers at this low point for complete deck drainage. All other scuppers are located progressively farther aft

A sailing awning shades the cockpit from intense sunlight. This one is simply rigged from the boom gallows and backstay and has three athwartship battens. Note air slot between the dodger and awning for visibility offshore and ventilation in hot weather.

of the low point—none forward. Install two primary water tank fills about six-inches forward of the first scuppers—one on each side of the boat for maximum catchment—as close to the bulwarks or toerail as practical.

When it rains, wait a few minutes for the salt and dust to be flushed off the decks, then roll up wet toweling to form dams between the deck fills and the first scuppers. Presto! Rainwater goes into the tanks instead of over the side, a very satisfying state of affairs while at sea or anchored in a remote lagoon.

If you wish to use your aft decks for raincatching too, plug all the deck scuppers, and in this instance no towel dams are necessary as rain has nowhere to go but down the fills. Think about using round scuppers that are easy to plug with rubber stoppers or corks, rather than traditional oblong-shaped scuppers that are difficult to block off.

Incidentally, cabintop catchment systems aft of the mast look good on paper, but are usually ineffective because they are generally sheltered by an all-weather awning. Ideally, the awning itself is rigged for raincatching, or it simply drains onto the side decks for catchment with the plugged scuppers.

MINI-AWNINGS

A couple of tarps about six feet square with grommeted edges pull their weight on a cruise. At sea under a hot sun, there'll be times when you want to jury rig additional cockpit shelter. At anchor, a tarp proves handy stretched over a forehatch to ward off sun or rain, allowing the hatch to be kept fully open for maximum air transfer. A small tarp also keeps rain out of a supervent or other ventilation aid without a water-trap feature. They are occasionally useful to cover supplies and half-done deck projects, too.

First-class cockpit shelter for sailing or harbor use. The entire rig folds down compactly in front of the dodger. Note generous slot above dodger for cockpit cooling and visibility.

OTHER NATURAL VENTILATION AIDS

Let's look at ways to make your ventilation features work overtime. When the wind dies to a whisper and the mercury soars, even wide-open ports and hatches, shade from the awning, and an army of cowl vents may not keep the accommodation as cool as you'd like. Experienced cruising sailors take along special gismos to force air through the accommodation in borderline circumstances. Without these additional bits and pieces, your comfort will be left in the hands of the gods—and they are not always kind!

Hatch Windscoops

A hatch windscoop is a canvas funnel that supercharges the air flow in the cabin spaces. It snaps to three sides of a hatch's outer coaming and is held upright by a bridle connected to a halyard and/or a piece of standing rigging. The bridle attaches at the ends of a wooden dowel sewn in a pocket on the upper edge of the scoop.

Windscoops can be fashioned with a closed throat encompassing all four sides of a hatch opening, their mouths resembling a giant cowl vent. In practice, however, this type of windscoop complicates the issue and doesn't perform much better than simple three-sided affairs, the back sides of which simply angle into the wind to deflect it below. And in a fresh breeze or gust, big windscoops need to be struck, whereas a strong three-sided scoop can be left up.

Regardless of its configuration, the scoop must allow the hatch to be raised or lowered while it's rigged for easy air-flow control.

Three-sided scoops are dead simple to make and fit to a hatch coaming. A drawstring sewn into the lower edge grips lashing hooks screwed to the hatch coamings.

Windscoops are an asset on every hinged hatch aboard, so make several. Like cowl vents, they can be positioned with their backs to a breeze to extract air, too. An extracting scoop is of particular benefit over the galley; heat, steam, and smoke shoot out of the boat!

Opening Porthole Scoops

Scoops for portholes increase air flow into the cabin spaces of an anchored or moored boat. If your yacht has round opening ports, making scoops for them will be a breeze. Locate some PVC pipe that just fits through a port. Cut a bevel or scallop on one end to catch the wind. Glue a length of half-inch PVC pipe across the inner end for a crossbar handle. Foam weatherstripping cemented around the outside of the inboard end acts as a stop to wedge the scoop in place so it won't fall overboard.

Rectangular opening portholes can be fitted with scoops, too. Three-sided

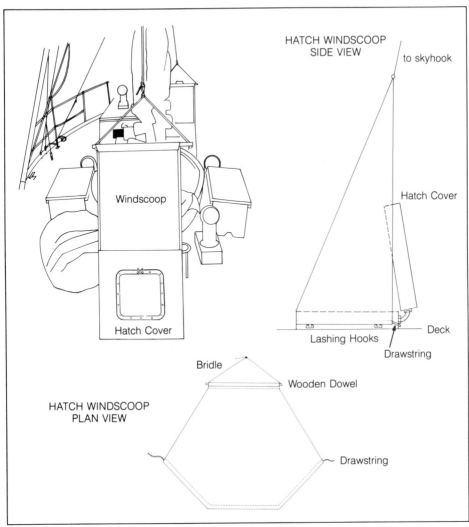

HATCH WINDSCOOP
SIDE VIEW

to skyhook

Hatch Cover

Windscoop

Hatch Cover

Deck

Lashing Hooks

Drawstring

Bridle

Wooden Dowel

HATCH WINDSCOOP
PLAN VIEW

Drawstring

A simple and effective hatch windscoop that's quick to rig, stands up to squalls, and easily made. The hatch may be adjusted to any position for air-flow control, or dogged, independent of the windscoop. Make windscoops of stout acrylic or canvas, not flimsy spinnaker material.

scoops can be bent to shape from Plexiglas or Lexan (by applying heat gently and slowly, making the material bend around a form). They look like little hatch windscoops lying on their sides. Make them so the top and bottom edges require some pressure to fit into the port aperture, and they'll hold themselves in place. Or cement on positioning tabs. Foam weatherstripping keeps them from rattling around. Scoops that might accidentally jump into the tide should be secured with a lanyard.

Porthole scoops have been made of stainless steel and aluminum, too, but plastic is cheaper and easier for the home handyman to work with.

Porthole Eyebrows

During a tropical downpour, the more the boat can remain open to the prevailing wind, the more comfortable the crew. Let's say you are down in the saloon writing a letter describing the lagoon where you're anchored to a friend back in suburbia. The ports are wide open, and a refreshing breeze flows through the cabin.

Suddenly, a black squall screams overhead, and there's a drenching cloudburst. Unless you have specifically prepared for this, you must leap up frantically to dog the ports and lower the hatches. Now your natural air-conditioning system is kaput; cabin temperature and humidity climb. Rain continues to thunder down on deck with no end in sight. You abandon the letter and escape to the cockpit for some fresh air under the awning.

Now take this a step further. What about a downpour when you're ashore? Either you return to soaked bedding, carpeting, and perhaps a washed down stereo system, or, if you anticipated the rain and dogged the ports beforehand, you return to an oven. Heads, you lose; tails, you lose.

This scenario introduces a treasured ventilation aid you'll love—mini-awnings called eyebrows. They shelter open ports all the time, rain or shine. You won't find them on many boats; just make sure yours is one of the comfortable minority.

Porthole eyebrows are simple and cheap to rig. They are fastened over a port or, better yet, over a whole row of opening ports, by a boltrope extrusion. The eyebrow slides into the extrusion by a rope sewn to its inner edge. Grommets in the outer edge provide attachment for shockcord leading to lashing hooks under the railcap out of sight. Once the shockcord is crimped to its grommets and eyes are crimped to slip over the lashing hooks in the initial fitting, an eyebrow can be rigged in seconds.

Eyebrows should slant downward about 20 to 30 degrees. Angle them as much as you can without cutting off the view from a port. This makes it more difficult for rain splattering on deck to jump in. Slanted eyebrows block a morning or hot, late afternoon sun from streaming through a portlight, too, whether it's open or closed. And for no extra charge, you get privacy from passers-by, afloat or afoot.

Hull ports are also served well by eyebrows. Since no railcap or bulwark is available to hold them out, lengths of fiberglass sail battens are sewn into pockets at three-foot intervals to cantilever them from the hull. Keeping the eyebrow in place requires rigging to tension the outer edge, so it stands proud. One line pulls the aft outboard corner back, but two lines are necessary up front— one pulling forward and slightly downward, the other pulling forward and a bit upward. This keeps the eyebrow from flapping in the wind. Lines from the batten ends to the railcap or lower lifelines keep longer hull eyebrows from drooping.

It's great to awaken in the night during a heavy rain and not have to worry about open ports.

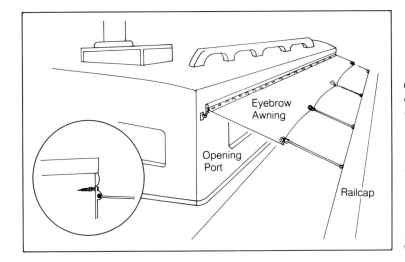

Opening port eyebrows. Portlight eyebrows keep rain and sun out of the accommodation in hot weather, 24 hours a day. They are indispensible! Boltrope extrusion on the cabin side makes them a breeze to rig. Cost: peanuts.

MATERIALS FOR CANVASWORK

Traditionally, canvas, a cotton derivative, has been used for awnings, windscoops, and the like. Today's synthetic acrylics have replaced it. Being inorganic, acrylics resist rot and mildew better than canvas, even treated canvas. An acrylic awning that's stowed wet out of necessity is not harmed.

Acrylic's Achilles' heel is lower chafe resistance; in this, canvas wins out. However, acrylics can be protected with chafing patches at wear points. It's claimed that acrylic won't stand up to sunlight as well as canvas, but you can expect years of service under a tropical sun.

Acrylics are lighter, strength for weight, and large acrylic items such as tropical awnings are easier to handle, especially when wet.

Don't be tempted to use nylon spinnaker cloth for any canvaswork, not even windscoops. It's too light and won't stand the strain in a blow. Spinnaker cloth doesn't always block sun or rain 100 percent, either.

MAKE YOUR OWN LUCK

Once you're out cruising, you'll thank your lucky stars for first-class climate control—not that luck has much to do with it. Cruising luck is made long before it's needed.

9 ▶ Laborsaving and Safety Equipment

Cruising security is earned through outfitting strategies that safeguard a boat and crew despite human limitations or the whims of Mother Nature. Security is not difficult to arrange, yet it eludes lackadaisical sailors by the hundreds. You, however, can enjoy safe passage wherever you sail *if* you view the cruising environment objectively and respect it with sound preparation.

Part One—Muscles Against Mother Nature

Most cruising crews begin a voyage knowing full well they are shorthanded. At sea, an extra hand would be welcomed, especially on a racing yacht, but at anchor, extra warm bodies only complicate shipboard life, just as boarders or long-term guests would do in a house.

YOUR CREW—ASSET OR LIABILITY?

Responsible cruising sailors compensate for their premeditated lack of manpower. Every chore aboard ship is examined critically to see if there's not an easier, faster, or simpler way of doing it. Tasks are organized so one person takes the place of two or three whenever possible. Time—and yes, money—spent on laborsaving features invest a crew with confidence to relax and sleep in rough weather, confidence to push the boat harder to make faster passages, and peace of mind from knowing everything is under control, at sea or in harbor. This self-assurance frees a crew to concentrate on the real purpose of the voyage—pleasure—rather than nervously biding their time between senseless episodes of high drama.

Smart sailors never have to be heroes.

Frequently, cruising yachts are built and/or outfitted by an adult male, either directly or in a supervisory role. As things progress, features are seen through a pair of eyes that often fails to acknowledge the abilities of others who will be charged with working the ship, too. The result: a disadvantaged crew. Bitching and moaning begin shortly after departure, when the crew discovers that nobody but the ignoramus who fitted out the vessel has the brawn to work her. This sort of tunnel vision during preparation is self-defeating and, in extreme situations, deadly.

In the final analysis, whether a crew ends up a valuable asset or a hopeless liability has little to do with people and a great deal to do with things: thoughtful, ingenious, sometimes powerful things, enabling a crew to function comfortably and competently despite their physiques.

Physical strength is no rational yardstick of a crew member's worth, anyway; it can't logically dictate who does what aboard ship. Certainly not on a family ship. Security depends on teamwork, and teamwork depends on specific, step-by-step preparation so everyone aboard can participate as an equal.

In other words, a boat outfitted for equal opportunity is a safe boat. And a happy one.

THE POWER WINDLASS

Every crew member—including half-grown children—must be capable of anchor handling without assistance. The mechanics of anchoring must not be left to the skipper, as is often the case on ill-prepared family boats. He or she has more important things to do, such as maneuvering out of an anchorage or figuring out the best place to drop the hook. If people with the most expertise are bogged down with menial chores, they isolate themselves from shiphandling duties, and the vessel is left to her own devices. In difficult circumstances, this results in chaos.

The way to select equipment such as windlasses is to imagine a tight spot and think about what it takes to save the day; drama on paper prevents drama in real life. For example, here's a scenario you may face someday:

The captain is incapacitated (flu, broken arm, bad back, food poisoning—you name it). Two hours after sunset the wind backs suddenly and starts to blow like stink. Black clouds march in from nowhere, and a torrential downpour blocks out the world. The boat swings 180 degrees, and a reef thought to be safely distant is suddenly dangerously close. It's hard to tell, but the anchor seems to be dragging.

The first mate and her eight-year-old daughter are left holding the bag. But whether they choose to save the ship by using their heads or get sidetracked into using their backs on a nonproductive, time-consuming, and possibly fruitless task is entirely academic. The outcome of this situation was preordained during outfitting.

A power windlass, either electric or hydraulic, must be forceful enough to pull the vessel up to the anchor against headwinds up to 50 knots—without help from the ship's propeller—so the boat can be kept into the wind for a controlled departure. Raising anchor must be done with dispatch, too, not the link-by-link, forever-and-a-day agony so common with manual windlasses. In an emergency, time is in scarce supply. Do not settle for chain speed under 40 feet per minute. Every sailor, sooner or later, gets blown out of an anchorage. When the chips are down, *the hook must come up fast.*

Install the largest windlass you can live with, perhaps a size or two bigger than you think appropriate. Don't let the counter staff in a ship's chandlery lead you astray. If they've never anchored in wild conditions, they don't know beans. With a powerful windlass, you'll never be tempted to anchor in shallow water just because it's such a bastard to pull the hook in deeper water. Instead, you'll be free to anchor wherever it's safest for the ship, regardless of depth. And when you feel the boat should be moved to another anchorage due to deteriorating weather, you'll do it straightaway, because the job is effortless. When you drop

Vertical capstan windlasses keep a low profile on deck, and motor components are protected under the deck. Pictured is Maxwell-Nilsson's model V4000. Photo by Maxwell-Nilsson, Auckland, New Zealand.

the hook and accidentally drift too close to another boat, you won't think twice about pulling the pick rather than fool yourself that you're okay because you just can't bear the thought of another wrestling match with a manual windlass. If another crew crowds you by anchoring too close, it's easy to move.

For maximum security, every cruising boat should have a power windlass. Please don't consider it an option. When Mother Nature gets tough, anchor tackle on any size cruising boat is dangerous or impossible to manipulate by hand.

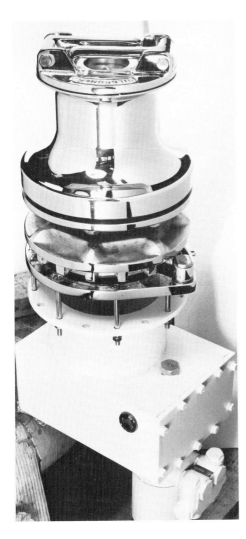

Maxwell-Nilsson V4000, showing the gear box and hydraulic motor. This powerhouse has a line pull of 4,000 pounds, coupling to a ten-gallon/ minute hydraulic pump with a working pressure of up to 2,000 psi. Chain size: up to one inch. For further information in North America, contact Dickinson Marine Products (U.S.) Inc., Seattle, WA. Photo by Maxwell-Nilsson, Auckland, New Zealand.

A Plath hydraulic windlass on a 45 footer. A stump-puller, and absolutely reliable over the years, although the spray-on finish was shortlived. Waterproof master switch selects foot switch (not shown) or disables it. (A foot or "step" switch can be dangerous if stepped on accidentally.) Operation is via electromagnetic clutch on engine-driven pump. Note handy mooring bitt and husky handwheel for controlling wildcat clutch.

A windlass must offer hands-off operation at the touch of a button. The anchor should self-stow, at least partially, so you can get cracking at the drop of a hat. Cable must self-feed into the locker without a hitch. Only a power windlass and all-chain rode meet the test for crew equality. Anything else is a compromise that could someday cost you dearly.

PRESSURE DECK WASHDOWN

At first glance, a washdown system seems a frivolous luxury, but there's more to it than you might think.

The old-bucket-and-long-handled-brush routine for cleaning anchor chain is cumbersome and time consuming. Nothing blasts mud off chain like pressure water from a hose. Without a washdown system, you'll be hauling heaps of sand and mud onto the decks and into the chainlocker; there isn't always time for a leisurely scrub while weighing anchor.

When your head's down scrubbing chain, it's harder to concentrate on seamanship, so the vessel loses another pair of eyes to needless labor. A deck-washdown system lets just one person pull the hook (with a power windlass, of course) *and* clean chain while watching chain tension, signaling the helmsperson about the ship's position relative to the anchor tackle, and keeping an eye out for other dangers the helmsperson may miss.

Aside from these practicalities, a washdown system sure beats the old bucket brigade for sluicing off the decks, washing out dinghies, hosing sweat off crew members, and cleaning topsides. And bucket marks on topsides become a thing of the past.

Washdown pumps are direct-driven from the main engine or powered from the 12-volt system. Since the engine is normally running when you pull the hook to power the windlass and maneuver the ship, a direct-drive setup pumps water when you most need it. Direct-drive taps the ship's power plant for all the horses needed for forceful water blasting, too. Washdown facilities are available while charging batteries, pulling down refrigeration, and motoring, as well.

Twelve-volt setups are a bit more flexible. They can be switched on and off whenever the mood strikes without running the engine, although power is limited to the size of the pump's 12-volt motor.

A faucet on deck is not necessary; the system is simply switched (or clutched) on or off as required. For best performance, use three-quarter-inch-diameter garden hose and plumbing instead of the more commonplace (and more restrictive) half-inch. Select a pump powerful enough to clean chain without a nozzle. Then the end of the hose can be left bare, eliminating an annoying hunk of hardware that dings decks and bruises brightwork.

Washdown pumps draw from their own seacock or tee into the engine's cooling inlet, providing it's sized with washdown in mind. The pump's inlet may be valved and plumbed to act as an emergency bilge pump, too.

Pressure deck washdown. Note three-quarter-inch-diameter hose without a nozzle. Stainless guard is a nice touch.

BOW THRUSTERS

Recreational powerboats are noted for gutsy maneuverability, making them easy to park, even with modest skill. On the other hand, seasoned skippers jockeying big sailboats into awkward places sometimes end up with egg on their faces. Yachts, at least fully-found cruising boats laden with fresh water, fuel, supplies, provisions, and a seemingly endless array of extra equipment, are not the most nimble creatures in tight quarters. They are hampered further by windage from rigs and hull/deck structures and deep keels that are easy prey for contrary currents.

Bow thrusters let you even the score with the powerboat folks by taking the worry out of tight spots. The equipment is suited to larger, heavier vessels lacking flexible maneuvering qualities, but there's no law against installing thrusters on any boat to improve handling.

A bow thruster is a fiberglass tube housing a propeller. The tube or tunnel is installed athwartships, a few feet below the waterline near the bow. A pair of thrusters will push the bow sideways in either direction by cockpit control. Sailboat bows often have a mind of their own, particularly in crosswinds; control of the bow usually means control of the ship.

Thruster apertures cause a smidgen of drag when the boat is underway, but not enough to lose sleep over. Power is either hydraulic or electric (all shipboard voltages available). They also work when the boat is underway to tighten the turning circle. In congested waterways, this is reassuring.

On a long-distance voyage, you don't go back to the same familiar slip everyday. Most mooring and piloting efforts are adventures into strange territory. If the day ever comes when you tire of maneuvering on a wing and a prayer, it might not be your fault so much as your boat's lack of response. However, a ship that is a dream to sail offshore can be a dream in close quarters, too—with a bow thruster.

AUTOMATIC STEERING

Most cruising yachts have between two and four crew members aboard, including the skipper. This means singlehanded watch keeping, particularly at night, so everyone gets enough sleep. Although automatic steering does not replace vigilance, it frees the watch to study the stars, brew a cup of tea, get a snack, navigate, adjust sheets, reef a sail, change a jib, chat on the radio, or visit the head. These things are difficult when you're a prisoner at the helm. Besides, manual steering on long passages is exhausting, especially in rough weather near land, when navigational and shiphandling duties are most demanding.

Like other cruising equipment, automatic steering has to function efficiently in adversity. It serves no purpose to have a system that steers when the going is easy and then goes on strike when the going gets tough. Any automatic steering system is charged with precise course holding on all points of sail in all weather. Only then will the crew be free to manage the ship.

In times past, autopilots were considered the domain of large yachts or commercial vessels with massive electrical generating capacity. Even now, windvane self-steering is seen by the majority of cruising sailors as obligatory. But there are compelling reasons to choose an electric autopilot for *any* size cruising sailboat. Advances in electrical generating systems and pilot technology have made the old problem of feeding them history.

Reliability

Windvane self-steering gear is fully exposed to the marine environment; maintenance is a factor with every system. Vane setups are susceptible to fouled servo blades or auxiliary rudders; they are vulnerable to damage from birds, people, and underwater obstructions; and they are subject to corrosion and electrolysis. This means periodic maintenance and periodic repairs for damage and natural deterioration. It's hard to keep moving parts properly lubricated when they are constantly washed by rain and sea and baked by the sun. So it's no mystery why a vane's moving parts—tiller lines, sheaves, cables, pivot joints, bearings, etc.—require frequent attention.

Good autopilots are fully protected from the environment, and the best are practically maintenance-free. The pilot I used for my last Pacific voyage (Wood Freeman, model 420) required a drop of oil on one bearing once a week during continuous use, and not one second of maintenance during 10,000 miles and three years. Such reliability cannot be matched by any windvane steering gear ever made.

Practicality

Windvanes sit back there on the transom, creating a nuisance. They add length to the vessel, and they interfere with activities like fishing, boarding dinghies, and negotiating gangplanks. Perched on the stern unprotected, they are subject to collision with other vessels, pilings, docks, you name it. And some windvanes eat inflatable dinghies for breakfast.

By contrast, an autopilot is installed out of sight inside the vessel, creating none of these problems. (Autopilots designed for cockpit installation are not part of this discussion. Exposed moving machinery in the cockpit work area is not conducive to offshore safety. Electrics and electronics subjected to saltwater baths are bound to have a shorter service life—despite manufacturers' claims—than equipment installed below decks. Also, steering motors connected to steering wheels load up the entire steering system. This wears cables, chains, sheaves, bearings, and other linkages faster, and it introduces more friction for the steering motor to overcome. A steering motor driving the rudder quadrant directly relieves steering components of strain, and more power is available to turn the rudder. Direct rudder operation also offers backup steering via autopilot in case of linkage or component failure between the wheel and quadrant. Finally, recreational pilots with cockpit steering motors lack muscle for blue-water service. A good offshore pilot is stronger than any helmsperson.)

Performance

Windvane steering creates extra drag and to some degree reduces a vessel's rate of progress (types with large auxiliary rudders have more wetted surface than the more powerful servo-pendulum vanes). Autopilots cause no drag whatsoever.

Although faster passages are beneficial, course keeping is of greater concern to cruising welfare. Accurate DRs, the estimated position between navigational fixes, depends dearly on precise steering. If the guess-timate of a vessel's average course is haphazard, the estimated position at any given time will be equally haphazard. This is of utmost relevance to security; in some instances, notably tricky landfalls, the quality of navigational input is critical.

Windvane steering holds the boat on a course relative to the prevailing wind conditions. Variations in wind velocity and direction cause course changes, burdening the navigator with guesswork. Like the helmsperson, autopilots steer by compass, but autopilots do it better. Sophisticated pilots even compensate automatically for changes in weather helm as wind strength varies.

Some autopilots are available with a wind-sensor option so course keeping

A servo-pendulum self-steering gear with the blade cocked out of the water and the vane stowed away. Windvanes add length to a boat, suffer from direct exposure to the environment, and are a hassle when moored stern-to. They also chew up inflatable dinghies. Think how nice this vessel's transom would look without one.

may be switched to respond to wind direction rather than compass heading. This is a curious option, wiping out precise course keeping. Why trade the accurate input of a magnetic compass for the vagaries of the wind?

There are sailors who believe an automatic steering apparatus of any kind should follow the wind to keep sails trimmed. In terms of vessel security, this is a startling viewpoint. When a wind shift prompts sail adjustment, surely it's the person on watch who's responsible, not an automatic steering system. A crew works a ship, and whatever or whoever steers, steers toward a definite objective over the horizon. Yachts left to the whims of the wind too often find reefs.

Just when the wind dies down and you wish to motorsail to keep the ball rolling, many vanes go on vacation. But an autopilot stays on the job.

In addition, autopilots have remote controls enabling you to steer from the foredeck or the spreaders. This can be handy in coral lagoons. The remote handset acts as inside steering in doghouses without manual steering, too.

Before choosing a pilot, talk to a few owners of commercial fishing boats to see what they have and how they like it. As I've said before, a product that reliably survives commercial marine service is right at home on a cruising boat. Fishermen are not in the habit of praising rubbish!

CONTROLLING SHEETS AND HALYARDS

Sailhandling must be organized for efficiency and equal opportunity. Again, it's adversity that tells what's needed. Rough weather is either a temporary annoyance or a more desperate affair of worry and hardship—outfitting largely determines which.

The peace of mind enjoyed every time a task is quickly dealt with will, in time, be almost taken for granted, but the irritation and disruption from shaking out sleeping shipmates to help momentarily on deck is soon dreaded. Also, awakening the offwatch to assist with chores that could be done singlehandedly depletes a ship's human resources. Sailing's enemy, fatigue, increases the risk of accident and opens the door for human error, especially in navigation and landfall tactics.

Sheet-winch power is as vital for cruising as it is for racing—maybe more so, since the cruising crew is likely to be composed of normal individuals, not muscle-bound athletes. A hard-pressed, closehauled vessel imposes tremendous loads on headsail sheets. These strains must be dissipated by mechanical advantage to minor loads within human control.

It's impossible to err by fitting too large a winch. When you cut costs with smaller winches, safety and convenience will be compromised throughout your cruising days. A good winch is a lifetime investment; they do not wear out. The investment repays itself every time the winch is used, and someday, when you sell your boat, a prospective purchaser won't be disadvantaged by compromise winches.

Don't consider old-fashioned single-speed winches, and shy away from ones with bottom action. Powerful, top-action, multispeed sheet winches are the answer to crew equality. Whether or not you decide on self-tailing winches is a matter of personal preference. If it's a toss-up between affording self-tailing ones or the next size up without self-tailing, go bigger. Regardless of winch type, a handy cleat should be through-bolted in line with the barrel and sheet. Don't skimp on cleat size, either; it must handle imposing loads and large-diameter sheets.

Sheet winches are used for more than sailhandling. They apply force to kedge a boat off the mud with a stern anchor; they haul in and tension stern anchor rodes; they are used to adjust and hold stern lines when moored stern-to; and they are superb attachment points for mooring lines when a mooring cleat is not convenient. As such, sheet winches must be bolted down solidly. Winches cantilevered over thin air on thin stainless steel brackets are not always anchored well enough to take it. It's best to bolt winches on an integral pad with fasteners running through the deck, reinforced by healthy backup plates to spread the load.

Sheet size is determined by the grip a given size gives a human hand or winch. On boats up to 50 feet, a comfortable sheet is strong enough by default. Consider nine-sixteenths-inch Dacron braided line a minimum, and think seriously about three-quarter-inch. Don't use half-inch; your hands won't like it. Traditionally, sheets are attached to a sail's clew with a snap shackle. If you outlaw such hardware, you can save money and improve safety. A flapping metallic missile is a menace; secure sheets to sails with a bowline.

By and large, halyard winches on cruising boats are too small for less athletic crew members to operate comfortably. A halyard winch should snug a luff with no more than firm pressure on the handle, not red-faced exertion. You'll use the winch for hoisting someone aloft in a bosun's chair, for launching and retrieving the ship's skiff, and for levitating heavy pieces of gear from dock to deck. A halyard might be pressed into service to lift an injured person from the water, too. So think big. And always think two-speed.

Wire halyards are not for cruising; they are a racing gimmick. Wire wakes the dead as it slaps against an aluminum spar; with paint or anodizing, it raises Cain. Burred wire cuts hands. Band-type brakes on wire winches are less reliable than open-barrel ratchets (pawls). And only the foolish trust their luck to band brakes in a bosun's chair.

Like sheet winches, halyard winches should be open-barrel types using the same braided Dacron for a comfortable and safe grip. Nine-sixteenths-inch is fine; half-inch is too small.

Avoid using fairleads on the mast to keep halyards in place. They chafe years off a halyard's life. Worse, when it blows, a halyard pinned to the mast whips up a clatter heard for miles. Halyards attached to nothing but their block aloft can be silenced by tying them clear of the mast. If everybody did this, you could walk down a marina dock on a windy day and hear yourself think. When chafe is a problem under sail, use smooth chafing patches where halyards rub.

To lower a sail singlehandedly, ease the halyard with one hand while simultaneously pulling the sail down the stay with the other. This keeps excessive slack out of the halyard and prevents fouling on a rolling boat. A halyard held captive at the mast with fairleads makes this impossible. Furthermore, cruising sailors who lead halyards to the cockpit, racing-style, don't do themselves any favors. Halyards terminating in cockpits presume there'll be at least two people working the boat. For cruising, this presumes too much.

ROLLER-FURLING HEADSAILS

Sailing adversity doesn't always mean gale-force conditions. When it blows, the ship is reefed down for extended periods, allowing the crew to settle into a routine. More wearing to shorthanded crews on long passages are widespread squalls. The mean wind speed may be moderate, say 15 to 25 knots, but gusts of 40 to 50 knots periodically buffet the boat as a squall marches past. Each time a squall approaches, the ship must be reefed.

One way to cope with persistent squalls is to proceed under shortened sail so the offwatch is not disturbed. This strategy has two things against it. First, most of the time the boat's traveling at reduced speed, and the passage is prolonged. Second, a vessel that's undercanvased can be damned uncomfortable—rolling is more pronounced, doing little for the offwatch's comfort.

Ideally, sail reduction takes place from the cockpit through the efforts of one crewperson. Then the vessel can be trimmed down for the odd blast and spread her wings again smartly when the wind abates to keep the average speed up. Singlehanded, spur-of-the-moment sail reduction takes the pressure off everybody. It's no comfort to lie in bed with a nagging feeling that your assistance will be shouted for any second. Sleep for the offwatch comes with peace of mind. Peace of mind depends on confidence that all is under control on deck.

A roller-furling headstay is a blessing, since the foredeck is the least desirable place to visit in rough weather. If a vessel is cutter rigged, the inner forestay could be fitted with a luffspar, too. Then a yankee or genoa jib on the forestay can be struck and a heavier staysail unfurled instantly in its place. Roller furling is at its best as all-or-nothing gear, but sail reduction by partial furling is feasible with good equipment, particularly off the wind, where sail shape isn't critical. The hitch is that as a sail rolls up on its luffspar, more belly is introduced, reducing windward efficiency (and straining the sail).

A cutter with a small, heavy, roller-furling staysail might be up to heavy-weather work—*might* being the operative word, depending on the size and weight of the sail and the quality of the furling system. Each case must be considered on its own merits. Naturally, compromise comes into it: a lighter weight, larger, furling staysail is more efficient under normal circumstances, and a smaller, more robust staysail stands up better to windier weather. To hedge their bets, some sailors fit another stay ahead of the furling gear, a stay that accepts a regular hanked-on sail specifically cut for rough weather (mandatory for offshore). Alternatively, furling gear is selected for easy sail changes right on the luffspar—a good idea regardless. Tender yachts need special attention; matching sail area to prevailing conditions is more critical with such boats.

All in all, bulletproof cruising furling gear is a godsend. But don't get involved with the racer/cruiser weekend equipment. Furling gear must be designed for severe service, or it won't last. And speaking of lightweight racer/cruisers: they offer more potential for trouble with roller-furling headsails offshore. Even

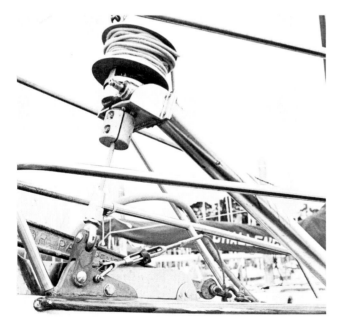

Custom headsail furling gear with a standard manual drum and drive shaft coupled to a below-deck electric motor. The sail is controlled from the cockpit by the push of a button.

furled sails present considerable windage. A light-displacement yacht can find herself blown off downwind by the windage of a furled jib in a gale despite attempts to steer her otherwise. If a lee shore is near, this could be curtains. Furling gear fitted to light-displacement, fin-keel craft must provide for quick and simple sail removal to reduce windage. The effects of furling-gear windage on more substantial cruising boats are less apparent.

All cruising headsail luffspars must rotate around a stay on evenly spaced, low-friction bearings. Roller-furling systems held aloft by halyard tension alone, those without the internal support of standing rigging, sag off badly on the wind and are not worth a hoot for deep-water cruising.

Larger furling drums reduce furling-line loads, but a cockpit winch is still advisable. Initially, a sail may seem easy enough to furl by hand, but in fresh winds a winch makes the job safe for everyone. Choose a system with a generous stainless steel halyard swivel and drum bearings for long life and low friction. Spar extrusions should be stout. Beware of cheap fastenings like pop rivets holding together short lengths of extrusion. If you have to take the thing to bits for maintenance out in the boondocks, pop rivets are hopeless.

REEFING THE MAINSAIL

As the wind freshens, the mainsail area is reduced first. This keeps the vessel balanced by reducing pressure on the boat's sailplan aft of the center of lateral resistance, and weather helm (the tendency for the ship to round up into the wind despite rudder to the contrary) is minimized. With weather helm under control, the helmsperson or automatic steering system has an easier job of maintaining a good course with minor variations in rudder angle. And of course, reduced sail lets the boat proceed once again at a safe speed and a reasonable angle of heel.

For crew equality and peace of mind, the mainsail should have powerful slab-reefing (or roller-furling) gear, which pulls a secondary clew down to its reefed position near the boom smartly. For this purpose, a reefing winch is bolted to the boom near the mast. This places it within reach anytime, even when the boom hangs out over the vessel's rail while sailing off the wind. Another winch on the mast for hauling down a secondary tack is usually not required if the mainsail slides move smoothly; the pull at the leech is sufficient to lower the sail en masse.

If you can't make friends with a platoon of reef-point ties, try weaving a continuous line through a reefing cringle, down under the foot of the sail, through the next cringle, and so forth. This forms a one-piece spiral that can be tweaked and tugged quickly, evening the strain at each cringle. With spiral reefing, a sail sets beautifully.

BOOM PREVENTERS

To reef a sail safely, the boom must be held rigidly while the sail is being manipulated; a secure boom offers the crew a vital handhold while standing on the cabintop, perhaps the only handhold within reach. If the boom is not held in check, the job of reefing can be dangerous in lumpy weather. To hold the boom securely, use a series of tackles that pull from three directions. A topping lift lends upward support, the mainsheet applies one downward component, and a third tackle called a boom preventer pulls at a tangent to the mainsheet.

The preventer attaches to a bail located about midway along the boom, underneath, and leads to a tang at the railcap. It's basically like a mainsheet, most likely with a four-to-one purchase. The bitter end of the preventer leads to the cockpit along the rail or side deck, where a free winch assists with fine tuning.

A preventer not only makes reefing safer but is used while the boat's under sail. In combination with the mainsheet, it keeps the boom and sail in check on a rolling boat, reducing chafe and increasing sailing efficiency. On downwind legs, it takes the slack out of the mainsail by pulling directly beneath a swung out boom, whereas a mainsheet leading to an outboard boom at a shallow angle is not capable of a direct downward pull.

The contribution to safety of firm boom control is beyond measure. A cruising preventer should not be confused with a hydraulic boom vang on a racing boat. A vang is not effective for securing a boom against a jibe and, because of its inferior lever arm, imposes ungodly loads on both mast and boom. Not that loads on cruising preventers are chicken feed. The tackle, the railcap tang, and the boom bail must be bull strong, capable of handling several tons. An accidental jibe and a backwinded mainsail will test the daylights out of it. But don't fret about the sail; the priority during a jibe, accidental or otherwise, is crew safety. The sail's health is secondary.

A parting shot on preventers: two are better than one. While sailing off the wind, it's convenient when one person can safely jibe a mainsail (due to a wind shift or a course change). With only one tackle, a crew member must physically leave the cockpit after the jibe is completed and resecure the boom to the opposite tang at the other rail. Meanwhile, the boom is uncontrolled. With two tackles, one is eased and the other taken up as the boom swings across. Total control prevails throughout the maneuver. It's a boon to cruising safety when a lone watchkeeper never has to leave the cockpit.

REEFING WITHOUT CHANGING COURSE

With husky hardware, a mainsail can be reefed without changing course. Just tighten the topping lift, ease the preventer a tad, and get to work. And that's how it should be—swift sail reduction without false moves. Changing course means fooling with automatic steering, first to relieve wind pressure on the sail and again after reefing to get back on course. It's a waste of time and energy. If you cannot reef your mainsail efficiently and safely without changing course, review the system and add power where necessary so you can. Maybe you need a bigger mainsheet winch, perhaps a more powerful preventer tackle, maybe a bigger slab-reefing winch, or possibly a topping-lift winch (often omitted on cruising boats, making life needlessly tough for small folks). The topping lift, like other reefing gear, should be controlled at the mast, too, not at the boom's end, out of reach.

ROLLER-FURLING MAINSAILS

Powerful slab reefing works well for cruising, but there's a better mousetrap: an encapsulated luffspar in the mast. With roller-furling mainsails, reefing is accomplished from the cockpit by one person. And that's something!

It's not possible for one person to reef a large cruising mainsail comfortably with slab reefing. Someone has to help, someone who often quits a warm bunk for the privilege. Once sail is reduced, it often stays that way for hours, despite a drop in wind strength, to give a harassed offwatch forty winks. Meanwhile, the boat progresses at reduced speed.

Another tactic of shorthanded crews is reefing down on speculation at sundown to give the offwatch an opportunity to rest in case the wind plays tricks in the night. Although safe and sensible, reefing on speculation is an inefficient way to run a boat. Those miles lost each night mean additional hours or perhaps days at sea. More time at sea equals less time to be savored in port.

Roller-furling mainsails are recognizable by a slot on the aft side of the mast; the sail rolls up inside the mast like a window shade. Freestanding systems lurking behind a mast, held aloft by halyard tension, are inefficient. The slot controls the sail by holding a straight luff, regardless of reef depth. Since the sail's leech moves forward as a reef deepens, the center of effort moves forward, too, minimizing weather helm. As long as the sail's cut fairly flat and is stout enough to perform reliably in a reefed state in heavier weather, the system has everything going for it. Slab-reefed mainsails operate under similar loads, so nothing extra is asked of a roller-furled mainsail.

Not only is a luffspar mainsail a cinch to reef singlehanded, but the sail stows in the blink of an eye. A vessel fitted with a furling headsail and a mainsail is a dream at the end of a sail or passage. No more bagging big jibs in the heat of the day. And no more striking and furling a mainsail by hand, the most hated job aboard! Just roll 'em up and forget 'em. The mainsail boot is dispensed with, too; the sail stays furled in the mast, out of the sun.

However, a failure inside the mast can jam a mainsail in an unfurled state. At best, it's embarrassing; at worst, it can create havoc in rising winds when the sail can't be doused. Improvements in equipment design and component durability have largely solved teething problems evident in roller furling's infancy. A good mainsail furling system must provide easy access for repairs and maintenance, however. Reliability is the number-one priority. If you decide on mainsail furling for offshore duty, cost cannot guide selection.

One more thing. When the sail is rolled up completely, a bare mast slot is exposed. This causes no difficulties with the wind on the bow. But when it blows across the slot from the beam, all hell breaks loose. You'll be assaulted by a wail

Roller-furling mainsail with sliding, self-aligning car for clew control. A boon to the shorthanded crew.

that sounds like a pipe organ giving birth to a tuba. To overcome this, organize a slot cover that can be hoisted by a halyard. If you don't have one, when the wind's just right, your neighbors will hate you.

GOING ALOFT

While underway, you may have to go aloft to fix a problem such as a burned out navigation light or a jammed halyard block. You may also climb the mast to con the ship. Obstructions like coral heads and shoal water are not always apparent at deck level, and piloting improves with a pair of eyes at the spreaders.

Going aloft, like most chores, can only be done promptly when need arises if it's simple and quick. If climbing the mast is arduous or scary, you won't always take advantage of the strategy, a lapse that someday could cost you your ship.

At sea, when the boat's rolling, a ride in a bosun's chair can be more than you bargained for. Imagine losing your grip on the mast or rigging and becoming a human pendulum. The chair is also awkward to hoist. Tackle must be rigged for

This 56-foot high-performance cruising cutter designed by Alan Warwick makes foredeck apes obsolete. The yankee, staysail, and mainsail all furl from the cockpit. Note high-aspect rig and modern profile— no slouch, this boat! Photo by Bruce Laybourn.

a person to inch himself singlehandedly up the spar (not easy on a rolling vessel, either). Alternatively, other crew members assist with a halyard winch, one person cranking the winch and another tailing the halyard. At best, this foolishness is strenuous. At worst, shipmates are needlessly placed in charge of each others' lives.

I've been dropped while high off a deck in a bosun's chair, fortunately fetching up abruptly on a spreader instead of plummeting to my maker. Others less lucky than I have dropped to their deaths. My adventure gives me incentive to discourage the use of a chair whenever there's an alternative.

Ratlines served to the lower shrouds for climbing look salty to some folks; others, myself included, think they look tacky. Aesthetics aside, they increase windage, require new serving every couple of years, and feel flimsy to people inexperienced at high-wire acts. Ratlines terminate under the spreaders, and swinging up onto the spreaders from them is best left to monkeys. And what about the rest of the mast?

Well-placed mast steps are the answer. They allow a person to climb with a minimum of exertion all the way up without superfluous gear and manpower. At any point along the way, it's convenient to sit on a spreader or carry out inspections or maintenance.

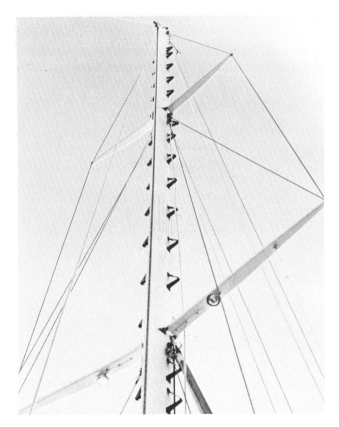

Polycarbonate (Lexan) mast steps on author's 45-foot cutter make going aloft easy. Safer by far than the deadly bosun's chair.

Preferable materials for steps are injection-molded Lexan or formed stainless steel. Pop rivets are not acceptable fasteners. Alloy masts should be drilled and tapped to take machine screws; wooden sticks should be carefully drilled with a tapered bit for wood screws.

Before choosing mast steps, make sure they are comfortable. The step should be at least one-and-a-half inches wide where you stand, or you won't like climbing in bare feet. Beware of sharp edges. Before committing yourself, buy two trial steps and fasten them to a tree or post at home. See if you can stand on them for 20 minutes without your feet screaming bloody murder. Then check them out for strength with a block and tackle. A loading of half a ton will not break a good maststep. Before bolting steps to the mast, have the stepping surfaces sandblasted. Otherwise, they'll be slippery when wet.

It's tempting to place steps too far apart. While this saves money, smaller folks with shorter strides have a hard time climbing. It's a shame to go to all the trouble of installing steps and then make life difficult by fitting too few of them. Near the masthead, position two steps level with each other so a person can stand normally on both feet for long periods to work. The masthead is where most maintenance takes place (halyard blocks, radio antennas, tricolor, strobe light, apparent wind speed and wind direction sensors, etc.). Don't install the top steps too close to the masthead, or you'll be cantilevered uselessly (and fearfully) out into space. It's easiest to work on equipment at the masthead that's around chin level.

Some sailors complain that steps foul halyards. This is only a minor annoyance if fairleads are not used; it's easy to flick a halyard free. But fouling often results in poor technique while raising sails. If you are hassled with this, fasten a tight, continuous line or wire along the outer edges of the steps to act as a guard.

While installing mast steps, check your spreaders. Will they be comfortable as a seat? Narrow spreaders need an oval-shaped plate of aluminum (or plywood in the case of wooden spreaders) about a foot by six or eight inches, either mechanically fastened or welded into place. Sitting comfort is important. You might have to perch up there for an hour while conning the ship through a pass or down a lagoon to an anchorage. Upper spreader surfaces and seats should be treated with nonskid paint or 3-M nonskid tape for a firm footing.

Once you have arrived at your work station, hook a line around the mast and tether yourself with a safety harness. The harness lets you work with both hands free at the masthead and adds confidence and safety when sitting on spreaders.

RUN THE SHIP WITH THE MIND, NOT THE BODY

Good equipment is not meant as a substitute for seamanship. Just the contrary. Anything that enhances physical shiphandling frees the crew to function as managers, rather than waste human resources with worrisome or dangerous

A sturdy crow's nest on the mainmast is handy for piloting around reefs and coral. Note teak grating and safety hoop.

When choosing aluminum deck hardware and equipment, beware of how it's finished. These windlasses, although still functional, both looked weary after Pacific voyages. Anodizing stands up to marine use; almost without exception, spray-on or dipped coatings don't.

tasks. Laborsaving equipment adds much to cruising safety and bolsters crew confidence. In turn, this helps safeguard the material investment in the boat.

How much mechanical assistance it takes to achieve a high level of shiphandling finesse on any given boat is immaterial, so long as it *is* achieved.

Part Two—Safety Equipment

Ashore, many human responses are born of caution. We look both ways before crossing streets, we wear white at night, airplanes land one at a time, and so on.

Sailing is no different from other outdoor pursuits. It can be a dangerous game for those who disregard their own safety.

SAFETY HARNESSES

If you sacrifice yourself to the sea, she'll not hesitate to accept. Without malice, of course, but the end result's the same—you buy the farm. For safety's sake at sea, the water flowing past the ship's flanks must be respected as if it were battery acid.

Safety harnesses are insurance against a watery grave. When you wear one, you are tied to the boat with something more tangible than blind luck. But like automobile seat belts, safety harnesses are useless unless worn.

Harnesses not only safeguard a person from being lost overboard, but they facilitate a quick rescue. Time could be critical. An injured or unconscious person needs help immediately to survive. There isn't always time for a search to save a life.

Some offshore sailors are slack about wearing safety harnesses during daylight hours when there is more than one person on deck, but it's not recommended. There is no guarantee a person will be found in broad daylight even if they were seen to go over the side. And sea state has little to do with falling overboard. Heavy weather is often safer for offshore cruising folks than relatively calm conditions. Sailors are more alert and cautious, and they take precautions to stay aboard. Accidents happen most frequently to people who have their guard down.

Harnesses should be clipped on when both feet are still firmly on the cabin sole below decks. Secure a set of harness tethers to a beefy fitting in the cockpit and hang the business ends on hooks inside the companionway for this purpose.

Rig a second set of tethers to slide along a fore-and-aft line tied between bow and stern mooring cleats. A spliced eye is the best attachment for sliding tethers; no metallic hardware scrapes deck paint and awakens the offwatch. With this system, a person has the run of the ship while being hooked up at all times.

Combination drink holder and safety harness anchor.

At sea, harnesses are life; there is no other way to look at them. Choose the best. Be wary of harness hardware. Is it bulletproof? Be wary of snap shackles that connect tether lines to harnesses, too. Some can accidentally unsnap themselves because of a sudden twist or jerk, or they may become dislodged as you go about your chores. The most foolproof attachment is a plain three-eighths-inch bronze screw-type shackle. Keep a nonferrous shackle key handy at the companionway to snug up shackle pins when you hook up. Harnesses and tether lines must be capable of taking fierce loads. Remember, it's not your weight that tests them but the sudden jerk when the slack's taken up during a fall. Pick gear that will withstand several tons.

Rules on safety harnesses must be enforced religiously. It's imperative that watchkeepers at night never venture on deck without a harness under any circumstances, even for a moment. A wise skipper insists all crew members use the ship's head, too. Sensible, safe sailing depends on reducing risks—all risks. There's a saying you'll hear in cruising harbors worldwide: *men who fall overboard usually have their flies open.* Think about it!

Falling overboard is the single major threat to life on a long-distance cruise (shipwreck, although intimidating, is rarely life threatening). If you think you are immortal, at least have some compassion for your shipmates who'll be faced with sailing on without you.

LIFELINES AND STANCHIONS

Lifelines are a barrier between the deck and the sea that can literally make the difference between life and death. They are your first line of defense against

A braced stanchion keeps the rest of the life-line system tensioned when the gate is open.

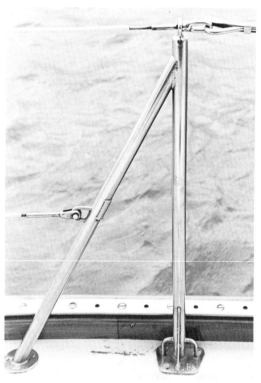

A grabrail and support for working at the mast. Note cleats for tying halyards away from the mast at anchor.

falling overboard. Safety harnesses come into play as a backup measure. Both systems are necessary to preserve offshore safety. When life is at stake, you don't put all your eggs in one basket.

Single lifelines are a token gesture; a shipmate could be swept under one in a flash. Double lifelines break up the gaping space between the railcap and a single upper. This not only helps people stay aboard but holds bagged sails and other gear.

Don't be tempted to use synthetic line for lifelines to save a few dollars. Wire rope won't stretch or chafe like Dacron or nylon, and it can be tensioned for a solid, safe handhold. Plastic-covered wire rope is easier on the hands than plain cable and looks better. The stainless part of the cable should be at least three-sixteenths of an inch. Swaged ends, Norseman fittings, or Castlok ends and regular turnbuckles anchor the wire to the pulpits; the system is tensioned just like standing rigging.

Lifelines are only as strong as the stanchions that support them. Generally, stanchions on yachts need upgrading to meet offshore conditions. Stanchion attachment to sailboats often relies more on wishful thinking than solid fact. Securement must have great integrity—a stanchion should bend over without ripping loose at the base. The tubing itself must be the weak link.

Stanchions are usually too short on recreational boats, and lifelines tend to trip people into the sea at the knees rather than retain them aboard. To do their job, stanchions should position the upper lifeline at least 30 inches off the deck.

One-inch stainless tubing is traditionally used for stanchions. Despite husky wall thicknesses, one-inch is too light. One-and-one-quarter-inch tubing is nearly twice as strong (wall thicknesses being equal) and offers greater rigidity. Watch out for stanchion placement. Remember: it only takes one more stanchion per side to close up the ranks, a small price to pay for security. Spacing should never exceed five feet.

Recreational yachts usually locate their lifeline gates back near the cockpit, so it's handy to leap on and off the boat from the dock at a marina. On your cruise, you may not spend much time in marina berths, and lifeline gates placed aft may be practically useless. Think instead about where you'll board the vessel from a dinghy or a swimming ladder, and put gates there. Normally, this is farther forward, around amidships, where the freeboard is lowest and mast shrouds offer convenient handholds for climbing.

Gate stanchions should have a diagonal brace to support the rest of the lifeline system when the gate is left open. The lifelines on each side of gate stanchions must be fitted with a stop or else terminated there so an open gate doesn't cause the rest of the system to sag. You might have laundry drying on the lifelines or they may be holding up eyebrows over hull ports. It's important to have a lifeline's help at anchor, too.

BOW AND STERN RAILS

Bow and stern pulpits or rails should rise at least 30 inches off the deck (or bowsprit). Again, one-inch tubing is used nearly universally on production boats, but a larger size is much more supportive. The crew should be able to stand on pulpits to dive off the boat at anchor. Offshore, many a white-knuckled hand will test a pulpit's strength. The stern rail is also a handy place to tie dinghies, which sometimes buck and tug fiercely.

Use only welded construction. Pulpits made with plumbing-type joints with setscrews work loose with pressure and vibration and become rickety. The same is true for pulpit bases: only welded construction ensures a rigid, lasting structure. The pulpits should match your lifelines with double rails so that no slot exists for people or gear to slip through. Double pulpits are also stiffer.

Before commissioning bow and stern rails, you should have your deck layout and operational tactics organized so all the necessary features and equipment can be consolidated with the pulpits. This includes the placement of lights (if any), brackets for man-overboard poles, horseshoe lifebuoys, anchors (the stern anchor lives happily on the stern pulpit), flagpoles, barbecues, fishing poles, perhaps a mounting point for a radio antenna, or whatever. Clamped-on bracketry isn't as pleasing to the eye nor as rigid as welded ones.

A strong pulpit on a bowsprit with double rails for stiffness and eight through-bolted attachment points. Note running-light placement.

PERSONAL SAFETY EQUIPMENT

Safety harnesses and lifelines dramatically reduce the risk of parting company with the ship, but it's naive to think that even the best equipment yields ironclad safety. Even good gear can fail in a freak accident. Therefore, some after-the-fact safeguards are necessary to protect life in case a crew member winds up in the drink in spite of precautions.

Each person on deck requires, in addition to a safety harness, a penetrating, loud whistle to attract attention (better yet, use those little aerosol horns ladies carry in their purses to scare off muggers); a personal waterproof strobelight that can be seen for many miles at night; waterproof, handheld flares and a dye marker; and some sort of flotation device. Armed with this gear, an unfortunate victim in the sea has a sporting chance.

Personal Strobelights

Powerful personal strobes can help guide the ship back to a person in the sea at night. Buying the less expensive and dimmer incandescent lights for man-overboard use is like saying your life is cheap. Each shipmate must have his or her own strobelight. There will be times when all hands will be working on deck after dark. Like harnesses, personal strobes are useless unless they're worn religiously. Nobody should be allowed on deck after dark without one. At the outset of every passage, renew the batteries and use the old ones in flashlights or somewhere less critical. Without fresh batteries, a personal strobe won't operate at peak duration. Choose one that flashes continually for 12 hours or more.

Flotation Aids

A wide range of flotation aids are available, from normal lifejackets to float coats resembling ski parkas and serving double duty as flotation gear and thermal protection. Retaining body heat is vital in cool regions, where hypothermia can be as deadly as drowning. Survival time in cold water is measured in minutes, not hours.

In the tropics, a flotation device can be a bother. If the decks are hot enough to fry an egg, nobody cares to don gear that makes life uncomfortable. But there's an alternative to more bulky lifejackets that will enhance safety in warm climates. This is the scuba diver's BC (buoyancy compensator), a thin, inflatable vest. The device may be worn comfortably deflated, then inflated orally in an emergency (*caution:* a victim must be conscious to do so). A snorkeling vest may be preferable to a scuba vest if a BC without inappropriate scuba fittings cannot be found. Vests are available from dive shops with both oral and automatic (by a small CO_2 cylinder) inflation.

A BC is not really meant as sailing flotation, but it beats going over the side with nothing if a person isn't comfortable wearing anything else. Most BCs and snorkeling vests have handy pockets for your whistle or horn, dye marker, flares, and strobelight. And they are designed to keep heads out of the water, as a flotation device must. As such, they come close to being the tool for the job.

Regardless of the type of flotation gear you choose, the color should never vary. They must be bright, international orange, so a person in the water can be spotted against the blues, whites, and grays of the sea.

THE SHIP'S EMERGENCY GEAR

Shipboard safety equipment complements personal safety devices and comes into play when a shipmate is observed going over the side. The basic strategy is the same as above—a strobelight to find the victim at night and a flotation device to keep the person safe until rescue. But there are a few additions.

Man-Overboard Pole

The man-overboard pole has a weighted end and a float so it stands upright in the water. An international-orange flag is attached to the pole's tip to mark the location. This facilitates daylight rescues when strobelights or flares are difficult or impossible to see.

The pole is stowed at the stern of the yacht, either in a specially designed tube leading into the transom, racing-style, or secured parallel to the backstay. If stowed against the backstay, a socket is fitted to the railcap or stern pulpit that accepts the weighted end. A length of PVC pipe is lashed or clamped to the backstay into which the upper part of the pole slides. The flag furls inside the tube so it won't fade. No lashings hold the pole in position—just the socket and tube. It must be ready to heave into the sea in a flash.

Many sailors tether a horseshoe lifebuoy to the pole with a length of line. The buoy is held in a quick-release bracket so it deploys automatically when the pole is tossed overboard. This makes sense, but an additional horseshoe lifebuoy that's independent of the man-overboard pole should be on hand at the stern for emergencies close to the boat. You can't toss a buoy very far if it's tethered to other hardware, and someday you may have to.

Man-Overboard Strobe

The ship's man-overboard strobelight differs from the crew's pesonal strobes. It's larger and more powerful, and it's designed to operate upright while floating, automatically flashing via a mercury switch when thrown into the sea. The strobe is stowed inverted in the "off" position. It's tethered to the horseshoe buoy and the man-overboard pole. This way, when the vessel steams toward the light or pole, the buoy and the person in it will be there, too.

Man-Overboard Alarm

Automatic Safety Products, Inc., in San Diego, makes a man-overboard system using a shipboard receiver and loud alarm horn. Each crewperson wears a small, water-activated transmitter, which trips the alarm automatically a few seconds after an incident, whether a person is conscious or not. There's an optional autopilot interface that makes the vessel heave-to, which benefits single-handers.

Man-Overboard VHF

At the time of writing, the ideal man-overboard signalling device had yet to hit the market. Perhaps some enterprising manufacturer will read this and apply for a patent.

The technology is here now. What's needed is a waterproof, compact VHF transceiver that operates on channel 16 only. The device must be capable of sounding a piercing warning tone on the ship's VHF radio to awaken a sleeping crew (shipboard VHF radios are left on 24 hours a day as standard procedure, anyway). Then direct communications would follow enabling a rescue to proceed accurately. Such a product would close a big loophole in offshore safety.

FIRE EXTINGUISHERS

Yachts are potential Molotov cocktails. The engine room and galley present two danger areas. Some careful thought about fire-extinguisher location aboard your boat can save heartache in case of emergency.

First, ascertain where fire is most likely to occur. Then mount the extinguishers well away from the potential sources of flame and heat so you can safely lay your hands on them in an emergency. A fire extinguisher engulfed in flames is no asset.

An engine room fire-control system that automatically (and manually) protects the compartment is a good investment. At least provide a knockout port into the engine room so a fire-extinguisher nozzle can be poked safely into the machinery space without having to open doors or remove the companionway stairs first. Someone might get burned in the process.

Once each year, inspect and recharge the fire extinguishers. Before taking them in for refilling, use the opportunity to practice with them. Children and adults alike need direct experience to be competent in an emergency. Children are particularly intimidated by the roar of CO_2 extinguishers, but a few practice sessions with small fires at home in the backyard give them confidence.

Arrange at least three extinguishers below decks and position a fourth somewhere easily reached on deck so a mishap with a barbecue or a blazing outboard motor can be dealt with quickly.

Carbon dioxide extinguishers are general-purpose units, leaving no mess. Dry powder extinguishers are particularly effective for stove, engine room, and electrical fires, but they leave a residue that is difficult to clean up.

Superior to both dry chemical and CO_2 for general cruising needs are the Halon extinguishers (1211 or 1301). Halon, weight for weight, has several times the fire-control capability of CO_2. It uses a bottle similar to the dry chemical type, not the heavy, more expensive high-pressure cylinder required for CO_2. Halon has greater range, can be aimed precisely, and halts combustion chemically—CO_2 stops combustion by displacing oxygen. Consequently, discharging Halon below decks is less likely to affect respiration. And Halon leaves no residue.

YOU ARE YOUR OWN GUARDIAN ANGEL

Laborsaving gear lets each crew member efficiently work the ship, whatever his or her physique. Safety equipment removes the element of chance. Together, both strategies prevent accidents and maximize human resources.

Racing sailors are so willing to risk their hides for a trophy that committees have to cram offshore safety down their throats. Cruising, however, is still an individual pursuit, mostly free of bureaucratic meddling. Your safety is entirely in your hands.

10▶ Dinghies Are Freedom

In home waters, the logistics of a cruise are relatively easy, simplified by automobiles, a slip at the marina, and a scattering of docks, piers, and handy marine facilities. You can also lean on home workshops, shoreside stowage, and a diversity of industrial and supply organizations.

However, in remote cruising areas, these crutches are notably absent. This burdens dinghies with a new responsibility: they must be true support vehicles.

A LOOK AT LAGOON LIFE

Imagine being anchored in a distant lagoon far from civilization. Half a dozen cruising neighbors swing on their hooks close by, and visiting them is no problem. But the plot thickens. The nearest beach landing is 300 yards away; the village where you like to shop daily for fresh vegetables, bread, and odds and ends is two miles down a stretch of lagoon churned by blustery tradewinds. There's a tourist hotel two miles farther that lays on a humdinger of a smorgasbord. It's been ages since you had a restaurant meal, but it's too far to walk by land. On the far side of the lagoon, about a mile over open water, is a reef with fantastic snorkeling. Around the other side of the island, there's an abandoned movie set where *Hurricane* was filmed. You hope to visit it, but shallow water won't let the mothership within a mile. Then there's a little motu (islet) five miles from the ship that would be perfect for picnicking. And an unspoiled section of the barrier reef a few miles past the motu that you heard has superb shelling.

But today it's work, not play. You need 50 gallons of diesel fuel from the village service station—three or four trips in the dinghy with jerry jugs. You're bunkering ship before guests arrive from the States in the morning. After meeting them at the airport and treating them to a sightseeing tour of the lagoon, you'll settle them in on the boat for some cruising. The airstrip is on a motu four miles away—water miles, naturally. You wonder about your guests' luggage. And hope they travel light.

This describes Bora Bora, French Polynesia. Stir in a few variations, and it could be any of thousands of tropical islands or atolls worldwide. Cruising circumstances are similar everywhere. Without flexible water-borne transportation, you're dead in the water.

THE DINGHY'S RESPONSIBILITIES

Water Taxi

A dinghy must be an efficient people carrier so the entire ship's company can hop in at the drop of a hat to be comfortably shifted to a neighboring yacht for dinner or to terra firma anywhere in the anchorage. There must be room for a few friends, too. A taxi for a crew of four should carry six, minimum. Otherwise, you'll have to make several trips to move a mob, a hassle that spoils the fun.

As a taxi, a dinghy should have seating for each passenger. Nobody should pay their fare with wet feet, either. Taxis have to travel far and wide at a decent rate of knots so you don't grow old getting places. And a water taxi must deliver its passengers to their destination in good condition, not soaked to the skin and colder than mackerels.

Cargo Lighter

Sometimes a dinghy is used as a lighter for transporting supplies and gear to the ship from shore, or vice versa. As a mini-freighter, the dink must pack a load; you never know what piece of equipment (generators, batteries, etc.) might need shifting ashore for repair or replacement, or what provisions or supplies (water, fuel, food) need hauling to the boat. A cargo dinghy, like a taxi, must cover great distances. The best anchorages are seldom handy to a source of goods or services.

Usually, it's the other way around. To function as a freighter, a dinghy must be both robust and seaworthy.

Mother's Helper

Occasionally, a dinghy acts as an assistant or escort to the mothership in times of maneuvering and anchoring need. It's asked to run out another anchor and length of chain if the tackle can't be deployed by the mothership. As such, the dinghy must take choppy water and brisk headwinds in stride. Mother's helper totes breast and stern anchors, too. In tight quarters, the dinghy may see service as a little tugboat to nudge the mothership into position against a current or breeze or help the ship make an impossible turn into an awkward docking or berthing location in safety.

Recreational Vehicle

Finally, the ship's boat is used (and abused) as a recreational vehicle for pleasure and sport. This includes diving expeditions; fishing trips; rowing and sailing outings around the anchorage; and picnicking, sightseeing, and shelling trips to distant points of interest. In this guise, a dink accommodates passengers and packs loads of recreational gear and provisions. A recreational dink must be stable, seaworthy, and easily boarded by swimmers.

Even in protected waters, a stiff breeze and a mile of fetch can build up quite a chop. If your recreational tender can't handle some adversity you may be marooned someday until the weather calms down. Or an ill-conceived passage may end in a swim.

DINGHY OPTIONS

Dinghies come in two basic flavors: rigid skiffs and inflatables. Each type is designed for either displacement or planing operation. Displacement dinks are supposed to be good to row or sail, whereas planing tenders are used with an outboard motor for speed and range. A straightforward choice? If only it were!

Rigid planing tenders—really small runabouts—are ungainly things to stow aboard all but the largest cruising boats. And inflatables aren't known as nimble performers under oar or sail. To muddy the waters further, small rigid dinghies are more bathtub toys than practical tenders. Loaded down in rough water, they are candidates for Davy Jones's locker.

Given that cruising depends on transportation that rows easily and maybe sails, something seaworthy for lugging heavy loads of people and/or supplies, and something capable of traveling far from the mothership and back again quickly and safely, what one dinghy works best? Unfortunately, not a single one! A jack-of-all-trades tender is guaranteed to excel in none of its duties. Several dinghies, though, each with a different skill, work with panache. Dinghy choice, then, is a matter of specialization.

THE RIGID SKIFF

A rigid displacement skiff with sweet lines and a modest beam-to-length ratio is the number-one choice for rowing around a bay. The same skiff, when fitted with a centerboard, rudder, and mast, makes a good sailing dinghy. Because of its easily driven, fine form, it's only capable of minor ferrying chores over short distances in reasonably calm conditions. Slender skiffs are not intended as heavy-weather load carriers; they move through the water at the stroke of an oar or a puff of wind, and that's what makes them fun. You don't use greyhounds to pull plows.

A skiff is built of GRP or of fiberglass-sheathed cold-molded timber for low maintenance. It should be lightweight for launching convenience and lively performance.

Dinghies, dinghies, and more dinghies—but most of these are sluggish performers. Short and fat dinghies are the norm, because they need to fit aboard recreational boats not designed to carry them.

This skiff has sweet lines for rowing or sailing. Photo by Nautical News *Magazine.*

Anything under ten feet won't cut the mustard. Short skiffs are built-in headwinds, because to carry a minimal load they are compromised by flat aft sections, broad transoms, and high beam-to-length ratios. Tiny skiffs won't row or sail worth a damn compared with ones having longer waterlines and more graceful shapes. The longer the dinghy, the more it can be designed for performance; the shorter the dinghy, the more its design concentrates on buoyancy at the expense of performance.

Don't buy a skiff without rowing and/or sailing it first. A vivacious personality is worth searching for. There's nothing like a spirited skiff for a solitary row around a quiet anchorage at dawn or an afternoon's sail in a fresh tradewind.

Disadvantages? Only one: a good skiff is hard to pry away from the kids when you want it yourself.

INFLATABLE DINGHIES

Your skiff will be a trusty companion, but it won't do heavy jobs. A second tender, an inflatable, takes care of passenger and cargo work. An inflatable's forte is stability; you can step on it practically anywhere, and it sits there, unmoved. Good ones are extremely seaworthy, and, by virtue of inbuilt buoyancy, unsinkable.

Since they deflate for stowage, larger inflatables are the way to go. Anything less than 12 feet is more toy than workhorse. Length increases versatility—to take you where you want to go, with whom, whenever you like. Swiftly!

Just any old inflatable won't support your lifestyle. First, choose one with rigid flooring of stiff inflatable tubes or plywood. A firm floor provides a solid footing for boarding. That's necessary for hauling supplies and equipment and, importantly, for maintaining bottom shape for efficient planing performance.

If you decide on a dinghy with a plywood floor (as opposed to an inflatable one), assemble and knock it back down a few times before writing a check. If the task takes a couple of wrestlers with tire irons, it'll scuttle your sense of humor on a hot day in paradise.

Side tubes must be large in diameter for massive reserve buoyancy and generous freeboard for a dry ride under load. The bow must be upswept, too, so the dinghy climbs over waves diligently without digging in and tossing salt water over the crew. A dry ride is all-important. You can't let choppy water tie you down; when you want to go, you want to go. And it's no fun arriving at a destination drenched.

Give rapt attention to the overall quality of the inflatable's construction. In particular, eyeball the moldings that make up the oarlocks, the mooring-line strong points, the outboard-motor-bracket anchoring points, carrying handles, and surrounding grabline-attachment points (a nice feature). Make sure they look permanent, well laid out, and as a result, practical. Most inflatables are ponderous to row, but this doesn't mean you should ignore rowing performance. Examine the oars to see if they came out of a cereal box or are actually meant for

A cold-molded skiff shaped nicely for rowing and sailing. Photo by Nautical News *Magazine.*

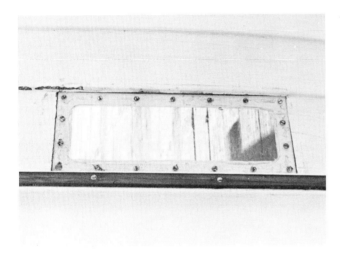

A Lexan viewing port in a dinghy's hull for checking anchors and observing coral and fish life.

cruising use and abuse. Even though your inflatable will have outboard power (yes, it will!), you'll want to row it on short trips around the anchorage to visit neighbors or the beach.

Check out the outboard motor brackets. Two general types exist: permanently bonded ones and removable ones. In a toss-up between two dinghies, one with and one without a removable bracket, you may want to choose the former on the premise that it's easier to stow two smaller packages.

Look at the air pump, repair kit, and pressure gauge (exact pressure is important for longevity, and a gauge is the only way to tell). Is the gear stout and well designed, or cheap and nasty?

Don't for a minute consider a displacement inflatable, and *never* buy one without a reinforced floor. Although little eight-to-ten-footers with waterbed floors are commonplace in the cruising world, their popularity is undeserved, a

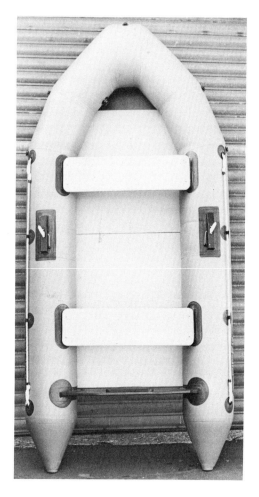

This Piper inflatable exhibits good cruising features such as a solid floor, strongly attached oarlocks, grablines, seats, and a transom for an outboard.

case of the blind leading the blind. Their barge-like bows drench passengers when bashing against a chop and headwind. The flimsy floors are a perpetual swamp of mud, water, and sand, and the goo pools in the low spot wherever you step. Folks with clean decks and carpeting don't appreciate visitors climbing aboard with muddy, dripping feet. Nor is a swamp kind to provisions and equipment in transit.

OUTBOARD POWER

Without outboard power clamped to a workhorse inflatable, there will be places you never see and people you never meet. An outboard gives you freedom to explore distant places—places where the action is, places less frequented by casual visitors, unique places a stone's throw from the mothership yet miles beyond rowing range. Why sail thousands of miles and miss out on points of interest only a few miles farther?

Horsepower depends on the number of passengers you wish to carry at planing speeds at about three-quarters throttle. Seven-and-a-half to ten horsepower will plane two adults at 12 to 15 knots in a 12-foot inflatable. Fifteen horsepower gets four people up and away. Twenty horsepower lets you water-ski—until your neighbors get sick of the noise and sugar your gas. Another advantage in choosing a bigger inflatable is motoring efficiency. A 12- or 13-footer, because of its larger planing surface area, takes *less* power to plane than a similarly designed ten-footer, particularly while carrying a load.

Planing ability is important. A dinghy mushing along off the plane makes five knots, or thereabouts, instead of 12 or better. On long excursions, extra speed means more time spent at the destination (or the ability to reach more distant places).

But don't go overboard with an outboard. You have to be able to feed it, manhandle it without getting a hernia, and stow it somewhere, too.

Pleasure aside, outboards are practical. They allow access to goods and services otherwise out of reach. For example, an anchorage in Rangiroa, French Polynesia, lies on one side of a pass, and the village where supplies such as fresh bread, butter, and diesel fuel are found is on the other side. Currents in the pass exceed five knots occasionally; without outboard power, there's no use making out a shopping list!

Tugboat and anchor-setting chores mentioned earlier are not always feasible without an outboard, either. In adversity, muscles are no substitute for mechanical might.

PROTECTING THE INFLATABLE

Most inflatables are reasonably sturdy, but if you expect them to last the distance they need loving. A little care adds years to their life, and that's money in the bank.

Chafe is the killer. Inflatables are designed for the open water, where they are supported evenly without stress, even when heavily laden. However, when beached, they are vulnerable to pokes and scrapes from jagged rocks, coral, and broken glass, and they don't like gear and supplies thrown into them willy-nilly.

Careful handling during launching and retrieval saves wear and tear, too. Use a bridle and lift the dinghy with a halyard over potentially damaging hardware such as lifeline stanchions.

Out in the cruising grounds, it's not unusual to see inflatables grinding themselves to death in a wicked surge against rugged seawalls, crude commercial wharfs, or amidst a pack of rafted hard dinghies or primitive native craft. A perfectly good inflatable can be ruined in hours by rubbing shoulders with rocks, barnacles, and jagged metal.

A few inexpensive mooring aids will keep your dinghy off the scrap heap. Equip it with three-eighths-inch nylon bow and stern lines, each at least 30 feet long; a folding, grapnel-type anchor with a fathom of smooth, vinyl-coated

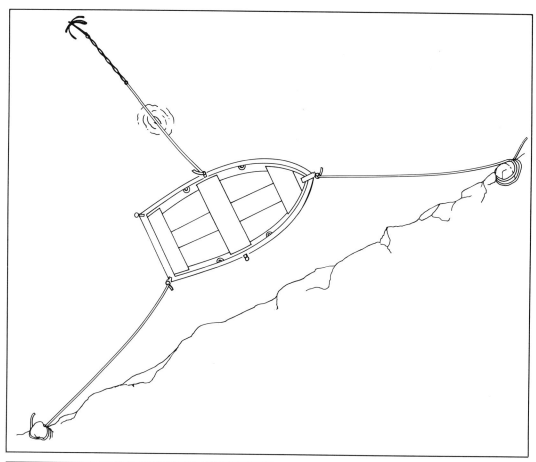

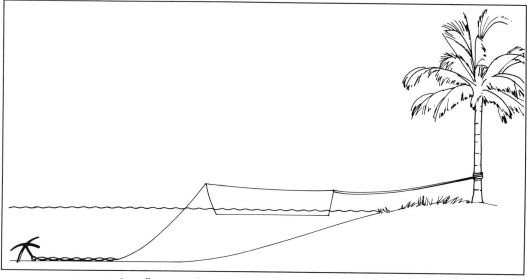

Some line, an anchor, an extra minute to tie them up right, and dinghies last twice as long.

chain; and 50 feet of three-eighths-inch nylon anchor line. Vinyl-coated chain is less abrasive when pulled over a gunwale, and a folding anchor won't poke or wear holes in a dinghy as it bounces along in a choppy seaway. With this simple, inexpensive gear, you can control your inflatable's destiny wherever you cruise.

Always refrain from tying an inflatable alongside a wharf or seawall, and try to keep it segregated from other moored boats. Usually, you can tie the dinghy across an inside corner of a dock or seawall with its bow and stern lines. If there's no practical way to keep the dinghy off obstructions with bow and stern lines, it's often possible to supplement the mooring lines with a breast anchor to hold the boat clear. Or anchor its bow off and tie the stern line ashore. The point is: the mooring gear lets you secure your investment in almost any situation without competing for space, because you are prepared, and most other sailors won't be. Most dinks are simply abandoned to their fate.

In remote areas, most landings are made on beaches. If you value your inflatable, you'll never drag it up on a beach over rocks, coral, or broken shells. Don't even drag it on sand. Carry it to a smooth place and gently set it down.

Whenever possible, leave the dinghy in its element by anchoring it off with a stern line leading ashore. Leave a little slack for tides and wakes from passing vessels, and it will bob contentedly. It's frequently more convenient to anchor off a beach than to haul a dinghy ashore, anyway. And an anchored dinghy is less of a temptation to native children, who sometimes frolic in them. Although meaning no harm, they may cause damage—jumping around in a beached inflatable is murder!

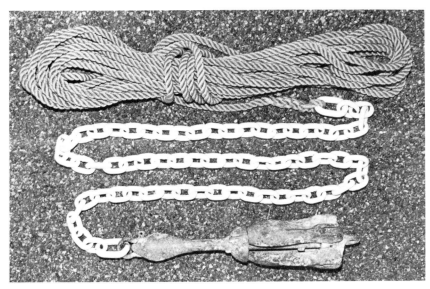

Dinghy ground tackle: 50 feet of three-eighths-inch nylon line, a fathom of coated quarter-inch chain, and a folding grapnel anchor.

Sailors who consider this level of care excessively fastidious fiddle most with repair kits. And patched dinghies are never as reliable as unpatched ones.

Naturally, the same mooring techniques will save your rigid dinghy wear and tear, too.

TYING DINGHIES TO THE MOTHERSHIP

When a breeze blows across the anchorage, dinghies trail off the stern of the mothership with no trouble if the painter is adjusted so they ride comfortably without snubbing or shipping water. But when the wind dies, dinghies are often attracted to the parent vessel like magnets. This tendency is aggravated when a tidal current holds the mothership's stern into the wind. Dinghies, unlike keel boats, are affected more by wind than tide, and instead of trailing peacefully, they thump in the night. Whatever the reasons, an inquisitive dinghy is annoying. And the wear from ramming and bumping takes a toll on the dinghy's health, not to mention the mothership's topsides.

Yachts with self-steering gear, particularly servo-pendulums with folded-up blades, can stab inflatables nudging curiously at the transom. In a surging anchorage, inflatables sneaking underneath vane gear can get gouged to death.

At times, a dinghy is more content when it's secured alongside by bow and stern lines, spaced from the topsides with fenders. So long as the lines have some slack, the dink nods and weaves happily. Tying dinghies alongside when weather permits is seamanlike: the yacht can be maneuvered instantly without fouling a painter in the prop. This lets a crew deal with the dinghy at leisure, rather than play games with it in the thick of weighing anchor.

Windless, lumpy anchorages are difficult. Dinghies won't trail off the stern, and they are equally unruly tied alongside, where they leap and buck, shipping water from wavelets surging between them and the ship. The more water the dink ships, the heavier it gets and the harder it struggles. In these circumstances, there are only two choices: haul the dinghy aboard or, if the yacht isn't rolling too much, rig a spar over the side from the mast to hold the dinghy at bay. A block at the end of a whiskerpole or downwind pole provides an adjustable mooring point for the painter. A slack stern line lets you retrieve the dink for use. A spar hanging out from the vessel at night can be a hazard to navigation, though, and should be rigged with a light.

Towing a dinghy offshore is chancy business, even on short passages in seemingly perfect weather. Sooner or later, the weather plays dirty, perhaps forcing you to cut your losses and abandon a dinghy if you can't manhandle it aboard. A freshening breeze or squall can quickly build seas that inundate or broach a towed dinghy. If this happens, you won't have to worry about cutting it loose—it will tear away by itself!

At the first sign of deteriorating weather, get your dinghies aboard the mothership smartly unless you plan to stick it out where you are and need a tender on standby for setting another anchor.

RIGID DINGHY STOWAGE

Designers don't always plan deck layouts around a good-sized skiff. Either they are more racing oriented, or their experience is limited to recreational jaunts in local waters, where dinghies play a lesser role.

However, once a boat is built, it either accommodates a decent cruising dinghy because of forethought, or it doesn't. Practically speaking, a fixed dinghy is chocked in a fore-and-aft position on the mothership's centerline, just ahead of the mast but not interfering with the foredeck work area. Dinghies positioned aft of mainmasts under a boom are more difficult to launch and retrieve, and they interfere with the working of a mainsail.

The skiff can be secured inverted or in an upright position, big-ship style, fitted with a ridgepole and a snug acrylic cover to keep out rain and spray. An upright dinghy provides deck stowage on passages for bulky items like awnings, deck chairs, extra cushions, and an inflatable dinghy or two—things that are put right back into service as soon as the boat makes harbor. An upright dink is convenient to launch with a bridle and a jib halyard. It doesn't require a laborious 180-degree roll first.

Athwartship dinghy stowage invariably interferes with the crew's free passage along the decks. Dinghies slung from stern davits are an obstacle to efficient vessel operations. They increase the effective length of a boat, always a

A ten-foot rowing skiff stowed upright, ready for launching. Deck space is made on the drawing board.

Stern davits are vulnerable appendages. If used, they should swivel or stow away for passages or for mooring stern-to. Carrying a dink this way offshore is risky.

disadvantage in today's crowded ports, and they are in the way when moored stern-to at a wharf or quay, making it difficult to rig and use a gangplank. Someday, a dinghy hanging from davits offshore will get the stuffing kicked out of it by a following sea. Davits also interfere with fishing and rear vision.

DINGHIES LEAVE YOUR OPTIONS OPEN

A cruising crew gets more out of life when members can pursue individual interests without competing for transport. If every social or recreational impulse is subject to mutual consent because of a dinghy shortage, individual freedom is stunted, and the ship's company at times gets bogged down in dissent.

While a rigid skiff and a workhorse inflatable are bare essentials for cruising, your fleet may include additional craft. Another, smaller inflatable gives a crew added flexibility. If dad is out diving for lobster in the big inflatable and junior is off sailing the skiff somewhere, a third, more modest craft offers those left aboard a chance to visit a neighbor or go ashore as they please, rather than being stranded. A third dinghy provides a backup, too, in case one of the primary dinks is damaged or shipwrecked.

11▶ Finding the Right Boat

Few material possessions tug the heartstrings like sailboats. People buy them because they look stately, graceful, cute—even because they *look* blue-water! If you want a conversation piece or a recreational toy, you can be frivolous or sentimental. Deep-water cruising is based on a more scientific approach.

Before you begin the process of selecting a boat, review your needs. Where do you plan to travel? For how long? Who's the crew? What's your anticipated standard of living? What amenities, features, and systems do you need to support your desired standard of living? Do you know what size boat will carry this lifestyle? What kind of boat copes best with the cruising environment? A patient search will reward you with a vessel that neatly fits your cruising plans; a hasty decision probably won't.

THE BUSINESS OF CRUISING

Let's face it: the cruising life is underwritten by time and money. Long-distance sailors often find cruising the most ambitious enterprise of their lives. Surely,

251

ventures of this magnitude deserve firm and thoughtful management from the outset. Think of your cruise as a business, because in many ways it is.

Cruising and business share similar principles. Both are set up with an expectation of profit. The cruising investment returns the freedom to pursue personal satisfaction and adventure—not the sort of profit you'll find on an accountant's ledger, but a kind of profit nonetheless.

Capitalization comes into it, too. Businesspeople don't set up a million-dollar factory to make a measly 20 bucks a week, and they can't expect to make a million bucks a week from a $20 factory. Investment must realistically match profit expectation (your desired lifestyle). False economy hurts the cruising life just as it does any other major enterprise. But by the same token, in business or cruising, throwing fistfuls of dollars at problems won't automatically make them go away. Profit depends a lot on good management, basic horsesense.

Finally, there's liquidation value. Nobody builds a million-dollar factory with the intention of sacrificing it a few years later for peanuts (unless they need huge tax write-offs!). Even if they enjoyed high profits meanwhile, the loss wouldn't compute. Same with a boat: resale value must reasonably reflect the time and money invested. Sooner or later, you and your boat will part company, and her selling price will influence your life after cruising.

WHAT SIZE?

Nailing down size is the first step toward owning a cruising yacht. Size depends a lot on the number, ages, and relationships of your crew, the duration of the voyage, how choosy you are about creature comforts, and the resources you bring to the project.

Generally, a more mature family of four—two adults and two teenaged children—needs more boat than a family with younger kids. And a crew of two adult couples strives for a larger vessel yet. As a rule, family units get by with less elbow room than adult groups, who have more diverse interests and social aims. The same can be said of three young men versus three older folks. As people age, they get stuck in their ways, and privacy becomes more important.

To a degree, the longer the voyage, the longer the boat. Short trips require less provisioning and can be confidently planned around compromises, whereas a voyage lasting years needs thorough support. Also, as time goes on, a boat seems to shrink in size; personal territory becomes more precious with every mile. The longer you sail, moreover, the more you collect—extra gear, personal possessions, mementos, and so forth.

Vessels selected for long voyages must be able to meet projected circumstances at the end of the voyage. For instance, an 11-year-old girl signing on for a three-year trip will become a teenager underway. Her needs will change under sail, and the boat must be of a size to absorb her growth. A sleeping cabin shared with a younger brother early in the voyage may become unbearable to her later. Forward thinking ensures lasting harmony.

Personal resources affect boat length. How much are you willing to donate to the cruising way of life? This does not necessarily mean the amount of money you have in the bank, but your willingness to sacrifice. Are you going to slave away seven days a week to have just the cruising life you want, or will you lower your standards to get away sooner? Bigger boats generally cost more, and all things being equal, bigger boats are more pleasurable to cruise on. Size and dedication usually go hand in hand.

Over the years, cruising yachts have steadily increased in length. Vessels under 30 feet were once common in remote cruising areas; now they're not. The average blue-water boat these days is around 40 feet. Bigger boats, many upwards of 45 feet, are being crewed by fewer people, too—sometimes just a couple—to maximize privacy and comfort at anchor. (But remember: overall length isn't the only indicator of size. Displacement has a lot to do with it, too.)

THE OPTIONS OF OWNERSHIP

Your personal circumstances will probably make one of the following ownership options attractive.

Buying Secondhand

A boat's replacement cost always exceeds its value as a secondhand vessel. The state of the economy determines the exact difference. When times are tough, used boats are cheapest. Geography affects resale value, too, not only because of local economic peculiarities, but due to the potential customer base in relation to the number of boats on the market. For example, a glut of cruising boats on the block in a small marketplace like Hawaii, where some burned-out sailors hang up their oilskins, can mean lower prices there than on the West Coast, boat for boat. The trouble is, discouraged sailors don't always have boats worth buying, because if they did, they mightn't be so discouraged.

The search for a used cruising boat could lead you overseas. Bargains are sometimes found in Tahiti due to forced sales. New Zealand's marketplace is traditionally underpriced by U.S. standards (both locally made and overseas yachts in transit). If this intrigues you, crank in the international rate of exchange, customs duty if applicable, transportation costs, and any delivery expenses. Traveling halfway around the world can pay off handsomely.

Buying secondhand saves time if you have a wad of money burning a hole in your pocket and a strong desire to go cruising *yesterday*. But it's not all smooth sailing. Used boats are like used cars; you could be buying someone else's problems. More to the point, you are buying someone else's lifestyle. A used vessel can suck up a bundle of bucks to refinish, re-equip, and outfit to your needs.

Prepare for mental fatigue when searching for a secondhand boat. You'll see countless vessels that don't measure up. This can lead to discouragement, or worse, a rash purchase. To guard against mental fatigue, eliminate wild goose chases by prequalifying boats over the phone. Long-distance phone bills are cheap at twice the price, saving time, aggravation, and travel expenses. Knowledgeable yacht brokers can save you legwork, too.

Buying New

Once you become set in your cruising ways, production yards will generally hold little interest for you. Few production boats make first-class offshore cruising vessels, despite marketing hot air to the contrary. And what the average yacht dealer knows about cruising isn't much. You'll soon discover your research has made you a comparative expert, and communication with salespeople, particularly about blue-water cruising, will be somewhat one-sided. What's more, some dealers purposely hire staff with minimal knowledge of boats. The rationale is that the less a salesperson knows about the product, the less he will have to apologize for.

If you decide to buy production, pick a local manufacturer so you can rubberneck the vessel's evolution. This might give you the opportunity to input a few ideas to create a semicustom boat. Being on the spot also gives you some control in case things begin to look a little too recreational for your liking. When you are offshore, it's comforting to know how a hull was built, whether a keel is full of lead or polyester resin, and whether the deck is joined to the hull with pop rivets or bolts. It's also comforting to know how the bulkheads are attached, where the wiring goes, what the chainplates are bolted to, what's inside the rudder skin, and whether the rigging is one size larger than it needs to be. A vessel built without your attention will always be a question mark.

Some of the saltiest looking production cruising yachts are built where labor is cheap. Trouble is, you pay peanuts and get monkeys. A boat can look the part perfectly, yet her beauty may only be skin deep. Some trusty-looking craft out of Taiwan, for example, sail lethargically, are a plumber's nightmare, and appear to have been wired by workers wearing blindfolds. Hardware is sometimes jerry-built locally; rigging may be swaged ham-fistedly. This does not imply that good boats can't be built in places like Taiwan; just be careful which yard you choose. Better yet, go over there to oversee construction personally.

The U.S., Canada, England, Scandinavia, the Netherlands, France, New Zealand, and Australia produce yachts of world-class quality. The cream of production yards in these countries may not cost you much more than a dubious bargain in the long run—resale value may square the account. Meanwhile, you've owned something you trust.

A custom vessel built to your exact specifications lets you input ideas and monitor progress to your heart's content. During construction, you have a chance to meet with your builder every day, if you wish, to hash out last-minute brainstorms. A good builder and a knowledgeable customer can form a close relationship, each benefiting from the other's experience. Before commissioning a project, do your homework. The more you know of the boat's features and systems and construction details, the more you'll be able to shape the boat to your needs. Homework saves a lot of false starts and wrong turns, too.

Naturally, a custom vessel is the most expensive way to go. But you get what you pay for. It's hardly economical for a production yard to build boats to offshore specifications for the recreational marketplace.

Building Your Own Boat

If you are good with your hands you can build your own boat at home. By doing so you'd save up to half the cash outlay of a new custom boat. Commercial yards have overheads—facilities and equipment to maintain, developmental costs, wages, and taxes, to name a few—which you won't have much of. And a yard must make a financial profit to stay in business. You are interested in another kind of profit. But wait! There's another side to the story.

Home builders face a few equalizers. One is time, which, as is often said, is money. Building and outfitting a good cruising boat singlehandedly takes years. If you plan to hold down a job and build the boat in your spare time, tack a few more years onto the project. Amateurs should also add their lost income while building to the overall cost, since lost revenue affects your balance sheet just as spending does. The financial benefit of home building is not so much monetary savings in real terms, as is sometimes thought, but the ability to pay the piper bit by bit over a period of years.

Time throws another wrench in the gears—inflation. During a four-year project, the price of materials and hardware may double. This must be plugged into cost projections. Figure on spending twice what you originally predicted, anyway. That's right—double your predictions. Otherwise, your bank manager may declare you *persona non grata* long before the mast is stepped.

Commercial yards buy in quantity and save on materials; you, as an amateur, will probably pay more. And commercial yards have a think tank and labor pool for problem solving and two-person tasks. You'll work in a partial vacuum, and an extra pair of hands won't always be available when you need it. Still, your standard of workmanship could exceed anything in the commercial sector for one reason: you care more.

Most amateur builders base their projects on commercial hulls or hull/deck combinations. This saves about a year. Building a one-off hull from scratch is extremely labor intensive. Unless you are dead keen, skip this part of it.

It takes a professional approach to build a good boat. The project should be set up as if a dozen boats were going to be built instead of one. Do not cut corners on machinery, tools, work areas, stairs, scaffolding, lighting, heating, ventilation, weather protection, and so forth. In the end, you can sell your surplus equipment; in the meantime, a well-equipped shop and pleasant working conditions more than pay for themselves in increased productivity, superior craftsmanship, and on-the-job safety.

Arrange the project as if you mean business, because you will be in business. Half an amateur builder's energies are expended on the telephone sourcing materials and equipment or in the car chasing after them. You'll need to be a diplomat, too. Cajoling goods out of wholesalers, sweet-talking tradesmen to put your little job first, and buttering up supply clerks to move paper faster are all part of the game. Good personal relations with your suppliers is important: they sell truckloads while you are after mere handfuls. Often, the only incentive they'll have to deal with you is a personal one. Building boats is not all cutting wood. Not by a long shot.

If you hanker to be an amateur builder, examine your motives. You are headed for grief if your primary motivation is economy. Only the best materials, the best equipment, and the best craftsmanship produce decent oceangoing boats. If your motives center around the love of work, the excitement of the challenge, and the desire to create an outstanding vessel that's as good or better than the pros can build—and you accept that it will cost you a small fortune—you're headed in the right direction. Amateur building is a creative experience, a gratifying achievement, and a sound investment if, and only if, you go into it with your eyes open. Otherwise, it'll be a fiasco.

Keep in mind the principle of investment reality. Cutting corners to save a few thousand dollars can bleed joy from your cruising life and ultimately cost you tens of thousands in resale value. Your financial and personal interests are best served by taking the long view.

CHOICE OF MATERIALS

The basic material options for an oceangoing cruising vessel are ferrocement, wood, steel, and GRP. Generally speaking, the weight-saving benefits of aluminum are not cost effective for family cruising boats under 50 feet. And exotics such as carbon fiber and Kevlar/epoxy composite laminates are not cost effective—period.

Material choice is grist for interesting armchair arguments. Personal prejudice stems largely from familiarity: a cabinetmaker turned sailor naturally favors wood, a boilermaker leans to steel, and many people who've owned recreational craft feel comfortable with GRP.

However, material choice has practical considerations with far-reaching consequences, particularly for the home builder. It pays to accept that an excellent vessel can be built from any of the basic mediums. A cruising boat's merit—structurally, aesthetically, and in terms of performance—is determined by the quality of construction materials, design, craftsmanship, and fittings and equipment, not by material type. The basic materials all require about the same expertise to craft, too. And similar one-off vessels of each material all cost about the same to build. In boatbuilding, you won't get blood from turnips.

Since cost and craftsmanship are constants, regardless of construction materials, other factors have a greater impact on choice. As a businessperson, you require optimum liquidation value versus invested capital; as a sailor, you need materials that stand up to the harsh marine environment for an untroubled cruising lifestyle.

Ferrocement

Scores of dreamers have been led down the garden path by propaganda inferring ferrocement somehow compensates for a lack of funds and/or skill. Many amateur-built boats suffer from internal hull corrosion, poor hull fairing and finish adhesion, and dangerous structural inadequacies. Loads on anchor windlasses in severe circumstances have been known to tear foredecks clean off amateur-built cement boats, and love taps from docks have punched cement right out of the mesh, leaving a hole a cat could crawl through.

The weight of hull/deck structures versus ballast density, mass, and position below the waterline has, in many abortive creations, produced boats that fall over on their sides under sail.

Frugal attitudes too often associated with backyard cementworks encourage the use of hardware, equipment, and fittings that are more agricultural than marine.

Setting up hull- and deck-reinforcing rod and mesh is a laborious epic. It can take a year for an amateur to get the hulk ready to plaster. The question is: how much money could the home builder make in the work force in the meantime? Enough to buy a commercial hull and deck of another material? Could be. And what about engines, winches, radios, masts, rigging, sails, stoves, outboards, sextants, and settee cushions? These cannot be made of ferrocement; they take hard cash. It's a pipe dream to think of ferrocement as a money saver.

Without doubt, professional yards and accomplished amateurs turn out quality yachts that compete favorably with boats built of other materials. Unfortunately, this is not relevant—the derelicts inflicted on the marketplace cripple the financial worth of every single ferrocement boat in the world, even those fully deserving to be called goldplaters. The medium quite simply has a terrible reputation.

All in all, building or buying a ferrocement yacht is a sure way to catch financial leprosy. As a businessperson, you can't afford it. As a sailor, you can do better.

Wood

Modern epoxies have revolutionized wooden boatbuilding. The traditional planked boats with bulky frames have given way to tighter structures built by the cold-molded, laminated process, an ideal way to construct one-off cruising yachts. One popular method, particularly outside the United States, uses thin, wide planks (⁵⁄₁₆- to ⅜-inch thick by four to six inches wide) in lieu of thinner veneers, which suits amateur builders perfectly. The planks are epoxy glued in one fore-and-aft and several diagonal layers over temporary and permanent frames. Conventional plywood decks and bulkheads and a network of laminated frames and stringers complete the structure. An outer skin of epoxy/ fiberglass and an inner epoxy sealing coat protect the wood from moisture.

Vessels constructed intelligently by this technique can be stiff, strong, lasting, and beautiful. This method, and its variations using thinner veneers, has a fine reputation, too, ensuring good resale value.

There is a temptation in some quarters to compromise overall strength for cruising purposes, because the more ordinary epoxy/plank method is used to build racing boats, too. Sometimes they are planked with only two skins over a framework of flimsy bulkheads and mainly thin air in the quest for lightweight performance. Offshore, a boat built to these extremes is hazardous to your health. But this is a self-inflicted problem faced by the racing crowd, not a criticism of the process.

Keels commonly fitted to cold-molded yachts are bolt-on lead castings. Care must be taken to use massive floor timbers, some that taper all the way up to the gunwales, to spread keel loads far and wide. Better yet, fit ring frames to absorb rigging and keel loads. Short keel floors terminating at settee fronts introduce a dangerous line of shear in the hull skin.

Laminated timber yachts are particularly pleasing below decks, and the natural inner hull surfaces don't usually need additional finishing. Hulls have a degree of inbuilt insulation and sound deadening, and they are blessed with bone-dry bilges.

Lamination suits both professional and amateur builders. Since the hull is a labor-intensive part of any one-off vessel, it cuts costs when several builders share temporary frameworks or male molds.

One other point to bear in mind regarding lamination: in the event of serious hull damage, repair is complicated by the need to dissect painstakingly the laminated skin before replanking. Localized problems often require the replanking of huge areas.

Steel

Steel is best suited to commercial vessels, pleasure boats over 60 feet in length, or smaller pleasure craft intended for severe service (i.e., voyages into ice-infested waters). It can't be beat for strength or abrasion resistance, but long-term maintenance is bound to be hindered by the material's potential for corrosion and electrolysis. Although modern building, finishing, and electrolytical-control know-how has largely conquered maintenance problems, steel still requires more attention to stay shipshape over the years than do boats of equal quality made of GRP or timber/epoxy.

Many steel cruising boats under 50 feet built by casual amateurs lack finesse. Even though there are plenty of beautiful boats professionally crafted of steel, the cruising fraternity has seen its share of eyesores, and the majority is not sold on the medium. While this general prejudice is unfair to those using steel competently, it's inescapable that resale value will be affected by the more limited marketplace.

Unless you have a special application in mind that demands the use of steel, don't jump in with both feet. Although steel is enjoying a resurgence for cruising, as an investor and a sailor you can do better.

GRP

The best GRP boats are built by the old hand-layup method. Precise quantities of catalyst are mixed evenly in resin manually for controlled gel times and cure rates. Panels are carefully saturated and thoroughly hand squeegied to keep the resin content low for a high strength-to-weight ratio. "Kick-off" (when the resin begins to harden) is timed to occur just before leaching (when resin begins to drain from the glass, leaving white air pockets). Slow cures allow the maximum opportunity for natural and mechanical saturation and reduce heat buildup, thus minimizing air bubbles, shrinkage, and distortion. Bulkheads, internal frameworking, and the deck are built in place before the hull is released from the mold. This produces a true, cured hull/deck structure of the highest quality. Boats are rarely built this way anymore.

For maximum strength (with conventional materials), a laminate should have alternating layers of three-quarter-ounce chopped strand mat and 24-ounce woven roving. Mat absorbs excess resin more readily than roving does, hence the desirability of keeping mat content down. However, this rationale can be carried too far. Layers of roving contacting each other directly should be avoided; thin mat interlayers provide a superior physical bond.

Laminating technique influences susceptibility to osmosis, a term coined for water blisters growing in GRP hull skins. Osmosis is accelerated by tropical conditions. Many boats in temperate climates show little sign of trouble until they are exposed to warm water and hot weather. Waterlines are particularly vulnerable. The combination of repetitive immersion and heat from the sun aggravates the condition. Osmosis repair is labor intensive. Each blister must be ground away, filled, and then the entire surface refinished. In extreme cases, when blisters bite deep into the laminate, it takes major surgery with a grinder, then complete refiberglassing over the diseased area to build it back up to strength. There are few jobs so miserable.

Although slam-bang workmanship with chopper guns and catalyst injection systems contributes to osmosis-prone, hygroscopic laminates, the industry at large cannot afford to admit it. Sometimes they don't have to, either. Problems often arise thousands of miles away from the boatyard. For example, osmosis-prone boats built in the U.S. that subsequently catch the pox in the tropics are often repaired in New Zealand or Australia, and builders in the U.S. are not held accountable. Some of the best production cruising boat manufacturers (in their lights, that is) build hulls that attract the pox like bees to nectar. Ask other owners about this before committing yourself.

Osmosis protection is straightforward if a yard cares to take the trouble. Underbodies are degreased, sanded, and sealed with epoxy resin before antifouling; topsides are painted with two-part polyurethanes. This seals out water. Traditional gelcoat finishes are porous and invite water into substandard laminates.

GRP has tremendous tensile strength and relatively poor stiffness. Thin laminates without proper internal support are flexible. Core materials such as PVC foam or end-grain balsa are sometimes used to increase stiffness. It has become generally accepted that a cored GRP hull is superior to a noncored hull. On paper and in testing laboratories, this is true; in the field, with conventional materials, not necessarily.

Poorly built or badly engineered cored hulls are subject to delamination from impact and stress. Once the outer fiberglass skin is breached by abrasion, strain, or impact, the core (and hence the hull) can fail catastrophically. Whenever the advantages of a core material (stiffness and insulation) are made secondary to expediency, there is cause for concern. Cored hulls are also more complicated to bore for bolts and through-hulls. The core material must be cut out around each hole and replaced with solid material, or the area will crush when a fastener is tightened. Water can infiltrate a sandwich skin around bolts and fittings, too. Turning out a quality cored hull requires a great deal of expertise. When weight saving is not a high priority, a stout, solid GRP hull will suit cruising use and abuse more reliably—the most robust core is GRP itself.

GRP is an ideal material so long as the builder knows what he or she is doing. Craftsmanship is the name of the game. Good fiberglass work ensures low maintenance, high strength, excellent long-term appearance, simple electrolytical control, and no worries about corrosion or rot (osmosis aside). These attributes are hard to beat in an offshore boat, hence the medium's wide popularity and high resale potential.

CRUISING YACHT DESIGN

A yacht costs about the same to build, size for size, whether she's designed as a dog or a thoroughbred. An outstanding design by a respected architect is well worth the price and is fairly insignificant as a percentage of overall cost. This is of particular relevance to one-off, custom-built, and home-built vessels that stand alone in the marketplace. They depend on three things to command good prices: high-quality materials and equipment, craftsmanship, and design credibility.

But let the buyer beware! Just because a yacht designer has made waves in the cruising arena does not guarantee his or her understanding of the life. Design popularity and offshore practicality don't always go hand in hand. No advertising, however optimistic or aggressive, can ever tame the sea or conjure comfort from a sow's ear.

BEWARE OF THE IOR (INTERNATIONAL OFFSHORE RULE)

Racing boats cross oceans regularly. But let's not be impressed! People have made ocean passages in U-boats, lifeboats, life rafts, balsa rafts, rowboats, and 12-foot sloops. Indeed, the English Channel and other large bodies of water have been spanned by swimmers, using no boat at all. Yet these same bodies of water can sink boats. Ocean-crossing potential per se is no recommendation—when conditions are favorable, almost anything that floats can cross an ocean. Your comfort and welfare rely on dead certainty, not potential.

A casual glance reveals obvious differences between a Formula One racing machine and a family car. An IOR racer and an ocean-cruising boat are at opposite ends of the spectrum, too, although the reasons are not quite as obvious. Factors contributing to good cruising design are most easily appreciated by taking the negative approach, that is, by concentrating on things to avoid. Then good features stand out.

Design and Strength

Shape has a lot to do with strength. Curves and gradual transitions are geometrically stronger than flatter surfaces and sharper angles, construction being equal. As a result, IOR boats with flat topsides forward and fin keels are more structurally vulnerable. Short fin keels bolted to flat bottoms impose a highly stressed hinge point on a small area. Cruising boats with geometrically stronger topsides and more deadrise, especially near the bow, take the sea more gently, pounding less viciously. Longer cruising keels with some curve at the garboard sections (transition between keel and hull) dissipate loads better, reducing localized strains. This is one reason racing boats are built of expensive, exotic materials: they have to be to hang together.

Hull Profile

Today's racing boats are designed with high-aspect fin keels and spade rudders (or rudders with minimal skegs). This serves to improve windward performance, reduce wetted surface area for maximum speed, and enhance agility around buoys.

While performance cannot be ignored for cruising purposes, such extremes in profile are detrimental to security and comfort. IOR boats often handle like a basket of snakes off the wind in a big seaway. Directional stability is further compromised when boats are built with asymmetrical waterline planes (pinched bows and wide afterbodies). When these boats heel hard over, they yearn to round up into the wind. Neither a shorthanded cruising crew nor an automatic steering setup can live with such squirrely behavior.

In heavy weather, a modern racing boat can be a menace; its slippery, light-displacement shape actually becomes a liability. These boats are difficult to slow down when running before a gale, even under bare poles, leaving the door open to pitchpoling, broaching, or screaming onto a lee shore. Heaved-to, they place their crews in hazard. They are easily knocked down, slower to recover, and have a higher degree of inverted stability. Light, flimsy construction (some racing boats have actually been built with *no-step* areas on deck and have been taken offshore—some haven't come back!) combined with vulnerable geometric shape invites disintegration.

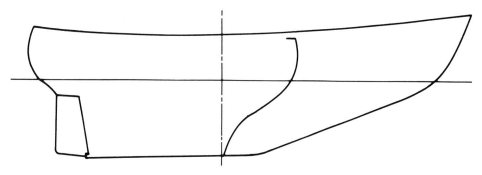

Typical heavy-displacement profile. The displacement-length ratio (D/L) of this hull type is commonly between 325 and 375. Full keels and slack bilges offer maximum underwater volume relative to length. This configuration is often unavoidable on long-distance voyages with vessels less than 40 feet long, when load carrying is critical and outright speed secondary. The design encourages bulletproof construction and docile handling offshore. Courtesy of Marine Design Services.

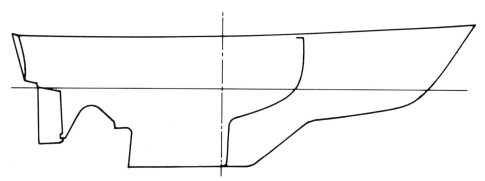

Typical medium-displacement profile—D/L's commonly between 250 and 300. Cutaway forefoot and skeg rudder reduce wetted surface and aid maneuvering. Flatter sections reduce the loss of underwater volume relative to heavier-displacement hulls. Suits long-distance cruising boats over 40 feet, where longer waterlines aid load carrying. Keel length is ample for taking the ground. Offshore handling is good. Design contributes to strong construction. Courtesy of Marine Design Services.

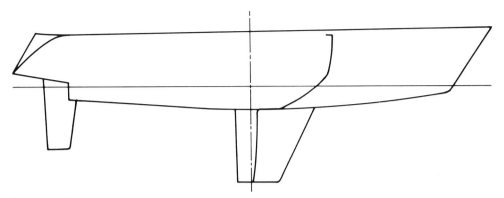

Typical light-displacement IOR profile with a D/L of around 180. High-aspect fin keels and spade rudders have a record of structural unreliability. Note flat bottom and hard keel hinge point. Also, note odd-shaped section for beating measurement rule. Load-carrying ability is nil, and handling offshore may be erratic. Profiles like this are not for cruising. Courtesy of Marine Design Services.

In practical terms, fin keel profiles don't suit cruising, anyway. They are tricky to haul out on anything but a Travelift. Collisions with Mother Earth are not taken lightly—the leading edges of fin keels are more nearly vertical, contributing to harsher impact. Longer keels tend to ride up over an obstruction, cushioning the shock, and impact loads are distributed over a wider area by design. A fin keel is more readily jammed between a rock and a hard spot, making extrication difficult.

Cantilevered rudders are more vulnerable to structural failure offshore even when they are well engineered, and being out in the open, are more likely to be damaged by an obstruction or while up on the bricks. Rudders hung on the backs of longer keels enjoy solid support and better protection. If the rudder's lower edge is located a few inches above the keel's shoe and angled slightly upward from the hinge point, it's unlikely to be touched by grounding.

Conversely, full-length keels have drawbacks. Namely, increased wetted surface causing more drag and, in some designs with a deep forefoot, ponderous maneuverability. Long keels combined with shallow draft reduce windward performance to wishful thinking, and excessive leeway on all points of sail except a dead run becomes the norm. Such compromises in performance are unacceptable for ocean travel.

When it comes to cruising, advocates of extremes, like most fanatics, miss the point. Sensible offshore boats for safe family sailing are middle-of-the-road craft, shying away from extremes—any extremes. The problem with single-purpose vessels like those spawned by the IOR is that they are designed to do one thing brilliantly and, as a result, do too many other things badly.

A cruising boat must do everything at least satisfactorily, and nothing badly.

Spade rudders continually try to bend and break their rud-
der shafts, and they sometimes succeed. Structurally speak-
ing, these rudders have all their eggs in one basket. Rud-
ders hung on keels or skegs with gudgeons and pintles are
more trustworthy, since the rudder shafts are under torque
load only.

Skeg rudders, although potentially super-
ior to spade rudders by design, must be
intelligently engineered and constructed.
Note stress cracks where this skeg joins
the hull, a sign the skeg is working. This
can lead to catastrophic failure far from
home.

Hull Shape

Racing boats have straight entries with low angles of attack offering less reserve
buoyancy than their fuller, more flared (or flammed) cruising counterparts. This
lets them cut deeper through waves rather than waste time riding over them. But

pinched IOR foredecks are wetter and offer poor work areas for family cruising. Dagger-like bows greatly restrict accommodation below decks, too.

Although the flat after sections of IOR-influenced boats cause less drag at high speed, this tends to be academic on a cruising boat; shorthanded crews usually lack the stamina to continually push a boat to her potential anyway. Besides, a cruising boat is likely to be too heavy to attain surfing speeds, so there's no sense designing them to do so. At anchor, flatter aft sections slap and pound in a chop, annoying the crew and the neighbors. A small thing, maybe—unless you have to live with it.

In a nutshell, cruising design should still recognize a seakindly shape, geometric strength, and cruising reality, not arbitrary rules for racing ratings. At the same time, cruising should not be held back by nostalgia and convention when the technology exists that encourages more efficient yet safe designs.

CRUISING DISPLACEMENT

Boats cost by the pound, not so much by the foot. Production yards compete in the marketplace by keeping weight down to a minimum, which suits weekenders and casual racers, hence the racer/cruiser. However, an extended-cruise vessel fitted out for self-sufficiency and maximum comfort must be heavier. A comfortable lifestyle depends on all kinds of things that weigh plenty—and they all add up.

Almost without exception, stock-designed so-called cruising boats head offshore riding lower in the water than they did on the drawing board. And the lower a boat's designed displacement-to-length ratio (D/L), the more overburdened she becomes in extended cruising trim. Why? Here's a sampling of things found on a long-range boat, and the approximate weights involved.

Books (reference, navigation, school texts, paperbacks, periodicals)	500 lbs.
A year's supply of canned goods, beverages, and general provisions	2,500 lbs.
Crew's total personal effects (clothing, hobby equipment, sports equipment, sewing machine, typewriter, stationery, whatever)	1,000 lbs.
Extra gear for extended cruising beyond that fitted for local sailing (another dinghy, bigger outboard, additional line, more anchor chain and anchors, bigger winches, roller furling, bigger windlass, awnings, extra tools, spares, etc.)	2,000 lbs.
Extra fuel and water tankage for remote cruising. Extra battery and generation capabilities	2,000 lbs.
Total	8,000 lbs.

Four tons later, the list goes on. But enough. Now for a gut feeling about the wet weight of various 40-footers:

Ultralight displacement racer	less than 10,000 lbs.
IOR two-ton racer	16,000 lbs.
Typical racer/cruiser	18,000 - 22,000 lbs.
Medium-displacement cruising yacht	26,000 lbs.
Medium-to-heavy displacement cruiser	30,000 lbs.
Very heavy displacement cruiser	36,000 lbs.

It doesn't take a computer to see which boats will be most affected by three or four tons of extra cruising gear.

For you number crunchers, the D/L ratio is computed by taking the weight of a boat in long tons (2,240 pounds) and dividing it by ten percent of the waterline length in feet, cubed. Boats with a D/L under 100 are considered ultralight; under 200, light; under 300, medium; over 300, heavy. Thus, if we pick the above 26,000-pound 40-footer and assign it a waterline length of 35 feet, its D/L is 271. This is fine as far as it goes, but don't get bogged down by a coarse classification. There are overlaps and shades of gray.

Compromises you'll face on too light a boat are: quicker motion at anchor and at sea (hull design affects motion, too, incidentally); less hull volume per foot, particularly at and below the cabin-sole level; reduced cabin-sole area, notably toward the bow; reduced load-carrying potential (less water and fuel, provisions, equipment, appliances, personal possessions, and sporting and hobby gear); and more difficulty building in a generous structural safety margin (in extremes, weight saving versus brute strength is a conflict of interest unless expensive exotic materials are used). Cruising safety, particularly in less predictable tropical lagoons, is compromised on boats without the displacement to carry all-chain rode, a variety of heavy anchors, and a wealth of laborsaving equipment.

On the other side of the coin, very heavy displacement boats have disadvantages, although of a different nature. They are more expensive to build per foot, less maneuverable in tight quarters (as mentioned), and generally slower for passagemaking.

I think you see the trade-offs. Simply put, light boats give away comfort and sometimes a margin of safety for a variety of reasons, and there's the possibility your quality of life will suffer—all in the name of performance. Conversely, heavier boats give away performance and maneuverability and construction economy for the prospect of longer life at anchor.

The displacement dilemma is solved by letting a vessel's form follow its function. A boat should displace enough to pack the lifestyle of your choice for the duration and yet be light enough to perform competently as a wind-driven machine. Extremes in displacement, too light or too heavy, should be avoided for cruising (although a bias toward lighter boats for local cruising is sensible, and a

Dolphin Queen *on the way to the water. Designed for seakindliness, massive load carrying, and brute strength, she provided a safe, comfortable lifestyle in remote cruising areas. LOA 52 feet; LOD 45 feet; LWL 39 feet; beam 13 feet 2 inches; draft 7 feet 2 inches; displacement 48,000 pounds (D/L 360). A handful to maneuver in the marina at times, but a pleasure to live on all the time.*

leaning toward heavier displacement is often inevitable for long-distance travel, particularly with shorter vessels).

Here's one more thing to chew on. Many things stowed or bolted aboard ship for extended cruising are constants in the weight equation. You'll want them aboard, regardless of your boat's size or design. Since boats cost by the pound, it could be to your advantage, for example, to build or buy a medium- or medium/heavy-displacement 40-footer rather than a very heavy 35-footer (or a medium or medium/heavy 45-footer versus a heavier 40-footer, as the case may be). Although both designs would carry the weight of your lifestyle equally well and cost similarly, the longer boat will likely be more spacious and will perform better. This is another reason why cruising boat length has increased over the years. Blue-water people want comfort *and* a degree of performance these days, and only longer vessels can supply both.

BALLAST/DISPLACEMENT RATIOS

There is nothing like sailing a boat that stands up to Mother Nature. And there's nothing so uncomfortable as sailing on your ear. Maybe a buried rail is a blast on a Sunday frolic, but the fun wears thin in everyday life. Sleeping, walking around, cooking, eating, going to the head—you name it—become onerous. Changing sails on a wet, seemingly vertical foredeck won't be family fun hundreds of miles offshore on a dark night, either. Nor is wrestling the helm a jolly pastime at high angles of heel (heeling usually increases weather helm).

Not only does stiffness give more comfort offshore, a stiff boat is likely to be drier and faster, too. Extreme heeling angles don't necessarily mean higher speeds; it just seems that way, because heeling is damned hairy. A stiff boat is appreciated at anchor, too—she'll stand up in squally weather.

A cruising boat is most comfortable if she is designed to sail hard on the wind at 15 and never more than 20 degrees of heel before she requires reefing. Off the wind, she shouldn't lean over more than 10 to 15 degrees before reefing (rolling excepted). Stiffness provides a more level habitat and work platform, and importantly, it reduces roll arc, which minimizes the sensation of rolling.

Cruising stiffness relies to some extent on high ballast-to-displacement ratios, usually at least 40 and perhaps 45 percent (computed with the boat laden, not ex-factory). Less, and the boat is liable to have round heels, other factors being equal. But ballast/displacement ratios in themselves are meaningless unless the center of gravity of the vessel as a whole is considered in relation to the center of buoyancy. And a sailboat's center of gravity depends a lot on where the center of gravity of the ballast is located, not just ballast mass per se. This strengthens the case for longer keels: the ballast's center of gravity can be positioned lower than is possible with a fin keel boat of equal draft. Deep draft gives the ballast a chance for more leverage yet, contributing greatly to overall stiffness and powerful knockdown recovery. And deep draft is an important contributing factor in windward performance.

Although racing boats and racer/cruisers depend quite a lot on form stability to resist initial heeling, an offshore cruising vessel should place less emphasis on it. Form stability won't snap a boat upright after a knockdown like a load of ballast down where it counts. A boat depending more on form stability and less on ballast will sooner or later get her mast wet offshore.

Interestingly, adequate stiffness for cruising encourages medium to heavy displacements, because a boat must be able to carry both her cargo and her ballast. Some production boats are too tender in cruising trim, because their ballast is lessened, as a percent of overall displacement, once they are laden. And, if ballast is reduced during construction to provide better load carrying, it's borrowing from Peter to pay Paul. This, in conjunction with shallow draft, makes boats pushovers.

THE RIG

Sailplan

For simplicity, economy, and optimum performance, any boat under 50 or 55 feet should have but one mast. A mizzen is an unnecessary expense that sometimes contributes more to windage than propulsion. It does allow a mizzen staysail to be flown and is a good place to mount radar. But radar can be mounted elsewhere, on a stern pylon or on a single mast, and if you have no mizzen staysail, you'll not miss it too much. For smaller boats, a schooner rig, although steeped with return-to-paradise nostalgia, is at its best on canvas over the mantlepiece at home. A schooner's worst point of sail is downwind. The large mainsail blocks the foretriangle, and reduced foretriangle height limits the area of downwind jibs.

Two-masted rigs of any configuration increase weight aloft, too, making a given boat more tender under sail. And two-masted vessels, all things being equal, don't point as high as they could with a single stick. Reasonable windward performance is critical when making landfalls against strong headwinds and sailing with land to leeward.

A cutter has practical advantages over a sloop. Sometimes a shorthanded crew is more interested in safety and conserving energy than in optimum boat speed, and quick, generous sail reduction fulfills this need. The jib or yankee can be doused and a smaller staysail quickly hoisted in its place. It's much easier to raise and lower sails than to unhank them and hank on replacements.

True cutters, as opposed to double-headed sloops, emphasize larger foretriangles by placing the mast farther aft. This allows more freedom for dinghy stowage, moves a considerable weight aft to make way for heavier ground tackle forward while preserving the boat's trim, moves a source of windage aft so the boat wanders less at anchor, and reduces the size of the mainsail—the sail shorthanded crews most love to hate. Shorter booms on cutters are safer to handle, too. And a mast closer to amidships is also closer to the cockpit, saving a step or two each time the crew visits it.

Cutter rigs have structural advantages, too. The mast may be located at maximum beam for a wider shroud base. The inner forestay gives the mast additional support, and whatever rigging backs up the inner forestay (running backstays, permanent intermediate backstays, or jumper struts and stays) lends further support.

The center of effort on cruising sailplans, regardless of configuration, should have a generous lead over the hull's center of lateral resistance, say between 15 and 18 percent. Lee helm is seldom a problem on a sailboat; it's weather helm that needs to be kept under control. Sailing a perfectly balanced boat is effortless for a crew or a self-steering setup.

The Mast

A mast is simply a column, and as such, works most reliably when asked to endure compression loads only. Fractional rigs force masts to bend outrageously, and anything that bends is closer to buckling. A masthead rig increases a mast's strength by helping it stay in column.

Double spreaders lend considerable support, too. One factor in a column's ability to withstand loads is the length of its unsupported panels. Reducing freestanding sections increases strength tremendously.

A mast secured by a deck *and* a step in the bilges has what's known in engineering terms as a *fixed end*, which helps it stay in column under

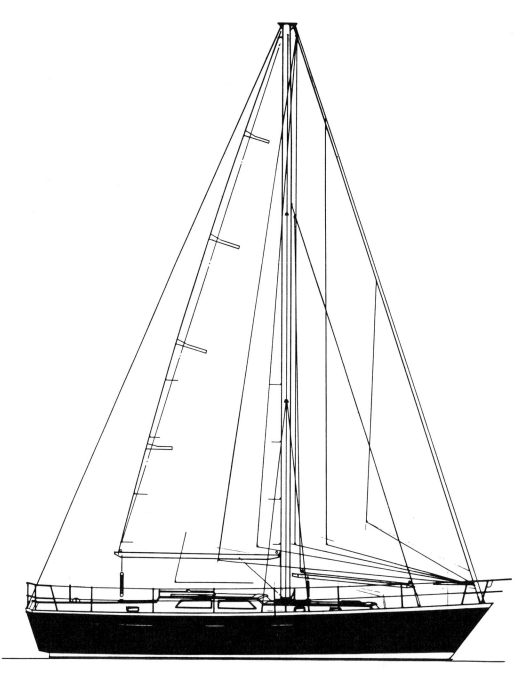

Well-proportioned cutter rigs offer cruising sailors flexibility and performance (see profile and layout of this boat on page 275). This design does away with intermediate backstays to counteract the forward pull of the inner forestay by using a stiffer mast section. When used, backstays should be fixed; running backstays are a complication best left to racing crews. Courtesy of Marine Design Services.

compression. Deck-stepped masts have no fixed end. Therefore, keel-stepped masts, configurations being equal, are inherently stronger. The advantages of stepping a mast on deck—watertight integrity, no rainwater invading bilges, increased spaciousness below decks—must be paid for by a larger mast section and slightly stronger standing rigging. However, it's a price worth paying if the benefits are important to you.

Obviously, a column's strength also depends a great deal on its sectional dimensions and wall thickness. For cruising, mast scantlings must be quite generous. A double-headed (cutter) rig with double spreaders should be matched by a spar of sufficient strength so that the loss of any single piece of standing rigging under normal sailing conditions leaves the mast intact. This is not as hard to engineer as it sounds, and it adds immeasurably to offshore reliability and peace of mind. A dismasting far from civilization can cost a packet, and it can stop a voyage in its track for months.

Standing Rigging

At the time of writing, a ketch had embarked from the east coast of New Zealand for Chile. Several hundred miles offshore, some shrouds came unglued from the mast. A crew member went aloft to try to fix the mess, at which time the vessel was dismasted, and he went overboard with the rig and became trapped underwater in the bosun's chair. He remained trapped beneath the sea for four long minutes while his shipmates struggled frantically to disentangle him. By the narrowest of margins, they wrestled him from his watery grave and resuscitated him. The voyage, of course, was aborted. While rigging your boat, keep this story in mind.

All standing rigging components must be stronger than the wire. Shroud chainplates should be stout enough to lift the boat. Fabricate mast tangs to sustain loads in excess of the breaking strength of the wire despite wear. Don't use racing gimmicks such as shroud fittings that hook in mast slots. Hang tangs on oversized bolts; beef up aluminum mast walls with welded bosses for increased bearing area.

Both ends of each piece of rigging must toggle on two axes to self-align. This eliminates side loads, which bend wire and/or components, contributing to metal fatigue and failure. Tang and chainplate angles must also align precisely with the wire. Tension loads on rigging are exactly opposite of those imposed on the mast, yet like the mast, they are best controlled when kept in line.

Terminal ends on standing rigging are potential weak links. Nicopress sleeves, although fine for other applications, are inferior for securing standing rigging. Wire is weakened by a tight radius around a thimble, and thimbles are not designed to withstand stresses imposed by a pin.

Proper swaged terminal ends, either forks or eyes, are a better bet for standing rigging, although they must be checked periodically for stress cracks. Don't trust

Beefy external chainplates are a simple, failsafe way to
anchor rigging. They also give the widest shroud base
for geometric strength. This one is attached with eight
half-inch stainless carriage bolts to a reinforced GPR
hull and bedded with Thiokol. No leaks, no worries.

Swaged fittings have been responsible for
many dismastings because of inexpert workmanship and internal corrosion. Can you see
the curve in the fitting to the right? A sign
somebody didn't know the score. This places
a bending load on the wire and the fitting,
inviting failure.

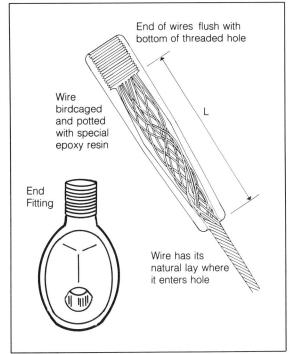

Castlok epoxy-filled sockets are reliable rigging fittings. The wire inside them is not stressed by compression or swaging. Internal corrosion is held in check (note sealing bead of epoxy acting as a water stop). This three-eighths-inch fitting has been tested over 10,000 offshore miles.

End of wires flush with bottom of threaded hole

L

Wire birdcaged and potted with special epoxy resin

End Fitting

Wire has its natural lay where it enters hole

Schematic of a Castlok fitting.

the job of swaging to just anyone, though. Go to a rigging shop certified by the government for commercial aircraft work. They know the score.

Terminal ends that hold wire without deforming or straining it are most reliable. This is accomplished two ways: by zinc-poured sockets or epoxy-filled sockets. The latter (manufactured under the trade name Castlok) are perhaps the perfect solution, particularly for home builders who wish to rig a boat themselves.

Those contemplating galvanized wire rope for standing rigging should examine their motives. Strength is not the issue, nor is fatigue resistance. Galvanized is better on both counts than stainless steel 1 x 19 wire, although stainless is 100 percent reliable when done right. The point is, galvanized wire and associated galvanized components need continual treatment against corrosion. And galvanized rigging lowers resale value. You can bet your boots a boat will fetch less with galvanized rigging—surely less than the additional cost of rigging with stainless and bronze in the first place.

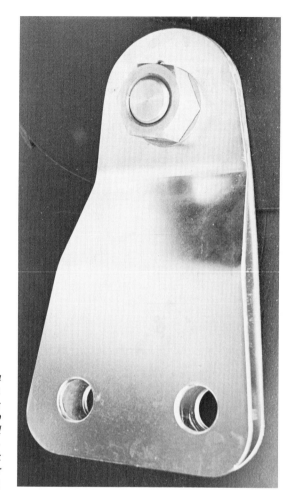

A lower shroud tang solidly bolted to a mast, the nut locked with a cotter pin. But double tangs have a disadvantage: under load, the bent piece is bound to stretch a little while the flat piece behind won't, throwing the pin out of perpendicular to the strain. It's better to use a thick single-piece tang and toggle forks, rather than toggle eyes and two-piece tangs.

ACCOMMODATION DESIGN

The foundations of comfort discussed earlier pertained mainly to accommodation layout—with one important exception. Although it's creative to invest your boat with your own brand of individualism, it pays to take the long view. Weird features and strange layouts cost dearly in resale value. Tens of thousands of dollars can go down the drain when a vessel deviates too far from accepted convention.

Make no mistake, there's plenty of room for creativity in achieving high levels of comfort. But creativity can be just as easily channeled to please a wide segment of the prospective marketplace as not. Unless you are wealthy and can afford to indulge yourself, always ask yourself how others will like your ideas.

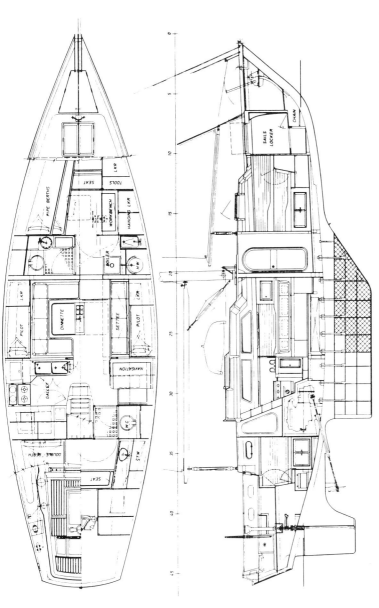

This substantial offshore cutter was designed for rounding Cape Horn (rig shown on page 270). Note the self-draining floor next to the companionway, the wet locker over the machinery space for drying gear by engine heat, the small toilet area aft, and the sink in the master stateroom. Although a single-purpose accommodation, the vessel has wide appeal. The workbench could be turned into a desk or a vanity; massive freezer and refrigeration space in the galley is always desirable; and the starboard upper in the saloon is easily converted to an entertainment center. Incidentally, the boat was built with a double berth forward instead of upper and lower pipe berths. Specs: LOA 45 feet 6 inches; LWL 36 feet; beam 13 feet 4 inches; draft 6 feet 2 inches; displacement 30,240 pounds (D/L 290). An ideal all-around cruising design. For more universal cruising service, the anchor windlass would be mounted on deck. Courtesy of Marine Design Services.

An example of how to turn a work area alongside the boom into a devil's playground. This kind of racing equipment hurts cruising safety.

CLEAR THE DECKS FOR ACTION

A stroll around the deck of a sailboat tells much about her designer or builder's affinity with the sea. Cruising boats must be designed and built specifically to be worked safely by their crews. Not all are—not by miles! When sailing conditions are gentle, helter-skelter deck layouts are just a nuisance; in adversity, nuisances can be killers.

Cruising safety and convenience are most important in four on-deck areas: the foredeck, the amidships space around the mast, the cockpit, and the afterdeck. These are action stations (which may someday become panic stations), where you handle sails, docklines, sheets, halyards, and anchor tackle.

KEEP HARDWARE OUT FROM UNDERFOOT

When a boat has just been decked, she presents, in many ways, the ideal platform for safety. No toe crunchers have been bolted down yet to slash and trip you in the night. Then outfitting begins, and safety is frequently forgotten in the clutter.

Often there's a conflict of interests: hardware needs to be positioned just so to do its job, or it's back to the drawing board. Since redesigning or rebuilding boats is out of the question, hardware sometimes gets nailed down, and to hell with it.

This block traveler is smack in the middle of the side deck. So are the chainplates and shrouds. Also, halyards led to a cockpit are no asset unless the vessel has roller furling so that singlehanded foredeck work is unnecessary. The vang tackle affixed to the base of the mast should be led to the railcap as a boom preventer instead, to control the boom off the wind better.

Put Vents in Their Place

Vents mustn't sprout on deck haphazardly like mushrooms. Define your work areas early in construction and make them off limits to ventilators, particularly the low-profile vents that are hard to spot at night. Place vents adjacent to deck boxes, dinghies, cabins—anywhere they fit snugly and safely out of the way yet scoop air efficiently.

Watch Out for Block Travelers

Tracks bolted on deck for headsail-sheet adjustment have no place on cruising boats; they are dangerous obstacles. Those lurking in confined quarters between the cabin sides and the railcap are accidents waiting for victims.

Sheet blocks fixed to cars sliding on tracks are a racing gimmick. With a bit of ingenuity in the sail loft, a cruising vessel can usually do without. Each foresail can be cut so its sheet leads to a fixed point. The same applies to sails bent on an inner forestay. Then a single block serving each stay can be positioned during sea trials and permanently fixed at the railcap, not inboard on deck if you can help it. Sometimes a railcap block limits a staysail's angle of attack when the boat is closehauled and an inboard block cannot be avoided. See if you can design the rig and the boat so the sheet leads to the cabintop instead of the deck.

Headsails sheeted to fixed blocks can be fine tuned by adjusting tack height. This alters sheet-lead angle. Once a sail's set up, you'll seldom have to fiddle with it. On a cruising boat, there's no sense having deck-hugging sails such as the racing crowd has. Your sails can be cut for visibility and practicality, not other people's rules. If your sailmaker and/or yacht designer can't help you eliminate a track, at least try to mount the menace where it interferes least with pedestrian traffic.

Downwind Poles

At night offshore, tippytoeing over poles chocked on deck is like walking blindfolded through a junkyard during an earthquake. Many sailors on larger boats refuse to subject their families to the dangers of handling big poles in tough, offshore conditions, preferring to jibe downwind, taking the wind comfortably on the quarter instead. However, if downwind poles are going to be included in your ship's inventory, secure them parallel alongside the mast or attach one end up the mast near the spreaders and the lower end to the railcap near the forward lower shroud. The slight added windage of vertically stowed poles is a small price to pay for greatly improved deck spaces. And you'll be saved the hassle and possible risk of injury when shifting them into position for use. The poles will be ready to go.

Anchors Away

Anchors chocked in the middle of foredeck work areas are a hazard. Yet such an arrangement is seen by some as seamanlike; the anchor *is* positioned where it's handy for use, right? But what is seamanlike on a recreational powerboat can be landlubberly on an offshore yacht. Powerboaters don't have to worry about sailhandling on their foredecks.

Invent homes for your anchors that keep your clear deck spaces sacred. Instead of placing anchors *close* to the action, it's better to chock them *ready* for action on a bow roller with their rodes attached. It's hard to beat two CQRs side by side at the stemhead (or alongside a bowsprit). Spare and auxiliary anchors can be secured vertically off the decks at the rail near where they are needed or stowed out from underfoot in deck lockers. Better yet, space your deck boxes off the deck so anchors stow beneath them.

Deck Camber

A safe action station requires a level footing. Excessive deck camber makes life difficult, particularly when the boat is rolling or heeling with wet decks and the crew has to work to leeward of the boat's centerline.

Camber serves two purposes: it increases a structure's strength geometrically, and it increases standing headroom below. Light-displacement racer/cruisers resort to rounder decks because they lack hull volume below the waterline for headroom, and they are built lighter and need more camber for stiffness. Due to hull-volume limitations, racer/cruisers seldom have the vertical clearance for proper deck beams, either, furthering the need for increased deck camber. A cruising yacht with three or four inches to spare for honest deck beams can structurally afford fairly flat decks, say a six-inch rise to 12 feet of beam.

Amidships work areas around the mast are on the cabintop, flush-deckers excepted. Cabintops often have more exaggerated camber than decks for reasons of headroom and strength. Like decks, flatter cabintops are easier to walk and work on. More critically, cabintop work areas are higher off the water than decks, and when the vessel rolls at sea, the motion is felt more keenly by the crew.

Although commonplace, excessive camber is a trend blue-water sailors should resist.

A Nonskid Surface

A reasonably flat deck (so far as structural considerations permit) free of impediments still won't be safe if the surface is like a skating rink. There are several good ways to texture a deck for a secure footing. Traditionally, sand is mixed with deck paint, producing a gritty, nonskid finish that grips bare feet and seaboots alike. But sand is cuttingly abrasive to foul-weather gear and sails.

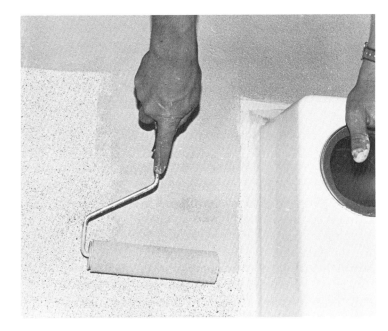

Coarse sand is sprinkled on a fresh underlayer of deck paint and the excess grit swept off after drying. A top coat or two completes the job for a nonskid surface that works.

Bonded nonskid sheeting makes a neat and effective deck surface.

Alternatively, organic substances such as crushed walnut shells can be mixed with paint. This produces a textured surface nearly as effective as sand, though not so long-lasting, without the harmful abrasive qualities. Organic nonskid decks should be resurfaced every year on a boat in constant service.

Coarse salt can be sprinkled on wet paint, then flushed with water after the paint dries. The salt dissolves, leaving pits and peaks that resist slipping and sliding. When the deck becomes a bit slick after a season's use, the process is repeated.

Prefabricated nonskid sheets can be bonded to the decks, too. They are attractive and effective in wet and lively conditions.

However you go about it, nonskid decks shouldn't feel like a gravel logging road. Just the contrary. Rough nonskid surfaces are difficult to scrub clean and hard on the knees. It's the sharpness of the nonskid substance that creates the friction, not so much the size.

Teak decks are considered by some as the ultimate for cruising. But they can be more slippery than a grit-in-paint finish; they are darker than a painted deck needs to be, which raises cabin temperatures in hot weather; they need wetting down daily to stay in shape; they require recaulking periodically; and they are tricky to lay over the primary decking material without causing leaks, rot, and/or corrosion. Teak is also less resistant to oil and fuel stains, etc. And teak decks are expensive and add unnecessary weight to a boat.

Mass-produced yachts built of GRP often have "nonskid" texturing molded into the deck gelcoat. Almost without exception, a molded nonskid deck offers poor or nonexistent purchase to feet in wet conditions. When making a mold, the pattern on the plug (mockup) is treated with mold-release agents, either wax and/or spray-on PVA, so the mold doesn't stick. Once the mold is put into service, the process is repeated to release each deck. Often, nonskid is polished with a cutting agent to reduce further the likelihood of the deck bonding to the mold. Each time the nonskid pattern is fooled with, it becomes microscopically smoother. Older molds suffer wear and damage to the nonskid pattern, too, and surfaces get slicker yet.

Gelcoat is a relatively soft substance, prone to rapid wear in daily service, and any marginal nonskid properties will be shortlived, anyway. Warm-weather sailors are most affected by slippery decks. Bare feet just don't grip wet decks as boat shoes do.

For offshore safety (or harbor safety, for that matter) a GRP-molded nonskid deck should be resurfaced. Sand it, degrease it, and apply a compatible deck finish such as two-part epoxy or polyurethane paint with a mixed-in nonskid compound.

The Vanishing Bulwarks

Fewer and fewer yachts are seen with shippy-looking bulwarks, the extension of the boat's topsides above the decks. They are formed by letting decks down in the hull or by fitting a false structure on top of the hull/deck joint. Bulwarks are becoming scarce because racer/cruisers rely on high topsides, along with considerable deck camber as previously mentioned, for minimal headroom. Since bulwarks visually add to freeboard, they go by the board. Eliminating bulwarks also saves money during construction.

Bulwarks serve many purposes, all of which improve the cruising life. They are a little fence between the deck and the sea, helping to halt sliding crew members and sails. When the boat heels, a bulwark provides a secure footing at the rail. They also keep wayward gear such as runaway winch handles from King Neptune's locker. The anodized aluminum extrusions you see bolted to racer/cruiser hull/deck joints are no substitute.

Without bulwarks, deck brackets are solely responsible for the vertical rigidity of stanchions. Stanchions supported this way are often insecure; it's a sure bet that a strong man could wander down to a marina and rip a truckload of them out by the roots—bare-handed! Bulwarks support stanchions by providing an elevated mounting surface for a secondary bracket. You can see the difference this makes yourself by holding a baseball bat vertically with one cupped hand and then using two hands spaced six or eight inches apart.

Bulwarks are also used for mounting mooring-line fairleads, and in some cases even mooring cleats, if strength permits. They are great for attaching boarding-ladder brackets, sheet-block and boom-preventer tangs, clips for a boathook, hooks for portlight eyebrows, padeyes to secure downwind poles, padeyes for stowed halyards, and so forth. All this stuff can be bolted down without drilling a single hole through the topsides that might cause a leak.

The Boom Gallows

Depending on a mainsheet and a topping lift to secure a boom when the mainsail is furled is asking for trouble. Leave that Mickey Mouse arrangement to the racing and recreational folks. Offshore, the boom must be firmly controlled every minute. The only way to hold a boom rigidly when it's out of service is by chocking it firmly in a gallows or horse.

Some aft-cockpit cruising boats have a gallows on the afterdeck near the boom's end. Trouble is, an afterdeck is an important work area and should be kept clear for docking, fishing, boarding when moored stern-to, and setting and retrieving stern anchors.

If possible, the gallows belongs on the cabintop, just forward or partially over the companionway hatch. Normally, this gives support to the boom about halfway along its length, which works fine. This way, the gallows is positioned forward of the helmsperson, who often assists striking the mainsail by working the mainsheet and helping guide the boom home. It's natural to face forward while doing this, rather than turn your back on the course you are steering and the person you're trying to help. A boom horse on the cabintop is also a handy thing to grab as you leave and return to the cockpit, and it's handy to rig a sailing awning from.

Center-cockpit vessels usually have an out-of-the-way place atop the aft cabin for the gallows. Yawls and ketches are not as lucky as sloops and cutters; horses for mizzens are not always feasible.

The Cockpit

Cockpits need unrestricted vision all around the compass for watchkeeping and plenty of swinging room for the helmsperson and crew to work the ship without scrambling all over one another.

Winches should be placed so they are close to hand for singlehanded sailing, handy to the helm, yet far enough apart so handles clear with knuckle room to spare and sheet cleats are easy to reach.

Full standing headroom off the cockpit sole must exist under the main boom—both under sail and when the boom is secured in the gallows. Offshore, in the event of an accidental jibe, a low boom is a widowmaker. In harbor, lack of headroom turns a boom into a daily headache.

Scuttle the Staysail Boom

A spar sweeping an important and sometimes precarious work area on the foredeck for the sake of tacking convenience under sail is a curious feature. Loose-footed staysails are safer and offer a superior airfoil for windward performance. It's also easier to use the inner forestay for heavy-weather sails with the loose-footed arrangement.

A staysail sheeted in normal headsail fashion disappears at anchor, where you spend most of your cruising life. A staysail boom does not disappear. It remains an ever-present fence on deck or another object to tie or stow out of the way.

A staysail boom is a menace at anchor or offshore; the self-tending advantage is not worth the trouble and danger. This foredeck is further compromised by chocking an anchor in the middle of the road. Larger running lights wouldn't hurt, either.

There is more than just a boom that clutters decks, too. The tackle and on-deck traveler confuse a foredeck as well.

If you have always sailed with a staysail boom, the safety and freedom you'll enjoy when you're rid of it could make you ask why it wasn't deep-sixed years ago. Besides, two extra sheet winches for controlling a loose-footed sail could be less expensive than the boom, its tackle, and the fittings.

Side Decks

The deck spaces between cabin sides and the railcaps are your sidewalks to and from the action stations. As such, they must never be dangerous bottlenecks in heavy weather. Wide side decks squeeze cabin sides closer together, reducing swinging room below decks. Because of this, side decks often feel the pinch on production boats—it's a compromise that puts minimal gains in below-decks comfort ahead of safety.

Side decks shouldn't be less than 20 inches wide; 24 to 30 inches is much more like it. Generous sidewalks not only contribute to offshore safety but also pave the way for pedestrians in harbor, such as boarding parties and shipmates lugging gear and supplies back and forth.

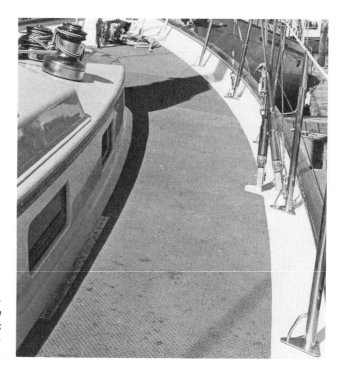

*A safe side deck is free of im-
pediments and wide enough to
walk on comfortably—virtues
that are created on the drawing board.*

Banish Inboard Shrouds

Racer/cruisers have flaunted inboard shrouds for years, and it's reached the point where these killjoys to offshore convenience and safety have become an established convention. This is tolerable if your only goal in life is to point higher than your competitors. But cruising has other priorities, namely unencumbered decks and a free work station around the mast.

At anchor, too, inboard shrouds are a pain in the neck. Maneuvering around them with an armload of groceries grows old fast. It's bad enough trying to get past them with your hands free.

Inboard shrouds place higher compression loads on the mast, geometrically. In turn, the shrouds themselves suffer greater tension, and wire, terminal fittings, chainplates, and toggles are all needlessly overworked. Like cancer, these strains spread to the vessel's structure. It's more difficult (in boatbuilding this means more expensive) to engineer and construct adequate strong points to back up inboard shrouds reliably with any peace of mind. Interior reinforcements for anchoring them interfere with below-decks accommodation, too, limiting design freedom for bulkhead placement.

Shrouds terminating outboard at the rail are opportune handholds where they are logically needed—between the deck and the sea. They help folks stay aboard, offer additional attachment points to secure lifelines, assist boarding parties from dinghies, support a tropical awning better, and importantly, are simple to anchor strongly to chainplates solidly bolted on the hull.

Mooring Cleats

Locate cleats so you won't stumble over them, yet so they are placed properly for the job. As a bare minimum, bolt a cleat on each side of the foredeck for bow lines and anchor snubbers, one to a side amidships for springlines and breast anchors (often omitted on production boats), and a pair astern. While this may sound like an army of cleats, it's only a starting point. On a cruise, there are times when a vessel is moored with a virtual cat's cradle of lines. And it's not handy to double up lines on a single cleat. The line underneath is always the one needing attention!

Undersized cleats are a perpetual pain in the backside. It might pay you to make a pattern and have husky custom cleats cast of bronze if no decent hardware is available over the counter. This not only saves money, but you end up with hardware that has brawn. Pay particular attention to cleat bases. A large bearing area is important to keep a cleat from digging itself into the deck or working its fastening, causing leaks and maybe rot. Do not bolt cleats down on sandwich core decks unless the foam or end-grain balsa has been replaced in that area with solid glass or plywood. Cleats countersunk for slotted flat-head machine screws, as most are, are harder to bolt down snugly. Fastening should be torqued tightly so a cleat doesn't get shifty later on. Normal hex bolts work well; carriage bolts are better—they have smooth heads that won't chafe line (a cleat base must be machined with square holes to fit carriage bolts).

It's not the overall strength of the fasteners that determines steadfast security so much as the bearing area of the softer deck material contacting the fasteners. If you decide to make your own cleats, it won't hurt to machine them to take six bolts rather than the usual four. Anything smaller than three-eighths-inch is a waste of time; use half-inch bolts if you can. If a cleat cannot be positioned to take advantage of a deck beam to distribute loads over a large area, then use hefty hardwood backing pads (ironwood or iron bark). Simply bolting cleats to deck skins won't cut it.

Mooring-line fairleads have to be secure. They are loaded to the gills when a line feeds through at a sharp angle, loads that can equal cleat loading. Open fairleads are unreliable. A sharp upward tug while the boat's moored to a high dock or seawall can free a line, raising havoc with lifelines or stanchions. Big-ship-style fairleads encapsulated by a bulwark control mooring lines positively. It's handy if each cleat has fairleads fore *and* aft for lines leading in either direction. To minimize chafe, fairleads should be highly polished with well-rounded edges.

Keep Garbage at Bay

It would be a shame to mess up your well-planned action stations with a clutter of rubbish, and yet some offshore cruising yachts look like flea markets. A tangle of gear on decks is unsightly and embarrassing—and bad PR for the cruising fraternity at large. Worse, it's against the interest of safe operation.

Build in ample fuel and water tankage so you don't have to resort to jerry jugs on deck; use fold-up bicycles that stow below instead of fixed ones; and organize below-decks racks or lockers for fishing gear, oars, diving equipment, and so forth. A deck box or two hides spare chain, mooring line, inflatable dinghy pumps, fenders, etc., and the boxes double as seats. When you sail with clear decks, you sail with a clear conscience.

EVALUATE ALL ADVICE

A cruising yacht must not be a stereotype; different boats are right for different folks. Every crew has unique needs, aspirations, and circumstances. To find the right boat, keep emotion, hearsay, and marketing ballyhoo out of it. As you sift information and advice from others, ask yourself how experienced they are at the kind of cruising you have in mind; how closely their needs, lifestyles, and resources resemble your own; and what axes they grind. Are they trying to sell something? Are they open minded? Or are they sounding off to justify prejudices or predicaments? If you relate personally to what you read or hear, it probably relates to you.

12▶ Making the Most of Cruising

Please take this to heart: the more a boat feels like home, the less a cruise feels like being away from home.

Many first-time participants mistakenly believe the excitement and freedom of cruising will sustain them, that their standard of living aboard is of secondary concern. They feel that departing is the objective, that once they are off and running everything will be roses. Unfortunately, they underestimate the impact self-sufficiency has on their futures. Cruising is a way of life, not a lark, and it either goes sour or goes on in fine style for the same reasons other ways of life do. It's naive to think any venture will succeed without a 100-percent effort behind it; certainly nothing worthwhile will.

If anything, cruising should be backed by a 110-percent effort to offset factors that can conspire against it: motion discomfort on passages, remote living away from the bright lights, friends and relatives left behind, the potential for boring diets, overly restrictive budgets, and discord from living like second-class citizens in confined quarters. These things don't affect crews on well-prepared boats, but on ill-prepared boats they are troublemakers.

THE TRAPPINGS OF CIVILIZATION

While it's practical to have things like plastic glasses and plates for casual meals at sea and at anchor, cruising gets tiresome without houseware to add atmosphere, romance, and a touch of class. Crystal wine goblets and liqueur glasses, stoneware or china plates, cut glass wine decanters, teak and stainless steel serving platters, decorative ice buckets, and smart cocktail accessories spruce up shipboard life. Instead of putting all your nice stuff to shoreside storage, why not cruise with some of it? Consider the little luxuries you take as expendable; if something bites the dust somewhere along the way, so what! It brightened your days while it lasted.

Even in the tropics, it's a pleasant change to dress for dinner now and then. Maybe slacks, pressed shirts, and blazers for menfolk and cocktail dresses for ladies (don't leave all the jewelry behind!). It's fitting to have hardware to complement an upmarket evening aboard, too: simple things like chunky candles, place mats, decorator salt and pepper mills, a set of attractive condiment bowls, a wooden salad-bowl set, pewter beer mugs, real cloth serviettes, and silverware to suit.

There's no reason why you can't cruise in the style you are accustomed to ashore. Preparations to maintain living standards are particularly rewarding far from civilization. Because out in the sticks, your boat is all the civilization you have.

HOLIDAY PREPARATIONS

On an overseas venture, it's part of the game to get involved in new customs and folkways. Yet, in spite of the excitement of new experiences, the farther you travel, the more nostalgic the old holidays of your homeland become. Remember this during preparation, or you'll feel let down later.

Arrange a compact kit for each occasion. For Christmas, pack away rolls of wrapping paper and ribbons for gifts; cards, candles, plastic holly wreaths; ornaments such as colored balls, Santas, and angels; a can of snow spray; a sprig of mistletoe; cassette tapes of Christmas carols; and so forth. It's amazing what fits in a small box when you choose decorations carefully. Include a little imitation fold-up fir tree and a string or two of miniature Christmas lights. Christmas isn't the same without them, and an inverter will run the lights for hours without denting the batteries. You may even decide to take along outdoor ones to decorate the rig.

Stow baskets, egg dye, and plastic grass for the Easter Bunny's visit. Halloween goes offshore with wigs, masks, false fangs, and makeup. Pack away party hats and surplus flares for New Year's Eve. Thanksgiving falls flat without the trimmings for a feast. Almost everything you need—turkey, cranberry sauce, yams, pumpkin pie filling, cream—is available in cans. Dehydrated mashed potatoes and packaged gravies are better than sad faces. Stow your favorite holiday drink ingredients, too. And a selection of festive paper plates and napkins.

The same principles apply whatever your background or preferences for celebrating holidays. Make a list of the items that liven up a particular event and sail with them. The joy of authentic get-togethers far from home repays preparatory efforts tenfold.

FAMILY CELEBRATIONS AND DIVERSIONS

When there are children on a cruise, family celebrations are of special importance. On long voyages, memorable birthdays are often made before departure. Pack away birthday candles, cards, wrapping paper, cake decorations, package mixes of icings and cakes, streamers, and a big roll of butcher paper and crayons to make banner headlines congratulating the birthday person.

Gifts are more appreciated out in the boondocks than in cities, where you can buy anything on a whim. Plan ahead by selecting presents to match your itinerary. Maybe a new swimsuit or a mask and snorkel for a tropical birthday. Or a diary, a book on shells, a new pair of thongs, or a pair of sunglasses. Something the recipient will put to immediate and grateful use.

Forethought will spice up your life. Try to cover all the bases: prepare for everything from wedding anniversaries to a party in King Neptune's honor when crossing the equator. Remember to stow a random selection of whacky greeting cards for new friends you'll meet along the way, too.

Stow a range of games like Scrabble, chess, dominoes, Monopoly, an assortment of card decks, and a few pairs of dice. These diversions come into play when your sailing adventure gets bogged down on rainy days or long passages. Bring along new ones to try when old ones lose their appeal. Small, magnetic board games are perfect for shipboard use.

LAST-MINUTE SHOPPING

If your voyage is to be a long one, say over six months, treat yourself to a shopping spree just before departure to stock up on extra personal gear and clothing. When a favorite item goes by the board during the cruise, it's a pleasure to pull a replacement out of storage. And it's frustrating to lose a deck shoe, a treasured shirt, or a favorite pair of shorts and have to live without.

Prepare for a high rate of attrition if you're heading for warm climates—the sun fades clothes quickly, particularly swimgear and towelling. Your wardrobe aboard ship won't be as extensive as it was ashore, either, and each item will get more use, accelerating wear.

THE SHIP'S LIBRARY

There never seems to be enough room on boats for books. Build extra bookshelves if necessary, and stock them with pertinent publications to suit your itinerary: books on geography, oceanography, cultural folkways, history, bird and fish identification, shells, diving, fishing, navigation, early voyages and explorations, and foreign languages, and reference books such as dictionaries and handbooks on medical care. Even if you don't read much now, you'll probably become a bookworm on the voyage. There'll be time to read and fascinating things to study.

Compile a scrapbook of magazine articles and copied material from libraries about your intended landfalls. Reading about a port of call just before arrival helps make the most of a short visit.

PROVISIONING FOR PLEASURE

The consumables stowed aboard ship largely determine your standard of living on the voyage. A thorough job of provisioning before departure saves money in the long run because you won't be faced with stopgap shopping where grocery prices are high. It's not always convenient to haul groceries back to the vessel in remote areas, either, assuming you stumble on something worth eating.

Before racing out to a wholesale grocer and buying case lots of fodder, do yourself a favor by doing some research. Bargain prices and enticing labels should never influence decisions. Only quality foodstuffs stand the test of time. Make sure the crew samples everything before you buy it in bulk, and while it's smart thinking to buy case lots of proven food on sale, never overdo it at the expense of diversity. An overkill of canned ravioli or Vienna sausages won't even make good ballast.

First-class provisioning can be best described in three words: variety, variety, and variety. Your lockers are your cruising supermarket.

The menu aboard ship should not differ significantly from what you eat ashore. A new life at sea requires enough adaptation as it is without the trauma of having to alter your eating habits radically. Naturally, it's part of traveling to eat as the natives do, but a steady diet of tacos, marinated seaworms, or raw sea urchin roe is hard to swallow. (As an aside, stock up on commercial toilet paper. Georgia Pacific's Verigood, 96 rolls to the case, *is* very good, with twice the sheets per roll of domestic varieties. It's also less fuzzy than household stuff, making it a better all-purpose tissue for cleaning sunglasses and lenses. If you hail from the States, where paper standards are high, foreign brands will feel like roofing paper.)

Basic foodstuffs are no problem to organize: you need the obvious things—sugars, flours, pastas, and so forth. These commodities can be replenished in most villages worldwide. It's frills and fancy foods that elevate a mediocre existence into a sparkling lifestyle. Provisioning should be planned with a heavy emphasis on entertaining— meeting interesting people and having the free time to socialize with them is one of the life's rewards.

Budget generously for hors d'oeuvres: things like tinned clams, smoked baby oysters, whole shrimps, smoked eels, sardines in various sauces, stuffed green olives, black olives, gherkins, dill pickles, tinned salmon, crab, tuna, chicken, turkey, a selection of tinned patés, jars and jars of nutmeats, a wide assortment of relishes, dozens of jars of mayonnaise, and boxes and boxes of crackers (decant them into sealed, plastic containers). Nibblies are your investment in good times ahead. Without them, socializing with fellow sailors and local residents can be a strain.

While a radical change in diet is disruptive, some spirit of adventure is necessary when selecting canned goods. Particularly if you, like most folks, don't eat out of cans ashore because fresh foods are readily available. See what you think of canned puddings, canned breads, canned fruitcakes, and canned cheeses. Premium-quality canned meats are the mainstay of meals far from civilization: things like ham, roast beef, and turkey. Canned bacon is another cruising favorite. And don't overlook canned goods from the local deli— things you haven't tried because they seem too extravagant. Steer away from cheap fillers like Spam and corned beef; why eat something afloat that you wouldn't feed a dog ashore? While you cruise, prices will keep escalating; soon your original purchases will be bargains, anyway, regardless of initial cost. And when your cook has the supplies to outdo any restaurant, you'll be happy to eat and entertain aboard more frequently, conserving cash reserves.

Give rapt attention to specialty foods and food indigenous to your region or nation. You may not see these things in foreign waters. Personal cravings might drive you to distraction unless you keep a private stash aboard. In particular, Americans should stock up on things like mustard, hot dog relish, hamburger relish, catsup, garlic dills, etc., all of which are hard to find overseas.

Home canning rounds out a provisioning program. Precooked, bottled hamburger is a tasty base for hundreds of dishes and is leagues ahead of store-bought substitutes. Canned smokies (sausages) add spice to casseroles. And canned pork chops or pork fillets are marvelous out in the boonies, too.

NUTRITION AT SEA

Sometimes the need to sleep during daylight hours at sea makes regimented eating schedules impractical. A spell of bad weather further limits formal cooking. Often, crew members meet for the main meal around sundown and fend for themselves the rest of the time. The cook cooperates by preparing brunch-type meals during the day that don't have to be eaten on the spot— things like sandwiches, which crew members gobble as they can.

An attack of the hungries at 0300 hours is another kettle of fish. On a passage, your crew works and eats 'round the clock. Trouble is, the sleeping offwatch shouldn't be disturbed by galley clatter, and hungry watchkeepers can't be distracted from their duties to rattle pans, anyway. Prepare for night watches by packing aboard a generous supply of nutritious snacks: breakfast bars, granola bars, instant breakfast drinks, mixed nuts and raisins, fresh fruit, dried fruit, candy bars, cookies, canned cold cuts and garnishes, eggs for boiling, individual packets of crackers and cheese or peanut butter (great offshore!), canned fruit and fruit cocktail, jars of cheese spreads, salamis, pepperonis, tinned brown bread, canned butter, and so on. Like armies, sailors travel on their stomachs.

Provide plenty of beverages to go along with the snacks: various cocoa mixes, a selection of teas, coffee, chicken and beef bouillons, instant soups, powdered fruit drinks, canned fruit drinks, canned milk, Milo, malted milk powder, Ovaltine, canned and powdered cream, cream substitutes, and so on. A few stainless steel thermoses mounted in the galley supply hot water for instant hot drinks all night.

SOFT DRINKS

Soda pop and mixers are heavy and bulky to stow in sufficient quantities for a lengthy voyage, and inflated prices in remote tropical areas discourage local buying. This makes life difficult for cruising folks who love whiskey and soda or gin and vodka tonics, or for those who hanker for a can of Coke or root beer now and then.

Home soda-makers solve the problem beautifully. A good appliance is the Soda Stream machine, which houses a big CO_2 cylinder to carbonate water in special bottles with reusable, gasketed screw caps. Soda water is made and refrigerated, to be flavored to taste with concentrated syrups on demand.

Since soda pop and mixers are practically all water, the flavored syrups take up a fraction of the stowage of ready-made drinks. A year's supply will fit aboard any vessel. The Soda Stream cylinder carbonates about 100 six-ounce drinks before expiring. A few spare cylinders keep a thirsty crew in fizzy drinks for months. The cylinders can be refilled anywhere they recharge fire extinguishers— and that's almost any small town in the world—so long as you have an adaptor fitting.

BEER

Few sailors turn down an ice-cold brew on a hot day in paradise. Even if you don't drink beer personally, you'll probably stock some to lubricate guests.

Beer costs the earth in many exotic ports, particularly tourist traps. Stocking up before departure can mean a big reduction in monthly cash outlays. If you are heading for the tropics, where consumption is high, plan on going through 50 dozen cans a year. Although this quantity looks formidable in one stack, it'll vanish without a trace when broken down into six-packs and individual cans and salted away in nooks and crannies below decks. Cram aboard all you can. You social life will raise your freeboard soon enough.

Buy only canned beer. It stows more efficiently, it won't break, and it cools quicker in the refrigerator. Avoid flimsy aluminum cans; sometimes beer mysteriously disappears from them over long periods of stowage (the same can happen with soda pop in aluminum cans). Steel cans are more robust and, although subject to superficial cosmetic rust, preserve contents more reliably long term.

Unlike premium wine, beer begins to go downhill the minute it leaves the brewery. But it'll be at least six months before there's noticeable deterioration in taste—according to conservative brewery experts, that is. In practice, you can confidently expect good canned beer to survive a year in your lockers, sometimes two, even three years. Premium beer has a longer shelf life than cheap suds.

WINE

If you hail from a wine-producing area, you'll be wise to stock up for the voyage right there, especially if you intend to sail to remote areas. The quality of bulk wine in far-away cruising areas such as French Polynesia is ghastly, and premium vintages cost a bundle.

Generally, a red wine cruises longer than a white, and bottled wine travels better than wine in casks or flagons. Run-of-the-mill quaffing whites in the three- to six-liter plastic-bladdered cardboard casks should last at least six months in your lockers. The casks stow efficiently, so buy plenty. You and your guests will probably drink the ship dry before it turns to vinegar.

A quality bottled vintage white such as a Chardonnay or Riesling can be expected to cruise for a year, and it's not uncommon for them to please the palate after two years in the locker.

Premium reds like Cabernet Sauvignon or Pinot Noir can delight taste buds two to three years over the horizon.

Three enemies of wine stowage are heat, light, and motion. Stowage temperature depends mostly on the climate you cruise in, but wine stowed under the waterline next to the hull will generally have a cooler environment than wine stowed in higher cabin lockers. Sunlight shouldn't be a factor; most lockers are dark. And motion? Well, there's little you can do about that on a sailboat. But wine stowed low amidships won't get quite the thrashing it would elsewhere. Leave bottled wine in the original divided cardboard cartons if you have the space; then the bottles will be safe from breakage without special preparation. Stow them horizontally to keep corks wet.

SPARKLING WHITE WINE

Champagne-type sparkling whites really come into their own on a cruise. Even if you don't drink much of it ashore, don't be surprised to find yourself popping corks afloat with a vengeance. A bottle of champagne adds a touch of class to birthdays, wedding anniversaries, and reunions with long-lost cruising friends.

A chilled glass of bubbly and a tropical sunset is an occasion in itself. Remember: good food and drink become more special the farther you sail from civilization.

A middle-of-the-road bubbly is heaven under the sun, so don't waste your money on premium sparkling whites unless you're a connoisseur. Expect a shelf life of around one year.

Champagne makes a thoughtful and special gift, too. During your cruise, you'll meet local residents who generously extend their hospitality. A bottle of sparkling white (or a bottle of still wine from your homeland) is a great thank you. It's all the more valued in less affluent island nations, where locals don't have the luxury of drinking good wine because of prohibitive cost or availability.

STOWING PROVISIONS

Most stowage spaces aboard are V-shaped, and canned goods nestle in an efficient, tight wedge. Foodstuffs can be stowed in any well-ventilated, insulated area free from moisture and condensation. Seeping seams, leaking portlights, dripping hatches, and weeping, uninsulated hull surfaces limit your options. Leaks must be dealt with before departure, or your foodstuffs won't last the distance. Go on a few sea trials in nasty weather to ferret out the wet spots. Be sure to live aboard for a time before departure, too. This tests locker and stowage spaces for condensation under real cruising conditions. Just because stowage spaces stay dry on an unattended vessel doesn't mean they'll be okay when there are additional sources of moisture.

Stow foodstuffs with convenience foremost in mind. A few handy lockers and bins near the galley should contain a cross-section of what's aboard, as your kitchen did ashore, to simplify the cook's job. Intermediate spaces should hold food in categories so things are logical to find. For example, one locker for canned meats, one for canned veggies, and another for canned fruit, soups in another, sauce mixes here, hors d'oeuvres there, and so on. When food's stowed by category, it's apparent at a glance as you cruise what needs replenishing.

Deep bins with top access are awkward when you want something buried at the bottom. Think about installing shelves halfway down tall bins. The lower section can be accessed by a vertical door or hatch in front, or designated for long-term stowage—next year's supply of rum and beer or rarely needed spares.

Bins and lockers should not be built too large. Smaller spaces allow more freedom to divide by category, items are easier to pack against shifting in a rolling seaway, and they are easier to reach.

Bilges are not ideal stowage spaces. Even if your vessel is made of GRP or cold-molded timber and has dry bilges, there's always the chance of accidental flooding from an open hatch or port. Nevertheless, space under floorboards cannot go to waste. The best candidates for the bilge are foodstuffs and beverages in glass jars or bottles. Things like marmalade, peanut butter, wine, and home-canned stuff. If they get a saltwater bath, they'll probably be no worse for wear.

Duty-free ship's stores for remote cruising add up. This pile will last a few months; a year's supply fills a truck. That's one reason why boottops are raised higher than they were on the drawing board.

Wrap individual glass containers in Styrofoam sheeting to protect against breakage.

Ashore, up is always up. On a boat, up may one day be down. Your bin and locker doors and access panels should be hinged and positively latched in case of a knockdown. Gravity is a fair-weather friend to sailors.

Inventory your provisions by stowage space with a card catalog. If you depend on memory, it's only a matter of time until treasure hunts begin, particularly for the more obscure items that don't fit basic categories.

SHELF LIFE

The shelf life of foodstuffs is variable. Assuming first-rate stowage conditions, a voyage of two or three years' duration won't have significant spoilage. As long as packaged goods such as cake mixes, bicarbonate of soda, and raisins are protected by heat-sealed plastic bags, they'll last indefinitely (make sure you use oxygen-barrier bags).

Canned food has a shelf life of one to ten years. Acidic items such as canned cherries and sauerkraut are most corrosive and go off first. Toss out a puffed or leaky can immediately. It's not worth risking your crew's health, even if the contents look and smell okay. Also, check the condition of your stores periodically. Leaky cans dribble over good cans, and if they're left to fester, the cancer spreads.

Dehydrated vegetables and fruits hermetically sealed in plastic food bags last years. Dry goods like flour and sugar keep well in wide-mouthed, plastic gallon jars. Apply stretchy vinyl tape to the lid/jar joint for extra insurance. Packaged soups, sauces, and gravies seem to last forever with no special packaging.

Don't let the prospect of spoilage keep you from buying out the store. Even if you lose a can of blueberries someday, think of all the pies the others made!

STEREO EQUIPMENT

High-fidelity stereophonic music is particularly appreciated on cruises to remote areas where FM stereo radio stations are scarce or nonexistent. The power of household setups is too great in confined cabins; a modest ten or 15 watts' output per channel should be enough to blow out your ports.

Most of the top-of-the-line automotive cassette players sound good aboard ship. But they have a drawback—few record. The ability to record on cassette lets you tape native music and special events en route and compose cassette "letters" to send back home, and it's handy to be able to tape memos, shopping lists, radio schedules, things-to-do lists, and so forth.

There's a lot to be said for a portable AC/D-cell cassette deck of professional quality hooked up to a separate 12-volt AM/FM stereo amplifier. The cassette deck can be used before departure to create a tape library, home reproduction being superior to pre-recorded tapes and cheaper, too. Make a bargain with your local lending library to have first option on new records as they come in. And borrow new records to tape from friends. This strategy has an additional advantage: once the deck goes to sea, it's already been tested. Don't forget a stereo microphone!

Hunt around for the best speakers and pay the price. Otherwise, the full potential of your sound system won't be realized. Some automotive speakers sound impressive in cars while disguised by road noise but lack depth and range in a quieter environment. Take your time comparing speakers in dealers' sound booths to narrow the choice. Make the final decision between the best of the bunch aboard ship to take into account your cabin's peculiar acoustics.

A second set of inexpensive speakers is handy for on-deck music. Then you won't risk exposing your high-tech (meaning high-bucks) equipment to the weather.

If younger children cruise with you, think about a second, inexpensive automotive stereo playback unit for their cabin. Armed with their own tape library, they're free to do their own thing without fumbling with your fancy system. Consider installing headphones in lieu of speakers so the kids can blow their brains out without driving you and the neighbors around the bend. Headphones are ideal on ocean passages, too. They let a person escape into the world of music without disturbing others.

Cassette-tape stowage between deck beams.

FUN IN THE SUN

A voyage to warm waters opens new horizons. Even if you like your water best in whiskey or in the shower, a clear lagoon is heaven—a cross between a swimming pool and a tropical aquarium. It doesn't take much skill to snorkel around coral heads to see the sights, either. Buy masks, snorkels, and fins from a recognized dive shop, not a department store, so that expert help is on hand to advise you on what's comfortable and practical. Good fit is everything. Chafing fins and leaky masks are worthless. Take along spares for guests and natural attrition.

Whether you are into scuba diving or not, it's handy to have someone aboard who's a certified diver, and at least one tank and regulator setup for emergencies. Scuba is great for scrubbing the bottom, retrieving a lost valuable in an anchorage, or freeing a jammed anchor. It's also a good way to catch dinner. Although snorkeling fills the bill for most underwater forays, it's limiting. Scuba lets a person go deeper, longer. It's almost essential if you want to try your hand at underwater photography. Snorkeling doesn't allow much leeway for composition; it's more a point-and-shoot exercise, shotgun style. Sealife doesn't pose for snorkelers, either. You have to be able to stay on location and wait for the action.

Shell collecting is exciting in outlying tropical areas. Some, such as cone shells, are poisonous, but simple equipment and a bit of book learning will keep you from getting stung. Use salad tongs to pick the critters off reefs or the seabed. Dentist picks are handy for cleaning. Soaking shells in bleach and water helps disguise the smell (and do they!), but go easy or the shells will fade. Divided cardboard cartons and cotton wool protect them in transit or storage. Shells are like stamps. Only perfect specimens, both in color and physical condition, are worth money. And the rarer they are, the more they're worth.

Kids like air mattresses for splashing around on. Cheap plastic ones are good enough.

Don't forget plenty of sun protection: visors, lotion, spare sunglasses, wide-brimmed hats. And some lightweight shirts and trousers for times when you've had enough.

CAMERA GEAR

All good things come to an end. Someday your voyage will be a fond memory and you'll be glad you recorded it on film. A 35 mm SLR (single lens reflex) camera outfit is ideal for cruising. With a few basic lenses, you can shoot up a storm. As a starting point, consider a wide-angle lens (28 to 35mm) and a telephoto zoom (about 70 to 200mm) to complement the standard lens (50 to 55mm). A wide-angle zoom is great for deck work, too (around 30 to 70mm). Extension tubes or close-up lenses are inexpensive accessories that let you shoot tiny subjects like shells and flowers. A strobe flash for below-decks and night work, a range of filters (UV and polarizing particularly), and you're in the photo business.

One of those zip-lock waterproof sports pouches protects your camera gear around water. They are especially important for taking an SLR out in a dinghy.

Serious photographers with sophisticated equipment often miss impromptu shots of people and sudden incidents. One of the automatic snapshot 35mm cameras (Nikon, Minolta, Pentax) is just the ticket for spur-of-the-moment, candid photography. They're compact with autofocus and auto-exposure for idiot-proof results, and they offer high resolution for enlargements or color slides—a far cry from lesser 110 cameras. And importantly, they're inexpensive enough to leave out on a shelf ready for the action. Forget disk cameras; their negative size is too small for decent resolution.

As mentioned, one of the attractions of tropical cruising is underwater exploration. Nikonos 35mm rangefinder-type cameras are perfect for shooting underwater scenery and marine life as well as above-water subjects in wet weather. They are totally waterproof and impervious to mud and sand. Improved models have through-the-lens metering so you don't have to carry around a separate light meter.

Unless you stick to shallow water, say less than ten feet, reds, oranges, and yellows are filtered out, and your color pictures will turn out mucky blue. An underwater strobe flash brings back the color.

CARPETING UNDERFOOT

Oiled teak and holly cabin soles are traditional and look salty. But why have polished wood floors aboard if you didn't favor them ashore? Teak cabin soles tend to be gloomy, and they're expensive and laborious to fabricate. They also need periodic refinishing to stay shipshape.

Sailors who take comfort seriously fit carpeting. It feels good to bare feet in hot weather and is cozy and warm in cold weather. Carpeting offers a secure footing offshore and adds color and a cheery feeling to the accommodation any time.

Velcro tape holds a carpet firmly in place yet allows quick removal on cleaning day (if the carpet is fitted in manageable sections). Synthetic nylon carpeting resists mildew and dries faster than wool. Make sure the backing is synthetic, too. Many less expensive synthetic carpets have organic jute backings that are susceptible to mildew. Short pile is great for sleeping cabins and saloons; water-resistant indoor/outdoor carpeting is better in the galley and companion-way areas, where water and cooking spillage are likely.

A carpeted (wall-to-wall, not throw rugs) vessel has cleaner bilges. Lint and hair stay above board to be vacuumed up rather than sneak down past cracks in flooring.

Carpet can be installed over painted plywood floors in a day and lasts years in liveaboard service. When it finally wears out, renewal is quick and relatively inexpensive, using the old carpet as a pattern. Restricted floor areas in boats concentrate wear. It's cheaper in the long run to buy for quality.

GEAR STOWAGE

Living aboard on the move involves a lot of gear, and it all has to live somewhere. If brackets, chocks, and holders are built for most of the things you use in daily life, the boat will be less cluttered, and things will be easier to find.

Houses are big enough to tolerate great disorder without actually looking a shambles; boats aren't. More to the point, orderliness is seamanlike. Tidy ships are usually the ones that are run most professionally. Neat is safe.

Offshore, an organized boat is quieter, too. When everything is securely stowed or chocked, it eliminates a symphony of clicks, clanks, and bangs. Organization isn't so much a matter of personal preference as it is ashore; it's a duty.

MORE APPRECIATED FEATURES

One or two doors aboard ship should be fitted with full-length mirrors made either of glass or break-resistant acrylic or polycarbonate. Otherwise, shipmates

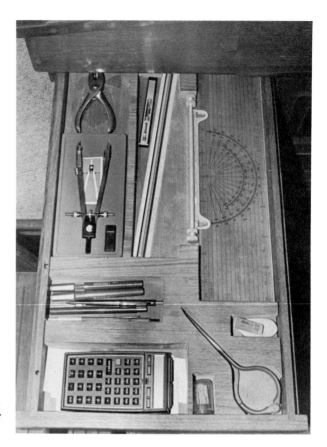

Custom-built drawer for navigation instruments keeps them secure and ready for use.

An attractive and functional wine-goblet rack. No, they don't jump out at sea!

will bemoan the omission. Mirrors also psychologically increase swinging room.

The captain will appreciate a quartz chronometer, a compass, and a depth-indicator readout berthside. They help keep him or her informed of the ship's status at sea and at anchor. When awakened in the middle of the night, particularly in an anchorage with all hands asleep, it's comforting to see the time, the ship's heading, and how much water's under the keel. One can go back to sleep in confidence, knowing nothing's changed, or leap on deck if it has.

Sextants can be stowed by sliding their boxes into a drawer-like space. All it takes is an opening, a pair of wooden guides, and a thumbscrew to secure the box in position. This keeps a sextant out of harm's way and frees shelf space at anchor for household purposes. At sea, the empty box slides back in its cubbyhole out of the line of fire while the navigator uses the instrument.

Fender boards are awkward to stow aboard anywhere. They look particularly ugly lashed to lifelines at the rail. If they are shaped to bolt to stern pulpit brackets for seat boards, they are unobtrusive, and you get a seat in the bargain. For no extra charge you have an on-deck workbench, too.

Companionway dropboards need a second home when the ship's opened to a tropical climate. If they slide into brackets flush with a vertical bulkhead adjacent to the companionway, they stay out from underfoot and can be reached conveniently from the cockpit or from below decks when needed. Dropboards dumped in lockers are always in the way.

It's well recognized that portlights should be fitted with lined curtains for privacy and/or daytime sleeping. Skylights and deadlights should have blackout covers, too.

Galleys often lack a shelf for cookbooks. A permanently mounted electronic timer/alarm is also appreciated by the cook. And regular egg timers come in handy; bring several so you always have one that works.

Master staterooms should be designed so the captain has a view of the helm from his or her berth through a port, hatch, or open doorway. It's comforting to see the watch safely on the job rather than wonder what's happening up on deck. This contributes to security and peace of mind at anchor, too; an intruder can't sneak aboard without being seen.

Additionally, the captain should be able to see a portion of the night sky through an open hatch and/or hatch skylight while in bed. This helps him or her keep tabs on the weather and the stars (it becomes a habit to check on the stars for rough time and bearings). The person in charge is on call 24 hours a day, at sea and at anchor. The more he or she is in tune with the boat and the environment—even while in the sack—the better.

Crews on boats with open deck spaces might consider taking folding deck chairs. At anchor, a good director's-type chair is a pleasant alternative to sitting in the cockpit. A portable chair lets you sit where the shade or the breeze or the view is best. They are also handy for picnics and shoreside potlucks.

If you don't mind LPG aboard, a stainless marine gas barbecue gives cooking another dimension without stowing bulky and messy solid charcoal briquettes. Make sure you take a small LPG cylinder specially for this, around five pounds, so the barbecue can be conveniently transported to the beach. The standard 20-pound bottles for galley stoves are too clumsy to cart around.

Five- or six-gallon plastic pails with removable pour-spout lids and carrying handles (such as those bulk chemicals come in) have advantages over regular

Dropboards need a home. Note Lexan inserts in boards and hooks for hanging safety-harness tethers at sea. Coiled cord is for an autopilot remote handset.

A handbearing compass stowed out of sight against infrequent use is no asset; mounted next to the skipper's berth, it's useful all the time.

jerry-jugs for ferrying water. They nest for stowing and make good laundry tubs. Buy new ones from a chemical wholesaler. Used ones might be toxic.

THE PRICE OF CRUISING

Cruising has social and economic ramifications that influence contentment over the horizon. Misconceptions about dollars and *sense* can make trouble in paradise. The following observations may help you firm up your socioeconomic strategies.

First, a look at the cost of cruising, which has various interpretations, depending on individual viewpoints:

Although cruising may seem to have a high price tag when total costs to

A stainless barbecue won't rust. Shoreside ones make crusty sailors.

achieve a departure and voyage are tabulated—acquiring the boat, outfitting, provisioning, month-to-month spending, etc.—remember that the burden is offset by the market value of the vessel. Shoreside folks wrap up huge sums in housing, cars, RVs, and the inevitable tangle of nonessential goods and services and think nothing of it!

Paying for food and shelter is part of life, whether you live ashore or afloat. These are fairly fixed expenses relative to certain standards of living that are not really cruising costs per se. And cruising, no matter how elaborately you go about it, tends to be more economical on a monthly basis than suburbia—even when the cost of initial provisioning is considered.

Some cynics say you have to add lost income and/or missed career opportunities to the cost (if you're not yet retired). Personally, I experienced more opportunities, financial and otherwise, after I got involved in cruising. You can miss plenty by taking root in one place.

An overseas cruise can represent five years of your life when you add up the time spent building a boat (or earning the money to buy a boat), outfitting and preparation, the voyage itself, and winding the affair up afterwards. The commitment is seen by some as a price, sometimes an intimidating one. But what's the alternative? Carrying on with a stale career and taking a few weeks off for good behavior each year? Working yourself silly on the suburban treadmill for no apparent purpose? Earning a heart attack for your trouble? Since cruising is a prolonged vacation with great potential for personal growth, why should the time factor be relevant? After all, you have to be somewhere!

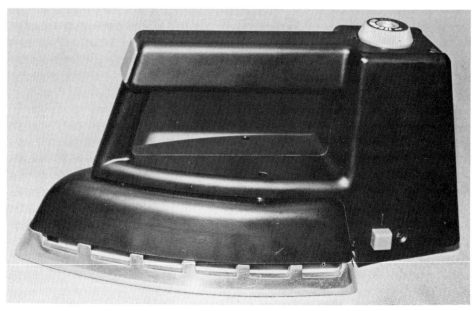

A butane iron is the ticket for cruising; it needs no electrical power source. This one self-starts electron-ically, and it has adjustable temperature regulation. For more information, contact Lyon Manufacturing Services, 4/5 Inverness Mews, London W2 3JQ, England.

ON COURSE FOR BANKRUPTCY?

On a balance sheet, cruising aspirations seldom tally. If an accountant examined my finances and cost projections before I built the boats I sailed away on extended voyages, or the finances of hundreds of others who've done the same, the verdict would have been bankruptcy. But dogged determination is a funny thing: it turns prophets of doom into liars. By taking it one step at a time, and by forging ahead relentlessly, you'll triumph in the end, even if on paper you don't have a snowball's chance. If this were not so, the cruising grounds of the world would be deserted.

BUDGETING TO MAKE THE MOST OF IT

My family and I have anchored in distant lagoons where we didn't spend a cent for months, and we've gone bananas in flashy resorts like Newport Beach, California; Puerto Vallarta, Mexico; and Tahiti.

So, although at times frugal, the average cost of a good cruising lifestyle can't be underestimated. It's no fun if you can't take advantage of a landfall by eating in some of its restaurants, renting a car to see sights you'd otherwise miss, taking an occasional scenic flight, buying local crafts, and, when the mood strikes, having a snort in a tourist trap.

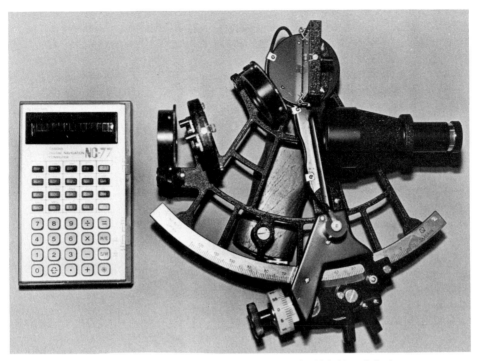

Sextants with rotating polarizing filters are preferable to ones with old-fashioned shades. A preprogrammed sight-reduction computer saves valuable time, reducing the chance of error when the navigator is tired. Shown is Tamaya's NC-77, a good one at a reasonable price.

Entertainment aside, there are running costs to budget for, notably diesel fuel bills (which can equal home heating costs) and fresh provisions bought along the way. Some countries such as French Polynesia require a cash bond for each crewperson aboard equalling the airfare back to their country of origin. This ties up funds temporarily. And there'll be port charges and clearance fees and moorage charges along the way, although these are chicken feed.

In other words, since life goes on while cruising, it's unrealistic to assume that expenses won't.

PREPARE FOR SOCIOECONOMIC REALITY

Cruising people today are obliged to face up to worldwide socioeconomic change. In the old days, landfalls were rare events, and not surprisingly, sailors were instant celebrities, treated like royalty. Nowadays, though, cruising boats venture routinely to remote places without raising an eyebrow. Coincidentally, distant lands and island nations are becoming more commercial, notably through tourism. This puts the onus on cruising people to pay their way.

What was once called living off the land is now stealing or bludging. Every banana tree, avocado tree, orange tree, papaya tree, and lime tree in the cruising grounds belongs to somebody. Shoestring sailors who lack the wherewithal to support themselves are simply oceangoing beggars.

All the old rewards are still there—the romance, adventure, and outright pleasure of visiting exotic places on a sailing yacht. So long as you don't expect free lunches.

YOUR IMAGE: YOUR CHOICE

While cruising, you'll attract the inevitable comment from the uninitiated: *you're so lucky!* Inferring you're lucky to be rich enough to mess around sailing the world while honest citizens keep the wheels of society greased. Luck probably had nothing to do with your fortunes, yet few land dwellers have any inkling of the struggles and sacrifices that go into a cruise. They just see the end result.

Whether cruising sailors are wealthy or not (and most are not) is beside the point—they *look* it to outsiders. Sure, it's an irony to work your tail off to realize a dream and feel you have to justify your success to the less motivated and bone lazy, but it's socially pertinent. Because, if someone from a similar socioeconomic background can be jealous of your accomplishments, think what residents of poorer island nations might feel. Particularly those who work all their lives to own a dugout canoe.

Incomprehensible wealth (real or imagined) is a cruising handicap that can be overcome by good manners. Arrogance, however, slams all the doors. Nobody from any walk of life has empathy for egotistical, apparently stinking-rich loudmouths. The point, at the risk of insulting your intelligence, is that the potential for resentment does exist in less affluent countries, and cruising people must compensate.

Here's another tricky one. Any student of human nature knows that first impressions are durable, regardless of their accuracy. It's a shame some cruising sailors don't understand this. Salty, crusty characters may fit *their* conception of the cruising image, but they lower themselves in others' eyes. Scruffy strangers of any kind are not esteemed by the public at large—any public anywhere. Well-presented strangers, by contrast, always have the advantage. The fact that personal appearance and individual worth have little in common is immaterial; the world reacts otherwise.

Dress and grooming are particularly relevant when conducting ship's business with officials. In discretionary matters, your appearance and attitude count considerably. For example, a freshly washed, clean shaven, neatly dressed crew on a tidy ship seeking pratique at a new landfall—in spite of a tough passage and a major effort to look human—is less likely to get nailed for custom's duty on liquor, may receive preferential treatment such as extended visas, and in extreme cases will be less liable to search. What's more, during your stay, you may be offered better mooring facilities and receive assistance or friendly advice on provisioning and fueling. In small towns, word spreads rapidly via the coconut telegraph. It's entirely your choice whether the gossip about you is good, bad, or indifferent.

Your reception in any port of call also depends to some extent on the sailors who came before you. Bad apples are sorely remembered, and cruising, like any other microcosm of society, has its stinkers. Generally, and thankfully, residents all over the world continue to accept sailors on their individual merits, despite increasing numbers. While they won't necessarily roll out the red carpet as in times past, they respond in kind on a one-to-one basis.

The few sailors I've met who complained about being ill-treated or harassed or overcharged or penalized by officials and/or merchants were themselves insufferable malcontents. They had it coming!

A pity, when tact and diplomacy cost nothing.

WAITING TO DO IT RIGHT

Each individual cruise is a one-off project, and it's difficult to schedule one-off projects of any kind accurately—they're done when they're done. Even if you've cruised before, a new voyage with a new boat is something of an experiment. You can't realistically expect clockwork.

Custom vessels are notorious for their reluctance to leave the womb. Even experienced builders, let alone amateurs, sometimes underestimate how long it takes to build them. So many things can screw up the works: key personnel walking off the job, overdue deliveries of vital materials and equipment, extra time spent ironing out wrinkles in systems, industrial disputes—even divorce, births, marriage, heat waves, and hard winters. Good boats are finished in their own good time.

The trouble is, a delay of a few months can mean a delayed departure of nearly a year to long-distance sailors who choreograph their voyages to global weather patterns. But so what? It's better to be philosophical and patient about delays and just keep putting one foot in front of the other. If necessary, a boat can be cruised locally and be better for it the following season. So will her crew.

When my brothers and I began planning our first offshore voyage years ago, we naively reckoned we'd build our 30-foot sloop and be on the high seas six months after taking delivery of the bare hull. Now that's optimism! Three years later (and much drier behind the ears), we finally left Seattle on a circumnavigation. At first, while building the boat, we'd give curiosity seekers the latest wishful departure date; later, after we had wised up, we said we'd stick around until the boat was built.

There are some cruising people who advocate setting a date for departure and leaving then, no matter what. This attitude is too casual for words. It means these people are prepared to go, prepared or not! Most folks who make haste pay later, the hard way.

Mind you, there's a difference between being unprepared and fiddling your life away on trivial projects. After all, you can only anodize your windvane or wax the mast so many times.

AS DEPARTURE NEARS

As departure nears, promote yourself from the boatbuilding business to the president of a private company specializing in expeditions. Because that's exactly what cruising is: a private expedition.

As president, you'll wear many hats. Preparation proceeds on several levels simultaneously: while you bolt on last-minute hardware, you provision, fine tune your itinerary, visit your lawyer, apply for passports and visas, sell shoreside material possessions, deed the family cat to a good home, appoint legal and business associates to carry the can while you're gone, find someone to collect and forward mail, maybe set up a school aboard for the kids, ad infinitum. What fun!

It pays to begin the extrication process well in advance. The longer the voyage, the more lead time you'll need. The most carefree world cruisers are those who made a clean break of it, knowing that, if they someday decided, it could be permanent. Lingering shoreside responsibilities are incompatible with cruising peace of mind.

Unless you are very experienced at cruising and outfitting, it's better to live aboard more or less exclusively some months before departure—at anchor mostly, not dockside. This helps identify and make good the final details to support your existence, and it gives you a chance to liquidate shoreside assets without being dependent on them right to the end. It's always a gamble to put homes and cars on the market at the last minute. Either they hold you up, or you are forced to sacrifice them to get the show on the road. Living aboard before departure eases the transition from shore to sea, too. You can test your independence afloat without fear of total commitment until you're convinced you have the lifestyle you want.

BON VOYAGE

Your cruising days will be the high point of your life so long as your needs and Mother Nature's whims are catered to by a boat that's a comfortable home and an efficient performer.

Someday well-wishers will wave and smile as you slip the lines to freedom. And you'll bid them all farewell to begin a new chapter in your life. But you won't be leaving civilization behind. You never do when you cruise in comfort.

▶ Index